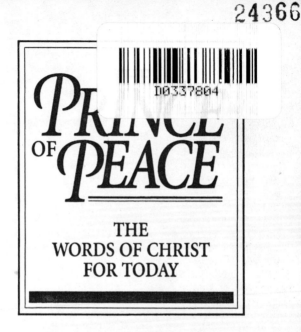

PRINCE OF PEACE

THE WORDS OF CHRIST FOR TODAY

Compiled by

Theodore Londos, Jr.

Publishers Since 1798

THOMAS NELSON PUBLISHERS

Nashville

Published in Nashville, Tennessee, by Thomas Nelson, Inc.

Scripture translations cited are

CEV CONTEMPORARY ENGLISH VERSION, © 1991, the American Bible Society. Used by permission.

KJV King James (Authorized) Version.

NASB THE NEW AMERICAN STANDARD BIBLE, © 1960, 1962, 1963, 1968, 1971, 1972, 1973, 1975, 1977, the Lockman Foundation. Used by permission.

NCV THE EVERYDAY BIBLE, NEW CENTURY VERSION, © 1987, Worthy Publishing, Fort Worth, Texas. Used by permission.

NEB THE NEW ENGLISH BIBLE, © 1961, 1970. The delegates of the Oxford University Press and the Syndics of the Cambridge University Press. Used by permission.

NKJV THE NEW KING JAMES VERSION of the Bible, © 1979, 1980, 1982, Thomas Nelson, Inc., Publishers.

NRSV NEW REVISED STANDARD VERSION BIBLE, © 1989, the Division of Christian Education of the National Council of the Churches of Christ in the United States of America. Used by permission.

Library of Congress Cataloging-in-Publication Information

Bible. N.T. Gospels. English. New King James. Selections. 1993.
    The Prince of Peace : the words of Christ for today / [compiled by] Theodore Londos.
    Includes index.
    ISBN 0-8407-6745-5
    1. Jesus Christ—Words. 2. Jesus Christ—Words—Concordances.
3. Bible. N.T. Gospels—Concordances. I. Londos, Theodore, 1948-.
II. Title.
BS2553.N49 1993
226'.03—dc20   93-11230
                                                      CIP

Printed in the United States of America
1 2 3 4 5 6 7 8 — 99 98 97 96 95 94 93

PREFACE

The Prince of Peace was compiled as a result of what I perceived as a void in Christian literature. For several years I had looked for a book which would serve as a concise reference of what Jesus said (as recorded in the Gospels). So many books have been written about Jesus and His Word, but I could find no satisfactory record of only His sayings.

During my research, I became engrossed in the power, beauty, and simplicity of what He had to say and, more importantly, Who He was. I also found within myself a hesitancy to leave anything out, along with a thought that almost stopped my work: *Can any book of sayings adequately present the true Christ?* Attempting to capture Spirit completely in words is futile—like holding a strong wind in a paper bag. The Spirit Who moved Jesus is not a commodity that can be packaged, owned, and stored for later use.

This humble book is not an effort to encompass all that Jesus said or was. Nor is it a scholarly work. But perhaps *The Prince of Peace* can be a useful guide to those on a spiritual path, a handy resource where one can find, on a page or two, Jesus' expressions about anger, forgiveness, God, materialism, violence, and so forth. While this book can be used for good or ill, I hope it will not be used to win religious arguments, but as a means to greater and higher spiritual ends.

One of my purposes has been to interest readers who grew up without the benefit of a traditional Christian vocabulary. In this, the decade of proclaiming Good News, I hoped to help those not part of any church to meet the Christ of Good News through His own words.

Because of the constraints of space, probably few entries list *every* saying of Jesus that might be relevant. But I have tried to achieve an adequate—if not complete—compilation in two ways: First, I have attempted to list the obvious and familiar sayings; and second, I have often referred the reader to one or more related entries where more sayings may be found. The Index at the end of the book will help readers discover even more related entries.

The sayings listed in any entry do not necessarily relate to the entry topic in the same way. All that I claim is that, to my mind, each saying does relate in a significant way. I leave to others the separate task of moving from a compilation such as this to a systematic presentation of Jesus' doctrine or theology. In the interests of variety, richness, and clarity, the sayings occur in several translations: the *Contemporary English Version* (CEV), the *King James Version* (KJV), the *New American Standard Bible* (NASB), the *New Century Version* (NCV), the *New English Bible* (NEB), the *New King James Version* (NKJV), and the *New Revised Standard Version* (NRSV).

I feel grateful to dear friends who helped me in this project: Pam Allen, Dan Bagby, Rosalie Beck, Bill Carden, Carla Butler, Katherine Blumenstetter, Theresa Collier, Katie Cook, Bob Darden, Diana Donovan, Lisa Freeman, Jamie Graham, Deborah Harris, Ralph Lynn, Jarrell McCracken, Nancy McNeil, Roger Paynter, Stuart Rosenbaum, Sharlande Sledge, Nathan Stone, Chris Surley, Valerie White, and Jeff Zurheide. Special thanks go to my editor, Mark Roberts, and to those ladies-of-light in my life, to whom this book is dedicated—Annie, Mabel, Mary, and Sandy Londos.

As the compiler, I have attempted to be objective, yet the entry headings and choice of sayings listed under each heading reflect my own values, inevitably biased perceptions, and spiritual blindspots. *The Prince of Peace* points to the Christ I know, the One who is forgiving, gentle, healing, humble, peace-loving, and merciful in judgment—the One Who invites us with His words, His life, and His Spirit "to be" as He is. I pray that this book may help others to know Him too.

Theodore Londos, Jr.

ABILITY (*also* FAITH, GREATNESS, POWER)

If you have faith and don't doubt, I promise that you can do what I did to this tree. And you will be able to do even more. You can tell this mountain to get up and jump into the sea, and it will. If you have faith when you pray, you will be given whatever you ask for.

Matthew 21:21–22 (Mark 11:23–24) CEV

With men this is impossible; but with God all things are possible. *Matthew 19:26 (Mark 10:27) (Luke 18:27)* KJV

Keep watching and praying, that you may not enter into temptation; the spirit is willing, but the flesh is weak.

Matthew 26:41 (Mark 14:38) (Luke 22:46) NASB

'If it is possible!' said Jesus, 'Everything is possible to one who has faith.' *Mark 9:23* NEB

She has done what she could; she has anointed my body beforehand for its burial. Truly I tell you, wherever the good news is proclaimed in the whole world, what she has done will be told in remembrance of her.

Mark 14:8–9 (Matthew 26:12–13) (John 12:7) NRSV

Strive to enter through the narrow gate, for many, I say to you, will seek to enter and will not be able.

Luke 13:24 (Matthew 7:13–14) NKJV

ABSTINENCE (*also* ADDICTIONS, CELIBACY)

John the Baptist did not go around eating and drinking, and you said, "That man has a demon in him!" But the Son of Man goes around eating and drinking, and you say, "That man eats and drinks too much! He is even a friend of tax collectors and sinners." Yet Wisdom is shown to be right by what it does. *Matthew 11:18–19 (Luke 7:33–35) CEV*

Not all men can accept this statement, but only those to whom it has been given. For there are eunuchs who were born that way from their mother's womb; and there are eunuchs who were made eunuchs by men; and there are also eunuchs who made themselves eunuchs for the sake of the kingdom of heaven. He who is able to accept this, let him accept it. *Matthew 19:11–12 NASB*

ABUNDANCE

But seek first the kingdom of God and His righteousness, and all these things shall be added to you. Therefore do not worry about tomorrow, for tomorrow will worry about its own things. Sufficient for the day is its own trouble.

Matthew 6:33–34 (Luke 12:31) NKJV

Give, and it will be given to you; good measure, pressed down, shaken together, running over, they will pour into your lap. For by your standard of measure it will be measured to you in return.

Luke 6:38 (Matthew 7:2) (Mark 4:24) NASB

Take heed and beware of covetousness, for a one's life does not consist in the abundance of the things he possesses.

Luke 12:15 NKJV

The thief comes only to steal and kill and destroy. I came that they may have life, and have it abundantly.

John 10:10 NRSV

ACCUSATIONS (*also* JUDGMENT)

God will bless you when people insult you, mistreat you, and tell all kinds of evil lies about you because of me.

Matthew 5:11 (Luke 6:22) CEV

But I say to you that if you are angry with a brother or sister, you will be liable to judgment; . . . and if you say, "You fool," you will be liable to the hell of fire.

Matthew 5:22 NRSV

John came, and he did not eat like other people or drink wine. And people say, "He has a demon." The Son of Man came eating and drinking wine, and people say, "Look at him! He eats too much and drinks too much. He is a friend of tax collectors and "sinners."" But wisdom is proved to be right by the things it does.

Matthew 11:18–19 (Luke 7:33–35) NCV

Woman, where are those thine accusers? hath no man condemned thee?

John 8:10 KJV

ACHIEVEMENTS

What will you gain, if you own the whole world but destroy yourself? What could you give to get back your soul?

Mark 8:36–37 (Matthew 16:26) (Luke 9:25) CEV

For which of you, intending to build a tower, does not first sit down and estimate the cost, to see whether he has enough to complete it? Otherwise, when he has laid a foundation and is not able to finish, all who see it will begin to ridicule him, saying, "This fellow began to build and was not able to finish."

Luke 14:28–30 NRSV

I cannot act by myself; I judge as I am bidden, and my sentence is just, because my aim is not my own will, but the will of him who sent me.

John 5:30 NEB

Don't work for food that spoils. Work for food that gives eternal life. The Son of Man will give you this food, because God the Father has given him the right to do so.

John 6:27 CEV

ACTION   (*also* SOCIAL ACTION, SOCIAL RESPONSIBILITY)

Therefore by their fruits you will know them. Not everyone who says to me, 'Lord, Lord,' shall enter the kingdom of heaven, but he who does the will of My Father in heaven. *Matthew 7:20–21 (Luke 6:44, 46) NKJV*

Therefore whosoever heareth these sayings of mine, and doeth them, I will liken him unto a wise man, which built his house upon a rock: And the rain descended, and the floods came, and the winds blew, and beat upon that house; and it fell not: for it was founded upon a rock.

Matthew 7:24–25(Luke 6:47–48) KJV

What do you think? A man had two sons; he went to the first and said, "Son, go and work in the vineyard today." He answered, "I will not"; but later he changed his mind and went. The father went to the second and said the same; and he answered, "I go, sir"; but he did not go. Which of the two did the will of his father? *Matthew 21:28–31 NRSV*

Why do you call me, 'Lord, Lord,' but do not do what I say?

Luke 6:46 (Matthew 7:21) NCV

ADDICTIONS (*also* ABSTINENCE, LIBERATION, PURIFICATION)

Be on guard, that your hearts may not be weighted down with dissipation and drunkenness and the worries of life, and that day come on you suddenly like a trap; for it will come upon all those who dwell on the face of all the earth.

Luke 21:34–35 NASB

If you keep on obeying what I have said, you truly are my disciples. You will know the truth, and the truth will set you free.
I tell you for certain that anyone who sins is a slave of sin! And slaves don't stay in the family forever, though the Son will always remain in the family. If the Son gives you freedom, you are free! *John 8:31–32, 34–36 CEV*

ADULTERY (*also* DIVORCE, FORNICATION, LUST, SENSUALITY, SEX)

It hath been said, Whosoever shall put away his wife, let him give her a writing of divorcement: But I say unto you, That whosoever shall put away his wife, saving for the cause of fornication, causeth her to commit adultery: and

whosoever shall marry her that is divorced committeth
adultery. *Matthew 5:31–32 KJV*

You must not murder anyone. You must not be guilty of
adultery. You must not steal. You must not tell lies about
your neighbor in court. Honor your father and mother.
Love your neighbor as you love yourself.

Matthew 19:18–19 (Mark 10:19) (Luke 18:20) NCV

Whoever divorces his wife and marries another woman
commits adultery against her; and if she herself divorces
her husband and marries another man, she is committing
adultery. *Mark 10:11–12 (Matthew 19:9) (Luke 16:18) NASB*

ADVERSITY (see AFFLICTION, TROUBLE)

AFFECTION (also LOVE)

Have you noticed this woman? When I came into your
home, you didn't give me any water so I could wash my
feet. But she has washed my feet with her tears and dried
them with her hair. You didn't greet me with a kiss, but
from the time I came in, she has not stopped kissing my
feet. *Luke 7:44–45 CEV*

The younger son got up and started back to his father. But
when he was still a long way off, his father saw him and
felt sorry for him. He ran to his son and hugged and kissed
him. *Luke 15:45 CEV*

AFFLICTION (also FEAR)

Blessed are the poor in spirit: for theirs is the kingdom of
heaven.
Blessed are they that mourn: for they shall be comforted.
Blessed are the meek: for they shall inherit the earth.
Blessed are they which are persecuted for righteousness'
sake: for theirs is the kingdom of heaven.
Blessed are ye, when men shall revile you, and persecute
you, and shall say all manner of evil against you falsely,
for my sake Rejoice and be exceeding glad: for so
persecuted they the prophets which were before you.

Matthew 5:3–5, 10–12 (Luke 6:20–23) KJV

Come to Me, all you who labor and are heavy laden, and I will give you rest. Take My yoke upon you and learn from Me, for I am gentle and lowly in heart, and you will find rest for your souls. For My yoke is easy and My burden is light.   *Matthew 11:28–30 NKJV*

AGGRESSION (see VIOLENCE)

AGING (also FAMILY)

Why do you disobey God and follow your own teaching? Didn't God command you to respect your father and mother? .... But you let people get by without helping their parents when they should. You let them say that what they have has been offered to God. Is this any way to show respect to your parents? You ignore God's commands in order to follow your own teaching.

Matthew 15:3–6 (Mark 7:9–13) CEV

Truly, truly, I say to you, when you were younger, you used to gird yourself, and walk wherever you wished; but when you grow old, you will stretch out your hands, and someone else will gird you, and bring you where you do not wish to go.   *John 21:18 NASB*

AGNOSTICISM (also FAITH, UNBELIEF)

Therefore by their fruits you will know them. Not everyone who says to Me, 'Lord, Lord,' shall enter the kingdom of heaven, but he who does the will of My Father in heaven.   *Matthew 7:20–21 (Luke 6:44, 46) NKJV*

Whoever is not with me is against me, and whoever does not gather with me scatters.

Matthew 12:30 (Mark 9:40) (Luke 11:23) NRSV

For he that is not against us is on our part.

Mark 9:40 (Luke 9:50) KJV

ALCOHOL, ALCOHOLISM (*see* ADDICTIONS, LIBERATION, PURIFICATION, WINE)

ALERTNESS (*also* VIGILANCE)

Watch and pray, lest you enter into temptation. The spirit indeed is willing, but the flesh is weak.

Matthew 26:41 (Mark 14:38) (Luke 22:46) NKJV

Therefore, be on the alert—for you do not know when the master of the house is coming, whether in the evening, at midnight, at cockcrowing, or in the morning—lest he come suddenly and find you asleep. And what I say to you I say to all, "Be on the alert!"   *Mark 13:35–37 (Matthew 24:42) NASB*

Be on guard that your hearts may not be weighted down with dissipation and drunkenness and the worries of life, and that day come on you suddenly like a trap; for it will come upon all those who dwell on the face of all the earth. But keep on the alert at all times, praying in order that you may have strength to escape all these things that are about to take place, and to stand before the Son of Man.

Luke 21:34–36 NASB

ALTRUISM (*also* SERVICE)

And whoever shall force you to go one mile, go with him two. Give to him who asks of you, and do not turn away from him who wants to borrow from you.

Matthew 5:41–42 (Luke 6:30) NASB

You have heard that it was said, "Love your neighbor and hate your enemies." But I tell you, love your enemies. Pray for those who hurt you. If you do this, then you will be true sons of your Father in heaven. Your Father causes the sun to rise on good people and on bad people. Your Father sends rain to those who do good and to those who do wrong.   *Matthew 5:43–45 (Luke 6:27–28) NCV*

Therefore all things whatsoever ye would that men should do to you, do ye even so to them: for this is the law and the prophets.   *Matthew 7:12 (Luke 6:31) KJV*

But it shall not be so among you: but whosoever will be great among you, let him be your minister; And whosoever will be chief among you, let him be your servant: Even as the Son of man came not to be ministered unto, but to minister, and to give his life a ransom for many.

Matthew 20:26–28 (Mark 10:43–45) (Luke 22:26) KJV

If any anyone wants to be first, he shall be last of all, and servant of all. *Mark 9:35 (Matthew 23:11) (Mark 10:44) NASB*

AMBITION (*also* TITLES, WORLDLINESS)

Satan, get away from me! You're in my way because you think like everyone else and not like God.

Matthew 16:23 (Mark 8:33) (Luke 4:8) CEV

If any man will come after me, let him deny himself, and take up his cross, and follow me. For whosoever will save his life shall lose it: and whosoever will lose his life for my sake shall find it. For what is a man profited, if he shall gain the whole world, and lose his own soul? or what shall a man give in exchange for his own soul? For the Son of man shall come in the glory of his Father with his angels; and then he shall reward every man according to his works.

Matthew 16:24–27 (Mark 8:34–38) (Luke 9:23–26) KJV

But so shall it not be among you: but whosoever will be great among you, shall be your minister: and whosoever of you will be the chiefest, shall be servant of all. For even the Son of man came not to be ministered unto, but to minister, and to give his life a ransom for many.

Mark 10:43–45 (Matthew 20:26–28) (Matthew 23:11) KJV

If anyone wants to be first, he shall be last of all, and servant of all. *Mark 9:35 (Matthew 20:27) (Mark 10:44) NASB*

Do not work for the food that perishes, but for the food that endures for eternal life, which the Son of Man will give you. For it is on him that God the Father has set his seal.

John 6:27 NRSV

ANARCHY (*also* GOVERNMENT)

Satan will not force his own demons out of people. A kingdom that fights against itself cannot continue. And a family that is divided cannot continue. And if Satan is against himself and fights against his own people, then he cannot continue. And that is the end of Satan.

Mark 3:23–26 (Matthew 12:25–26) (Luke 11:17–18) NCV

Now the brother shall betray the brother to death, and the father the son; and children shall rise up against their parents, and shall cause them to be put to death.

Mark 13:12 (Matthew 24:21) (Luke 12:16) KJV

ANGELS

The Son of man shall send forth his angels, and they shall gather out of his kingdom all things that offend, and them which do iniquity.

Matthew 13:41 KJV

Don't be cruel to any of these little ones! I promise you that their angels are always with my Father in heaven.

Matthew 18:10–11 (Luke 15:3–7) CEV

And he shall send his angels with a great sound of a trumpet, and they shall gather together his elect from the four winds, from one end of heaven to the other.

Matthew 24:31 (Mark 13:27) KJV

I tell you this: everyone who acknowledges me before men, the Son of Man will acknowledge before the angels of God; but he who disowns me before men will be disowned before the angels of God.

Luke 12:8–9 (Matthew 10:32–33) NEB

The people in this world get married. But in the future world no one who is worthy to rise from death will either marry or die. They will be like angels and will be God's children, because they have been raised to life.

Luke 20:34–36 (Matthew 22:30) (Mark 12:25) CEV

Very truly, I tell you, you will see heaven opened and the angels of God ascending and descending upon the Son of Man.

John 1:51 NRSV

ANGER (also FEAR, GUILT, JUDGMENT)

But I say to you that if you are angry with a brother or sister, you will be liable to judgment; . . . and if you say, "You fool," you will be liable to the hell of fire.

Matthew 5:22 NRSV

Judge not, that you be not judged. For with what judgment you judge, you will be judged; and with the measure you use, it will be measured back to you.

Matthew 7:1–2 (Luke 6:37) NKJV

If any of you have never sinned, then go ahead and throw the first stone at her! *John 8:7 CEV*

ANXIETY (also STRESS, WORLDLINESS, WORRY)

Therefore I say to you, do not worry about your life, what you will eat or what you will drink; nor about your body, what you will put on. Is not life more than food and the body more than clothing? Look at the birds of the air, for they neither sow nor reap nor gather into barns; yet their heavenly Father feeds them. Are you not of more value than they? Which of you by worrying can add one cubit to his stature? *Matthew 6:25–27 (Luke 12:22–25) NKJV*

But seek ye first the kingdom of God, and his righteousness; and all these things shall be added unto you. Take therefore no thought for the morrow: for the morrow shall take thought for the things of itself. Sufficient unto the day is the evil thereof. *Matthew 6:33–34 (Luke 12:29–31) KJV*

Martha, Martha, you are worried and bothered about so many things; but only a few things are necessary, really only one, for Mary has chosen the good part, which shall not be taken away from her. *Luke 10:41–42 NASB*

Let not your heart be troubled; you believe in God, believe also in Me. In My Father's house are many mansions; if it were not so, I would have told you. I go to prepare a place for you *John 14:1–2 NKJV*

I leave you peace. My peace I give you. I do not give it to you as the world does. So don't let your hearts be troubled. Don't be afraid.   *John 14:27 NCV*

APARTHEID (see BIGOTRY, RACE RELATIONS)

APATHY (also COMMITMENT)

Ye are the salt of the earth: but if the salt have lost his savour, wherewith shall it be salted? it is thenceforth good for nothing, but to be cast out, and to be trodden under foot of men.   *Matthew 5:13 (Luke 14:34–35) KJV*

But to what shall I compare this generation? It is like children sitting in the market places, who call out to the other children, and say, We played the flute for you, and you did not dance; we sang a dirge, and you did not mourn.
                                          Matthew 11:16–17 (Luke 7:31–32) NASB

Whoever is not with me is against me, and whoever does not gather with me scatters.
                                Matthew 12:30 (Mark 9:40) (Luke 11:23) NRSV

And because lawlessness will abound, the love of many will grow cold. But he who endures to the end shall be saved.   *Matthew 24:12–13 NKJV*

Why do you keep on saying that I am your Lord, when you refuse to do what I say?   *Luke 6:46 (Matthew 7:21) CEV*

No one, after putting his hand to the plough and looking back, is fit for the kingdom of God.   *Luke 9:62 NASB*

APOCALYPSE (see END TIMES, FINAL JUDGMENT)

APPEARANCE (also MATERIALISM, RELIGOSITY)

When you do good deeds, don't try to show off. If you do, you won't get a reward from your Father in heaven. When you give to the poor, don't blow a loud horn. That's what showoffs do in the meeting places and on the street corners, because they are always looking for praise. I promise you that they already have their reward. When you give to the poor, don't let anyone know about it. Then your gift will be given in secret. Your Father knows what is done in secret, and he will reward you.   *Matthew 6:1–4 CEV*

And whenever you fast, do not put on a gloomy face as the hypocrites do, for they neglect their appearance in order to be seen fasting by men. Truly I say to you, they have their reward in full.   *Matthew 6:16 NASB*

And why take ye thought for raiment? Consider the lilies of the field, how they grow; they toil not, neither do they spin: And yet I say unto you, That even Solomon in all his glory was not arrayed like one of these. Wherefore, if God so clothe the grass of the field, which today is, and tomorrow is cast into the oven, shall he not much more clothe you, O ye of little faith?

Matthew 6:28–30 (Luke 12:27–28) KJV

Woe to you, scribes and Pharisees, hypocrites! For you are like whitewashed tombs which indeed appear beautiful outwardly, but inside are full of dead men's bones and all uncleanness. Even so you also outwardly appear righteous to men, but inside you are full of hypocrisy and lawlessness.   *Matthew 23:27–28 (Luke 11:44) NKJV*

You make yourselves look good in front of people. But God knows what is really in your hearts. The things that are important to people are worth nothing to God.

Luke 16:15 NCV

If a man receives circumcision on the Sabbath that the Law of Moses may not be broken, are you angry with Me because I made an entire man well on the Sabbath? Do not judge according to appearance, but judge with righteous judgment.   *John 7:23–24 NASB*

ARROGANCE (*also* PRIDE)

You disobey God's commands in order to obey what humans have taught. You are good at rejecting God's commands so that you can follow your own teachings!

Mark 7:8–9 (Matthew 15:3–6) CEV

But many who are first will be last, and the last will be first.

Mark 10:31 (Matthew 19:30) (Matthew 20:16) (Luke 13:30) NRSV

You Pharisees are in for trouble! You love the front seats in the meeting places, and you like to be greeted with honor in the market. But you are in for trouble! You are like unmarked graves that people walk on without even knowing it.

Luke 11:43–44 (Matthew 23:2, 6–7, 27) (Mark 12:38–39) CEV

For everyone who exalts himself shall be humbled, and he who humbles himself shall be exalted.

Luke 14:11 (Matthew 23:12) (Luke 18:14) NASB

ART (see CREATIVITY)

ASCETICISM (also MYSTICISM, SELF-TRANSCENDENCE)

The thing you should want most is God's kingdom and doing what God wants. Then all these other things you need will be given to you. So don't worry about tomorrow. Each day has enough trouble of its own. Tomorrow will have its own worries. *Matthew 6:33–34 (Luke 12:31)* NCV

If any man will come after me, let him deny himself, and take up his cross, and follow me. For whosoever will save his life shall lose it: and whosoever will lose his life for my sake shall find it.

Matthew 16:24–26 (Mark 8:34–35) (Luke 9:23–24) KJV

ASSERTIVENESS

You are the light of the world. A city set on an hill cannot be hidden. Nor do men light a lamp, and put it under the peck-measure, but on the lampstand; and it gives light to all who are in the house. Let your light shine before men in such a way that they may see your good works, and glorify your Father who is in heaven.

Matthew 5:14–16 (Mark 4:21) (Luke 8:16) (Luke 11:33) NASB

Suppose one of you goes to a friend in the middle of the night and says, "Let me borrow three loaves of bread. A friend of mine has dropped in, and I don't have a thing for him to eat." And suppose your friend answers, "Don't bother me! The door is bolted, and my children and I are in bed. I cannot get up to give you something." He may not get up and give you the bread, just because you are his friend. But he will get up and give you as much as you need, simply because you are not ashamed to keep on asking. So I tell you to ask and you will receive, search and you will find, knock and the door will be opened for you. Everyone who asks will receive, everyone who searches will find, and the door will be opened for everyone who knocks.

Luke 11:5–10 CEV

ASSURANCE (*also* ENCOURAGEMENT)

And remember, I am with you always, to the end of the age. *Matthew 28:20 NRSV*

I tell you the truth. The things you don't allow on earth will be the things God does not allow. The things you allow on earth will be the things that God allows. Also, I tell you that if two of you on earth agree about something, then you can pray for it. And the thing you ask for will be done for you by my Father in heaven. This is true because if two or three people come together in my name, I am there with them. *Matthew 18:18–20 NCV*

The Spirit shows what is true and will come and guide you into the full truth. The Spirit does not speak on his own. He will tell you only what he has heard from me, and he will let you know what is going to happen. *John 16:13 CEV*

ATHEISM (*see* FAITH, UNBELIEF)

ATONEMENT (*also* COMMUNION)

For even the Son of Man did not come to be served, but to serve, and to give His life a ransom for many.

Mark 10:45 (Luke 22:27) NKJV

ATTACHMENT (*also* LOSS, POSSESSIONS)

Give to him who asks of you, and do not turn away from him who wants to borrow from you.

Matthew 5:42 (Luke 6:30) NASB

Whoever loves father or mother more than me is not worthy of me; and whoever loves son or daughter more than me is not worthy of me; and whoever does not take up the cross and follow me is not worthy of me. Those who

find their life will lose it, and those who lose their life for
my sake will find it.

Matthew 10:37–39 (Luke 14:26–27, 17:33) NRSV

"Then I'll say to myself, 'You have stored up enough good
things to last for years to come. Live it up! Eat, drink, and
enjoy yourself.' " But God said to him, "You fool! Tonight
you will die. Then who will get what you have stored up?"
This is what happens to people who store up everything
for themselves, but are poor in the sight of God.

Luke 12:19–21 CEV

There is one thing you still need to do. Go and sell
everything you own! Give the money to the poor, and you
will have riches in heaven. Then come and be my follower.

Luke 18:22 (Matthew 19:21) (Mark 10:21) CEV

So therefore, none of you can become my disciple if you do
not give up all your possessions.   *Luke 14:33 NRSV*

AUTHENTICITY (*also* SPIRITUALITY)

Beware of false prophets, who come to you in sheep's
clothing, but inwardly they are ravenous wolves. You will
know them by their fruits. Do men gather grapes from
thornbushes or figs of thistles? Even so, every good tree
bears good fruit, but a bad tree bears bad fruit.

Matthew 7:15–17 NKJV

Not every one that saith to me, Lord, Lord, shall enter into
the kingdom of heaven; but he that doeth the will of my
Father which is in heaven.   *Matthew 7:21 (Luke 6:46) KJV*

Believest thou not that I am in the Father, and the Father in
me? the words that I speak unto you I speak not of myself:
but the Father that dwelleth in me, he doeth the works.
Believe me that I am in the Father, and the Father in me: or
else believe me for the very works' sake.

John 14:10–11 (John 10:37–38) KJV

AUTHORITY   (*also* POWER)

You know that the rulers of the Gentiles lord it over them,
and their great men exercise authority over them. It is not

so among you: but whoever wishes to become great among you shall be your servant, and whoever wishes to be first among you shall be your slave;

Matthew 20:25–27 (Mark 10:42–44) (Luke 22:25–26) NASB

I also will ask you one thing, which if you tell Me, I likewise will tell you by what authority I do these things: The baptism of John—where was it from? From heaven or from men?

Neither will I tell you by what authority I do these things.

Matthew 21:24–25, 27 (Mark 11:29–33) (Luke 20:3–8) NKJV

All authority in heaven and on earth has been given to me. Go therefore and make disciples of all the nations, baptizing them in the name of the Father and of the Son and of the Holy Spirit, and teaching them to obey everything that I have commanded you. And remember, I am with you always, to the end of the age.

Matthew 28:18–20 NRSV

For the Son of man is as a man taking a far journey, who left his house, and gave authority to his servants, and to every man his work, and commanded the porter to watch.

Mark 13:34 KJV

And he said unto him, Well, thou good servant: because thou hast been faithful in a very little, have thou authority over ten cities. *Luke 19:17 (Matthew 25:21) KJV*

For just as the Father has life in himself, so he has granted the Son also to have life in himself; and he has given him authority to execute judgment, because he is the Son of Man. *John 5:26–27 NRSV*

BAPTISM (*also* REBIRTH)

You do not know what you ask. Are you able to drink the cup that I am about to drink, and be baptized with the baptism that I am baptized with?

You will indeed drink My cup, and be baptized with the baptism that I am baptized with; but to sit on My right hand

and on My left is not Mine to give, but it is for those for whom it is prepared by My Father.

Matthew 20:22, 23 (Mark 10:38, 39–40) NKJV

I have just one question to ask you. If you answer it, I will tell you where I got the right to do these things. Who gave John the right to baptize? Was it God in heaven or merely some human being?

Then I won't tell you who gave me the right to do what I do.   *Matthew 21:24–25, 27 (Mark 11:29–33) (Luke 20:3–8) CEV*

Go therefore and make disciples of all the nations, baptizing them in the name of the Father and of the Son and of the Holy Spirit, teaching them to observe all things that I have commanded you; and lo, I am with you always, even to the end of the age.   *Matthew 28:19–20 NKJV*

Go into all the world and proclaim the good news to the whole creation. The one who believes and is baptized will be saved; but the one who does not believe will be condemned.   *Mark 16:15–16 NRSV*

I came to bring fire to the earth, and how I wish it were already kindled! I have a baptism with which to be baptized, and what stress I am under until it is completed!

Luke 12:49–50 NRSV

Truly, truly, I say to you, unless one is born of water and the Spirit, he cannot enter into the kingdom of God. That which is born of the flesh is flesh; and that which is born of the Spirit is spirit. Do not marvel that I said to you, You must be born again.   *John 3:5–7 NASB*

BEAUTY (*see* APPEARANCE)

BELIEF (*also* FAITH)

Go your way; let it be done to you as you have believed.

Matthew 8:13 NASB

Do you believe that I have the power to do what you want?' 'Yes, sir', they said. Then he touched their eyes, and said, 'As you have believed, so let it be'.   *Matthew 9:28, 29 NEB*

If You can believe, all things are possible to him who believes.   *Mark 9:23 NKJV*

Whoever believes in me believes not in me but in him who sent me. And whoever sees me sees him who sent me. I have come as light into the world, so that everyone who believes in me should not remain in the darkness.

John 12:44–46 NRSV

Let not your heart be troubled: you believe in God, believe also in Me.   *John 14:1 NKJV*

Believe me that I am in the Father and the Father is in me; but if you do not, then believe me because of the works themselves. Very truly, I tell you, the one who believes in me will also do the works that I do and, in fact, will do greater works than these, because I am going to the Father.

John 14:11–12 NRSV

Thomas, because thou hast seen me, thou hast believed: blessed are they that have not seen, and yet have believed.

John 20:29 KJV

BEREAVEMENT (*see* GRIEF)

BETRAYAL (*also* DISLOYALTY)

The Son of Man is to go, just as it is written of Him; but woe to that man by whom the Son of Man is betrayed! It would have been good for that man if he had not been born.

Matthew 26:24 (Mark 14:21) (Luke 22:22) NASB

Now the brother shall betray the brother to death, and the father the son; and children shall rise up against their parents, and shall cause them to be put to death.

Mark 13:12 (Matthew 24:10) (Luke 21:16) KJV

Are you still sleeping and taking your rest? Enough! The hour has come; the Son of Man is betrayed into the hands of sinners. Get up, let us be going. See, my betrayer is at hand.   *Mark 14:41–42 (Matthew 26:45–46) NRSV*

Judas, are you betraying the Son of Man with a kiss?

Luke 22:48 NASB

BIBLE (see HEBREW SCRIPTURES, WORD)

BIGOTRY (also DISCRIMINATION)

The most important one says: "People of Israel, you have only one Lord and God. You must love him with all your heart, soul, mind, and strength." The second most important commandment says: "Love others as much as you love yourself." No other commandment is more important than these.   *Mark 12:29–31 (Matthew 22:37–40)* CEV

I am giving you these commands so that you may love one another.

John 15:17 NRSV

BIRTH CONTROL (see CELIBACY, SEX)

BLASPHEMY (also OATHS)

Therefore I say to you, every sin and blasphemy will be forgiven men, but the blasphemy against the Spirit will not be forgiven men. Anyone who speaks a word against the Son of Man, it will be forgiven him; but whoever speaks against the Holy Spirit, it will not be forgiven him, either in this age or in the age to come.

Matthew 12:31–32 (Mark 3:28–29) (Luke 12:10) NKJV

Are you still lacking in understanding also? Do you not understand that everything that goes into the mouth passes into the stomach, and is eliminated? But the things that proceed out of the mouth come from the heart, and those defile the man.   *Matthew 15:16–18 (Mark 7:15)* NASB

Is it not written in your law, "I said, you are gods"? If those to whom the word of God came were called "gods"—and the scripture cannot be annulled—can you say that the one whom the Father has sanctified and sent into the world is blaspheming because I said, "I am God's Son"?

John 10:34–36 NRSV

BLESSINGS (also GRACE, REWARD)

God blesses those people who depend only on him,
They belong to the kingdom of heaven!
God blesses those people who grieve.

They will find comfort!
God blesses those people who are humble.
The earth will belong to them!
God blesses those people who want to obey him more than
   to eat or drink.
They will be given what they want!
God blesses those people who are merciful.
They will be treated with mercy!
God blesses those people whose hearts are pure.
They will see him!
God blesses those people who make peace.
They will be called his children!
God blesses those people who are treated badly for doing
   right.
They belong to the kingdom of heaven.
God will bless you when people insult you, mistreat you,
   and tell all kinds of evil lies about you because of me.

Matthew 5:3–11 CEV

Then the King will say to those on His right hand, "Come,
you blessed of My Father, inherit the kingdom prepared
for you from the foundation of the world: for I was hungry
and you gave Me food; I was thirsty, and you gave Me
drink; I was a stranger and you took Me in; I was naked,
and you clothed Me; I was sick and you visited Me; I was
in prison and you came to Me."   *Matthew 25:34–36 NKJV*

You believe because you see me. Those who believe
without seeing me will be truly happy.   *John 20:29 NCV*

BLINDNESS—SPIRITUAL (*also* VISIONS)

The eye is the lamp of the body. So, if your eye is healthy,
your whole body will be full of light; but if your eye is
unhealthy, your whole body will be full of darkness. If then
the light in you is darkness, how great is the darkness!

Matthew 6:22–23 (Luke 11:34–36) NRSV

Let them alone; they are blind guides of the blind. And if a
blind man guides a blind man, both will fall into a pit.

Matthew 15:14 (Luke 6:39) NASB

You give God a tenth of the spices from your garden, such as mint, dill, and cumin. Yet you neglect the more important matters of the Law, such as justice, mercy, and faithfulness. These are the important things you should have done, though you should not have left the others undone either. You blind leaders! You strain out a small fly but swallow a camel.   *Matthew 23:23–24 (Luke 11:42)* CEV

The Lord's Spirit has come to me,
  because he has chosen me
  to tell the good news to the poor.
The Lord has sent me
  to announce freedom for prisoners,
  to give sight to the blind,
  to free everyone who suffers   *Luke 4:18* CEV

I came into this world so that the world could be judged. I came so that the blind could see and so that those who see will become blind.

If you were really blind, you would not be guilty of sin. But now that you say you can see, your guilt remains.

      John 9:39, 41 NCV

The light will be with you for only a little longer. Walk in the light while you can. Then you won't be caught walking blindly in the dark. Have faith in the light while it is with you, and you will be children of the light.

      John 12:35–36 CEV

BOASTING (*also* EGO, PRIDE)

It was this man, I tell you, and not the other, who went home acquitted of his sins. For everyone who exalts himself will be humbled; and whoever humbles himself will be exalted.   *Luke 18:12–14 (Matthew 23:12)* NEB

BODY (*also* PURIFICATION, WORLDLINESS)

Your eyes are like a window for your body. When they are good, you have all the light you need. But when your eyes are bad, everything is dark. If the light inside you is dark, you surely are in the dark.

      Matthew 6:22–23 (Luke 11:34–36) CEV

Do not fear those who kill the body but cannot kill the soul; rather fear him who can destroy both soul and body in hell.

Matthew 10:28 (Luke 12:4–5) NRSV

Keep watching and praying, that you may not enter into temptation; the spirit is willing, but the flesh is weak.

Matthew 26:41 (Mark 14:38) (Luke 22:46) NASB

If then your whole body is full of light, having no part dark, the whole body will be full of light, as when the bright shining of a lamp gives you light. *Luke 11:36 NKJV*

Destroy this temple and in three days I will build it again!

John 2:19 CEV

It is the Spirit who gives life; the flesh profits nothing; the words I have spoken to you are spirit and are life.

John 6:63 NASB

BORN AGAIN (*see* REBIRTH)
BORROWING (*also* MONEY)

Give to him who asks of you, and do not turn away from him who wants to borrow from you.

Matthew 5:42 (Luke 6:30) NASB

And if you lend to those from whom you hope to receive back, what credit is that to you? For even sinners lend to sinners to receive as much back. But love your enemies, do good, and lend, hoping for nothing in return; and your reward will be great, and you will be sons of the Most High. For He is kind to the unthankful and evil.

Luke 6:34–35 NKJV

BREAD (*also* COMMUNION, HUNGER)

It is written, "Man shall not live by bread alone, but by every word that proceeds from the mouth of God."

Matthew 4:4 (Luke 4:4) NKJV

Give us day by day our daily bread.

Luke 11:3 (Matthew 6:11) NKJV

Most assuredly, I say to you, Moses did not give you the bread from heaven, but My Father gives you the true bread from heaven. For the bread of God is He who comes down from heaven and gives life to the world.   *John 6:32-33 NKJV*

BROTHERHOOD (*also* LOVE, ONENESS)

Who is my mother? Who are my brothers? . . . See! These are my mother and my brothers. My true brothers and sisters and mother are those who do the things that my Father in heaven wants.

Matthew 12:48–50 (Mark 3:33–35) (Luke 8:21) NCV

BUDGET (*also* BUSINESS)

For which one of you, when he wants to build a tower, does not first sit down and calculate the cost, to see if he has enough to complete it? Otherwise, when he has laid a foundation, and is not able to finish, all who observe it begin to ridicule him, saying, "This man began to build and was not able to finish."   *Luke 14:28–30 NASB*

BUREAUCRACY (*also* GOVERNMENT)

You guide the people, but you are blind! You are like a person who picks a fly out of his drink and then swallows a camel!   *Matthew 23:24 (Luke 11:42) NCV*

Woe also to you lawyers! For you load people with burdens hard to bear, and you yourselves do not lift a finger to ease them.   *Luke 11:46 (Matthew 23:4) NRSV*

BUSINESS (*also* ECONOMICS, LABOR)

Do not lay up for yourselves treasures upon earth, where moth and rust destroy, and where thieves break in and steal. But lay up for yourselves treasures in heaven, where neither moth nor rust destroys, and where thieves do not break in or steal; for where your treasure is, there will your heart be also.   *Matthew 6:19–21 (Luke 12:33–34) NASB*

No one can serve two masters; for either he will hate the one and love the other, or else he will be loyal to the one and despise the other. You cannot serve God and mammon.   *Matthew 6:24 (Luke 16:13) NKJV*

Therefore I say to you, do not worry about your life, what you will eat or what you will drink; nor about your body, what you will put on. Is not life more than food and the body more than clothing? Look at the birds of the air, for they neither sow nor reap nor gather into barns; yet their heavenly Father feeds them. Are you not of more value than they? Which of you by worrying can add one cubit to his stature?   *Matthew 6:25–27 (Luke 12:22–25) NKJV*

What will you gain, if you own the whole world but destroy yourself? What could you give to get back your soul?   *Mark 8:36–37 (Matthew 16:26) (Luke 9:25) CEV*

A rich man's farm produced a big crop, and he said to himself, "What can I do? I don't have a place large enough to store everything." Later, he said, "Now I know what I'll do. I'll tear down my barns and build bigger ones, where I can store all my grain and other goods. Then I'll say to myself. 'You have stored up enough good things to last for years to come. Live it up! Eat, drink, and enjoy yourself.'" But God said to him, "You fool! Tonight you will die. Then who will get what you have stored up?" This is what happens to people who store up everything for themselves, but are poor in the sight of God.   *Luke 12:16–21 CEV*

There was a rich man who had a manager, and charges were brought to him that this man was squandering his property. So he summoned him and said to him, "What is this that I hear about you? Give me an accounting of your management, because you cannot be my manager any longer." Then the manager said to himself, "What will I do, now that my master is taking the position away from me? I am not strong enough to dig, and I am ashamed to beg. I have decided what to do so that, when I am dismissed as manager, people may welcome me into their homes. So, summoning his master's debtors one by one, he asked the first, "How much do you owe my master?" He answered, "A hundred jugs of olive oil." He said to him, "Take your bill, sit down quickly, and make it fifty." Then he asked another, "And how much do you owe?" He replied, "A hundred containers of wheat." He said to him, "Take your bill and make it eighty." And his master commended the dishonest manager because he had acted shrewdly; for the children of this age are more shrewd in dealing with their own generation than are the children of light. And I tell you, make friends for yourselves by means of dishonest wealth so that when it is gone, they may welcome you into the eternal homes. Whoever is faithful in a very little is faithful also in much; and whoever is dishonest in a very little is dishonest also in much.   *Luke 16:1–10 NRSV*

Take these things away! Do not make My Father's house a house of merchandise!   *John 2:16 NKJV*

CALLING (*also* MYSTICISM)

For many are called, but few are chosen.

Matthew 22:14 NRSV

One thing you lack: Go your way, sell whatever you have and give to the poor, and you will have treasure in heaven; and come, take up the cross, and follow Me.

Mark 10:21 (Matthew 19:21) (Luke 12:33) NKJV

Follow Me.   *Luke 5:27 (Matthew 9:9) (Mark 2:14) NASB*

If anyone wishes to come after Me, let him deny himself, and take up his cross daily, and follow Me. For whoever wishes to save his life shall lose it, but whoever loses his life for My sake, he is the one who will save it.

Luke 9:23–24 (Matthew 16:24–25) (Mark 8:34–35) NASB

A certain man made a great supper, and bade many: And sent his servant at supper time to say to them that were bidden, Come; for all things are now ready. And they all with one consent began to make excuse. The first said unto him, I have bought a piece of ground, and I must needs go and see it: I pray thee have me excused. And another said, I have bought five yoke of oxen, and I go to prove them: I pray thee have me excused. And another said, I have married a wife, and therefore I cannot come. So that servant came, and shewed his lord these things. Then the master of the house being angry said to his servant, Go out quickly into the streets and lanes of the city, and bring in hither the poor, and the maimed, and the halt, and the blind. And the servant said, Lord, it is done as thou hast commanded, and yet there is room. And the lord said unto the servant, Go out into the highways and hedges, and compel them to come in, that my house may be filled.

Luke 14:16–23 (Matthew 22:2–9) KJV

No one can come to me unless drawn by the Father who sent me; and I will raise that person up on the last day. It is written in the prophets, "And they shall all be taught by God." Everyone who has heard and learned from the Father comes to me. *John 6:44–45 NRSV*

You did not choose me; I chose you. And I gave you this work, to go and produce fruit. I want you to produce fruit that will last. Then the Father will give you anything you ask for in my name. *John 15:16 NCV*

CALLOUSNESS (also WORLDLINESS)

And many false prophets will arise, and will mislead many. And because lawlessness is increased, most people's love will grow cold. *Matthew 24:11–12 NASB*

Then he will say to those on his left hand, "You that are accursed, depart from me into the eternal fire prepared for the devil and his angels; for I was hungry and you gave me no food, I was thirsty and you gave me nothing to drink, I was a stranger and you did not welcome me, naked and you did not give me clothing, sick and in prison and you did not visit me." *Matthew 25:41–43 NRSV*

CAPITALISM (see ECONOMICS)

CAPITAL PUNISHMENT (also VIOLENCE)

Why callest thou me good? there is none good but one, that is, God: but if thou wilt enter into life, keep the commandments.

Thou shalt do no murder, Thou shalt not commit adultery, Thou shalt not steal, Thou shalt not bear false witness, Honour thy father and thy mother: and, Thou shalt love thy neighbor as thyself.

Matthew 19:17–19 (Mark 10:18–19) (Luke 18:19–20) KJV

CAREER (*also* CALLING)

You cannot be the slave of two masters! You will like one more than the other or be more loyal to one than the other. You cannot serve both God and money.

Matthew 6:24 (Luke 16:13) CEV

It is not so among you, but whoever wishes to become great among you shall be your servant, and whoever wishes to be first among you shall be your slave; just as the Son of Man did not come to be served, but to serve, and to give His life a ransom for many.

Matthew 20:26–28 (Mark 10:43–45) (Luke 22:27) NASB

Earthly food spoils and ruins. So don't work to get that kind of food. But work to get the food that stays good always and gives you eternal life. The Son of Man will give you that food. God the Father has shown that he is with the Son of Man.

John 6:27 NCV

CARELESSNESS (*also* RESPONSIBILITY)

God will be as hard on you as you are on others! He will treat you exactly as you treat them.

Matthew 7:2 (Luke 6:37) CEV

But I say unto you, That every idle word that men shall speak, they shall give account thereof in the day of judgment. For by thy words thou shalt be justified, and by thy words thou shalt be condemned. *Matthew 12:36–37* KJV

Then the king will answer, "I tell you the truth. Anything you refused to do for any of my people here, you refused to do for me."

Matthew 25:45 NCV

CELEBRATION (*also* ABSTINENCE, JOY)

When you give a dinner or a supper, do not ask your friends, your brothers, your relatives, nor rich neighbors, lest they also invite you back, and you be repaid. But when you give a feast, invite the poor, the maimed, the lame, the blind. And you will be blessed, because they cannot repay you; for you shall be repaid at the resurrection of the just.

Luke 14:12–14 NKJV

And the son said unto him, Father, I have sinned against heaven, and in thy sight, and am no more worthy to be called thy son. But the father said to his servants, Bring forth the best robe, and put it on him; and put a ring on his hand, and shoes on his feet: And bring hither the fatted calf, and kill it; and let us eat and be merry: For this my son was dead, and is alive again; he was lost, and is found. And they began to be merry.   *Luke 15:21–24 KJV*

CELIBACY (*also* SEX)

Only those who have been given the gift of staying single can accept this teaching. Some people are unable to marry because of birth defects or because of what someone has done to their bodies. Others stay single for the sake of the kingdom of heaven. Anyone who can accept this teaching should do so.   *Matthew 19:11–12 CEV*

CEREMONY (*also* BAPTISM, COMMUNION)

When you pray, don't be like the hypocrites. They love to stand in the synagogues and on the street corners and pray loudly. They want people to see them pray. I tell you the truth. They already have their full reward.
                    Matthew 6:5 NCV

Those who are well have no need of a physician, but those who are sick. But go and learn what this means: 'I desire mercy and not sacrifice.' For I did not come to call the righteous, but sinners, to repentance.
                    Matthew 9:12–13 (Mark 2:17) (Luke 5:31–32) NKJV

Now you Pharisees clean the outside of the cup and of the dish, but inside you are full of greed and wickedness. You fools! Did not the one who made the outside make the inside also? So give for alms those things that are within; and see, everything will be clean for you.
                    Luke 11:39–41 (Matthew 23:25–26) NRSV

CHANGE (*also* CONVERSION, SOCIAL CHANGE)

Ask, and it shall be given you; seek, and ye shall find; knock, and it shall be opened unto you. For every one that asketh receiveth; and he that seeketh findeth; and to him that knocketh it shall be opened.

Matthew 7:7–8 (Luke 11:9–10) KJV

No one patches old clothes by sewing on a piece of new cloth. The new piece would shrink and tear a bigger hole. No one pours new wine into old wineskins. The wine would swell and burst the old skins. Then the wine would be lost, and the skins would be ruined. New wine must be put into new wineskins.

Mark 2:21–22 (Matthew 9:16–17) (Luke 5:36–37) CEV

Very truly, I tell you, no one can see the kingdom of God without being born from above.   *John 3:3 NRSV*

I tell you the truth. Unless one is born from water and the Spirit, he cannot enter God's kingdom. A person's body is born from his human parents. But a person's spiritual life is born from the Spirit.   *John 3:5–6 NCV*

CHARACTER (*also* INTEGRITY, VIRTUE)

So then, you will know them by their fruits. Not everyone who says to Me, "Lord, Lord," will enter the kingdom of heaven; but he who does the will of My Father who is in heaven.   *Matthew 7:20–21 (Luk 6:44, 46) NASB*

If then your whole body is full of light, having no part dark, the whole body will be full of light, as when the bright shining of a lamp gives you light.   *Luke 11:36 NKJV*

CHARITY (*also* ALTRUISM, FORGIVENESS, LOVE)

Give to him that asketh thee, and from him that would borrow of thee turn not thou away.   *Matthew 5:42 KJV*

Beware of practicing your piety before others in order to be seen by them; for then you have no reward from your Father in heaven.   *Matthew 6:1 NRSV*

Then the king will say to those on his right, "My father has blessed you! Come and receive the kingdom that was prepared for you before the world was created. When I was hungry, you gave me something to eat, and when I was thirsty, you gave me something to drink. When I was a stranger, you welcomed me, and when I was naked, you gave me clothes to wear. When I was sick, you took care of me, and when I was in jail, you visited me." Then the ones who pleased the Lord will ask, "When did we give you something to eat or drink? When did we welcome you as a stranger or give you clothes to wear or visit you while you were sick or in jail?" The king will answer, "Whenever you did it for any of my people, no matter how unimportant they seemed, you did it for me."

Matthew 25:34–40 CEV

So give for alms those things that are within; and see, everything will be clean for you.　　　　*Luke 11:41 NRSV*

Sell your possessions and give to charity; make yourselves purses which do not wear out, an unfailing treasure in heaven, where no thief comes near, nor moth destroys. For where your treasure is, there will your heart be also.

Luke 12:33–34 (Matthew 19:21) (Mark 10:21) (Luke 18:22) NASB

When you give a dinner or a supper, do not ask your friends, your brothers, your relatives, nor rich neighbors, lest they also invite you back, and you be repaid. But when you give a feast, invite the poor, the maimed, the lame, the blind. And you will be blessed, because they cannot repay you; for you shall be repaid at the resurrection of the just.

Luke 14:12–14 NKJV

There was a certain rich man, which was clothed in purple and fine linen, and fared sumptuously every day: And there was a certain beggar named Lazarus, which was laid at his gate, full of sores. And desiring to be fed with the crumbs which fell from the rich man's table: moreover the dogs came and licked his sores. And it came to pass, that the beggar died, and was carried by the angels into Abraham's bosom: the rich man also died, and was buried; And in hell he lift up his eyes, being in torments, and seeth Abraham afar off, and Lazarus in his bosom. And he cried and said, Father Abraham, have mercy on me, and send Lazarus, that he may dip the tip of his finger in water, and cool my tongue; for I am tormented in this flame. But

Abraham said, Son, remember that thou in thy lifetime
receivedst thy good things, and likewise Lazarus evil
things: but now he is comforted, and thou art tormented.

Luke 16:19–25 KJV

CHILDREN (*also* PARENTS)

Is there anyone among you who, if your child asks for
bread, will give a stone? Or if the child asks for a fish, will
give a snake? If you then, who are evil, know how to give
good gifts to your children, how much more will your
Father in heaven give good things to those who ask him!
In everything do to others as you would have them do to
you; for this is the law and the prophets.

Matthew 7:9–12 (Luke 6:31) NRSV

I promise you this. If you don't change and become like this
child, you will never get into the kingdom of heaven. But
if you are as humble as this child, you are the greatest in
the kingdom of heaven. And when you welcome one of
these children because of me, you welcome me. It will be
terrible for people who cause even one of my little followers
to sin. Those people would be better off thrown into the
deepest part of the ocean with a heavy stone tied around
the neck!   *Matthew 18:3–6 (Mark 10:15) (Luke 18:17) CEV*

Take heed that you do not despise one of these little ones,
for I say to you that in heaven their angels always see the
face of My Father who is in heaven. For the Son of Man has
come to save that which was lost.   *Matthew 18:10–11 NKJV*

If anyone accepts a little child like this in my name, then he
accepts me. And when he accepts me, he accepts the One
who sent me. He who is least among you all—he is the
greatest.   *Luke 9:48 (Matthew 18:5) (Mark 9:37) NCV*

Permit the children to come to Me, and do not hinder them,
for the kingdom of God belongs to such as these. Truly I
say to you, whoever does not receive the kingdom of God
like a child shall not enter it at all.

Luke 18:16–17 (Matthew 19:14) (Mark 10:14) NASB

Humans give life to their children. Yet only God's Spirit can change you into a child of God. Don't be surprised when I say that you must be born from above.

John 3:6–7 CEV

When a woman gives birth to a baby, she has pain, because her time has come. But when her baby is born, she forgets the pain. She forgets because she is so happy that a child has been born into the world. It is the same with you. Now you are sad. But I will see you again and you will be happy. And no one will take away your joy.   *John 16:21-22 NCV*

CHOICE (*also* FREEDOM)

No one can serve two masters; for either he will hate the one and love the other, or he will hold to one and despise the other. You cannot serve God and mammon.

Matthew 6:24 (Luke 16:13) NASB

Go; let it be done for you according to your faith.

Matthew 8:13 NRSV

He who loves father or mother more than Me is not worthy of Me. And he who loves son or daughter more than Me is not worthy of Me. And he who does not take his cross and follow after Me is not worthy of Me. He who finds his life will lose it, and he who loses his life for My sake will find it.   *Matthew 10:37–39 (Luke 14:26–27, 17:33) NKJV*

Not all men can accept this statement, but only those to whom it has been given. For there are eunuchs who were born that way from their mother's womb; and there are eunuchs who were made eunuchs by men; and there are also eunuchs who made themselves eunuchs for the sake of the kingdom of heaven. He who is able to accept this, let him accept it.   *Matthew 19:11–12 NASB*

A man once gave a great banquet and invited a lot of guests. When the banquet was ready, he sent a servant to tell the guests, "Everything is ready! Please come." One guest after another started making excuses. The first one said, "I bought some land, and I've got to look it over. Please excuse me." Another guest said, "I bought five teams of oxen, and

I need to try them out. Please excuse me." Still another guest said, "I have just gotten married, and I can't be there." The servant told his master what happened, and the master became so angry that he said, "Go as fast a you can to every street and alley in town! Bring in everyone who is poor or crippled or blind or lame." When the servant returned, he said, "Master, I've done what you told me, and there is still plenty room for more people." His master told him, "Go out along the back roads and fence rows and make people come in, so that my house will be full."

Luke 14:16–23 (Matthew 22:2–10) CEV

CHRIST (also FALSE PROPHETS, ONENESS, PURPOSE)

All things have been handed over to me by my Father; and no one knows the Son except the Father, and no one knows the Father except the Son and anyone to whom the Son chooses to reveal him. Come to me, all you that are weary and are carrying heavy burdens, and I will give you rest. Take my yoke upon you, and learn from me; for I am gentle and humble in heart, and you will find rest for your souls. For my yoke is easy, and my burden is light.

Matthew 11:27–30 (Luke 10:22) NRSV

I must go to Jerusalem. There the nation's leaders, the chief priests, and the teachers of the Law of Moses will make me suffer terribly. I will be killed, but three days later I will rise to life.   *Matthew 16:21 (Mark 8:31) (Luke 9:22) CEV*

Just as the Son of Man did not come to be served, but to serve,and to give His life a ransom for many.

Matthew 20:28 (Mark 10:45) NKJV

But do not be called Rabbi; for One is your Teacher, and you are all brothers. And do not call anyone on earth your father; for One is your Father, He who is in heaven. And do not be called leaders; for One is your Leader, that is, Christ.   *Matthew 23:8–10 NASB*

Then the King will answer, "I tell you the truth. Anything you did for any of my people here, you also did for me."

Matthew 25:40 NCV

All authority in heaven and on earth has been given to me. Go therefore and make disciples of all the nations, baptizing them in the name of the Father and of the Son and of the Holy Spirit, and teaching them to obey everything that I have commanded you. And remember, I am with you always, to the end of the age.

Matthew 28:18–20 NRSV

Which is easier, to say to the paralytic, "Your sins are forgiven," or to say, "Stand up and take your mat and walk"? But so that you may know that the Son of Man has authority on earth to forgive sins . . . I say to you, stand up, take your mat and go to your home.

Mark 2:9–11 (Matthew 9:4–6) (Luke 5:22–24) NRSV

When you welcome even a child because of me, you welcome me. And when you welcome me, you welcome the one who sent me. Whichever one of you is the most humble is the greatest.

Luke 9:48 (Matthew 18:5) (Mark 9:37) CEV

For the Son of Man has come to seek and to save that which was lost.   *Luke 19:10 NASB*

No one has ascended into heaven except the one who descended from heaven, the Son of Man. And just as Moses lifted up the serpent in the wilderness, so must the Son of Man be lifted up, that whoever believes in him may have eternal life.   *John 3:13–15 NRSV*

I have food to eat that you know nothing about. My food is to do what the One who sent me wants me to do. My food is to finish the work that he gave me to do.

John 4:32, 34 NCV

Very truly, I tell you, the Son can do nothing on his own, but only what he sees the Father doing; for whatever the Father does, the Son does likewise. The Father loves the Son and shows him all that he himself is doing; and he will show him greater works than these, so that you will be astonished. Indeed, just as the Father raises the dead and gives them life, so also the Son gives life to whomever he wishes. The Father judges no one but has given all judgment to the Son, so that all may honor the Son just as they honor the Father. Anyone who does not honor the Son does not honor the Father who sent him. Very truly, I tell you, anyone who hears my word and believes him who sent me has eternal life, and does not come under judgment, but has passed from death to life.

John 5:19–24 NRSV

For just as the Father has life in himself, so he has granted the Son also to have life in himself; and he has given him authority to execute judgment, because he is the Son of Man.

John 5:26–27 NRSV

I am the bread that gives life! No one who comes to me will ever be hungry. No one who has faith in me will ever be thirsty. I have told you already that you have seen me and still do not have faith in me. Everything and everyone that the Father has given me will come to me, and I won't turn any of them away. I didn't come from heaven to do what I want! I came to do what the Father has given me to do.

John 6:35–38 CEV

No one can come to me unless drawn by the Father who sent me; and I will raise that person up on the last day. It is written in the prophets, "And they shall all be taught by God." Everyone who has heard and learned from the Father comes to me.

John 6:44–45 NRSV

My teaching is not Mine, but His who sent me. If any man is willing to do His will, he shall know of the teaching, whether it is of God, or whether I speak from Myself. He who speaks from himself seeks his own glory; but He who is seeking the glory of the one who sent Him, He is true, and there is no unrighteousness in Him.

John 7:16–18 NASB

When ye have lifted up the Son of man, then shall ye know that I am he, and that I do nothing of myself; but as my Father hath taught me, I speak these things. And he that sent me is with me: the Father hath not left me alone; for I do always those things that please him.   *John 8:28–29 KJV*

I do not have a demon; but I honor my Father, and you dishonor me. Yet I do not seek my own glory; there is one who seeks it and he is the judge. Very truly, I tell you, whoever keeps my word will never see death.

John 8:49–51 (John 7:18, 8:54) NRSV

I tell you the truth. Before Abraham was born, I am!

John 8:58 NCV

Do you believe in the Son of God?
You have both seen Him and it is He who is talking with you.   *John 9:35, 37 NKJV*

I am the gate. All who come in through me will be saved. Through me they will come and go and find pasture. A thief comes only to rob, kill, and destroy. I came so that everyone would have life, and have it in its fullest.

John 10:9–10 CEV

Therefore doth my Father love me, because I lay down my life, that I might take it again. No man taketh it from me, but I lay it down of myself. I have power to lay it down, and I have power to take it again. This commandment have I received of my Father.   *John 10:17–18 KJV*

The Father and I are one.   *John 10:30 NCV*

In your Scriptures doesn't God say, "You are gods?" The scriptures cannot be destroyed, and God spoke to those people and called them gods. So why do you accuse me of a terrible sin for saying that I am the Son of God? After all, it is the Father who prepared me for this work. He is also the one who sent me into this world. If I don't do as my Father does, you should believe me. But I do what my Father does, you should believe because of that, even if you don't have faith in me. Then you will know for certain that the Father is one with me, and I am one with the Father.

John 10:34–38 CEV

I have come as a light into the world, so that everyone who believes in me should not remain in the darkness. I do not judge anyone who hears my words and does not keep them, for I came not to judge the world, but to save the world. *John 12:46–47 NRSV*

But everyone who rejects me and my teachings will be judged on the last day by what I have said. I don't speak on my own. I say only what the Father who sent me has told me to say. I know that his commands will bring eternal life. That is why I tell you exactly what the Father has told me. *John 12:48–50 CEV*

Do not let your hearts be troubled. Believe in God, believe also in me. In my Father's house there are many dwelling places. If it were not so, would I have told you that I go to prepare a place for you? And if I go and prepare a place for you, I will come again and will take you to myself, so that where I am, there you may be also. And you know the way to the place where I am going. *John 14:1–4 NRSV*

I am the way, the truth, and the life: no man cometh unto the Father, but by me. If ye had known me, ye should have known my Father also: and from henceforth ye know him, and have seen him. *John 14:6–7 KJV*

Father, the hour is come; glorify thy Son, that thy Son also may glorify thee: As thou hast given him power over all flesh, that he should give eternal life to as many as thou hast given him. And this is life eternal, that they might know thee the only true God, and Jesus Christ, whom thou hast sent. I have glorified thee on the earth: I have finished the work which thou gavest me to do. *John 17:1–4 KJV*

You say rightly that I am a king. For this cause I was born, and for this cause I have come into the world, that I should bear witness to the truth. Everyone who is of the truth hears My voice. *John 18:37 NKJV*

Don't hold me. I have not yet gone up to the Father. But go to my brothers and tell them this: 'I am going back to my Father and your Father. I am going back to my God and your God. *John 20:17 NCV*

CHURCH (*also* INCLUSIVENESS)

Who is my mother and who are my brothers? . . . These are my mother and my brothers! Anyone who obeys my Father in heaven is my brother or sister or mother.

Matthew 12:48–50 (Mark 3:33–35) (Luke 8:21) CEV

Blessed are you, Simon Bar-Jonah, for flesh and blood has not revealed this to you, but My Father who is in heaven. And I also say to you that you are Peter, and on this rock I will build My church, and the gates of Hades shall not prevail against it. *Matthew 16:17–18 NKJV*

And if your brother sins, go and reprove him in private; if he listens to you, you have won your brother. But if he does not listen to you, take one or two more with you, so that by the mouth of two or three witnesses every fact may be confirmed. And if he refuses to listen to them, tell it to the church; and if he refuses to listen even to the church, let him be to you as a Gentile and a tax-gatherer.

Matthew 18:15–18 (Luke 17:3) NASB

I tell you the truth. The things you don't allow on earth will be the things God does not allow. The things you allow on earth will be the things that God allows. Also, I tell you that if two of you on earth agree about something, then you can pray for it. And the thing you ask for will be done for you by my Father in heaven. This is true because if two or three people come together in my name, I am there with them. *Matthew 18:18–20 NCV*

Take these things away! Do not make My Father's house a house of merchandise! *John 2:16 NKJV*

I am the good shepherd. I know my sheep, and they know me. Just as the Father knows me, I know the Father, and I give up my life for my sheep. I have other sheep that are not in this sheep pen. I must bring them together too, when

they hear my voice. Then there will be one flock of sheep
and one shepherd.   *John 10:14–16* CEV

Father, I am not praying just for these followers. I am also
praying for everyone else who will have faith because of
what my followers will say about me. I want all of them to
be one with each other, just as I am one with you and you
are one with me. I also want them to be one with us. Then
the people of this world will believe that you sent me.

John 17:20–21 CEV

CIRCUMSTANCE (*also* TROUBLE)

Love your enemies and pray for your persecutors; only so
can you be children of your heavenly Father, who makes
his sun rise on good and bad alike, and sends the rain on
the honest and the dishonest.

Matthew 5:44–45 (Luke 6:27–28) NEB

So I tell you, don't worry about the food you need to live.
Don't worry about the clothes you need for your body. Life
is more important than food. And the body is more
important than clothes. Look at the birds. They don't plant
or harvest. They don't save food in houses or barns. But
God takes care of them. And you are worth much more
than birds. None of you can add any time to your life by
worrying about it. If you cannot do even the little things,
then why worry about the big things?

Luke 12:22–26 (Matthew 6:25–27) NCV

CIVIL DISOBEDIENCE (*also* SOCIAL RESPONSIB-ILITY)

Blessed are the meek, for they will inherit the earth.
Blessed are the peacemakers, for they will be called
   children of God.
Blessed are those who are persecuted for righteousness'
   sake, for theirs is the kingdom of heaven.

Matthew 5:5, 9–10 NRSV

I am sending you like lambs into a pack of wolves. So be as
wise as snakes and as innocent as doves. Watch out for
people who will take you to court and have you beaten in

their meeting places. Because of me, you will be dragged before rulers and kings to tell them and the Gentiles about your faith. But when someone arrests you, don't worry about what you will say or how you will say it. At that time you will be given the words to say. But you will not really be the one speaking. The Spirit from your Father will tell you what to say.   *Matthew 10:16–20 CEV*

Do not fear those who kill the body but cannot kill the soul; rather fear him who can destroy both soul and body in hell.

Matthew 10:28 (Luke 12:4–5) NRSV

CLARITY (*see* PERCEPTION)

CLEANLINESS (*also* APPEARANCE, HYPOCRISY)

But what comes out of the mouth proceeds from the heart, and this is what defiles. For out of the heart come evil intentions, murder, adultery, fornication, theft, false witness, slander. These are what defile a person, but to eat with unwashed hands does not defile.

Matthew 15:18–20 (Mark 7:21–23) NRSV

How terrible for you, teachers of the law and Pharisees! You are hypocrites! You wash the outside of your cups and dishes. But inside they are full of things that you got by cheating others and pleasing only yourselves. Pharisees, you are blind! First make the inside of the cup clean and good. Then the outside of the cup can be truly clean.

Matthew 23:25-26 (Luke 11:39) NCV

CLOTHING (*also* MATERIALISM)

And why take ye thought for raiment? Consider the lilies of the field, how they grow; they toil not, neither do they spin: And yet I say unto you, That even Solomon in all his glory was not arrayed like one of these. Wherefore, if God so clothe the grass of the field, which to day is, and tomorrow is cast into the oven, shall he not much more clothe you, O ye of little faith?

Matthew 6:28–30 (Luke 12:27–28) KJV

They do all their deeds to be seen by others; for they make their phylacteries broad and their fringes long. They love to have the place of honor at banquets and the best seats in the synagogues, and to be greeted with respect in the marketplaces, and to have people call them rabbi.

Matthew 23:5–7 NRSV

I tell you not to worry about your life! Don't worry about having something to eat or wear. Life is more than food or clothing. *Luke 12:22–23 (Matthew 6:25) CEV*

CODEPENDENCE (*also* LIBERATION)

Always treat others as you would like them to treat you: that is the Law and the prophets.

Matthew 7:12 (Luke 6:31) NEB

Don't think that I came to bring peace to the earth! I came to bring trouble, not peace. I came to turn sons against their fathers, daughters against their mothers, and daughters-in-law against their mothers-in-law. Your worst enemies will be in your own family. If you love your father or mother or even your sons and daughters more than me, you are not fit to be my disciples. And unless you are willing to take up your cross and come with me, you are not fit to be my disciples. If you try to save your life, you will lose it. But if you give it up for me, you will surely find it. *Matthew 10:34–39 (Luke 12:51–53, 14:26–27, 17:33) CEV*

Love the Lord your God with all your heart, soul and mind. This is the first and most important command. And the second command is like the first: "Love your neighbor as you love yourself." All the law and the writings of the prophets depend on these two commands.

Matthew 22:37–40 (Mark 12:29–31) NCV

You can be sure that anyone who gives up home or brothers or sisters or mother or father or children or land for me and for the good news will be rewarded. In this world they will be given a hundred times as many houses and brothers and sisters and mothers and children and pieces of land, though they will also be mistreated. And in the world to come, they will have eternal life. But many who are now first will be last, and many who are now last will be first.

Mark 10:29–31 (Matthew 19:28–30) (Luke 18:29–30) CEV

COERCION (*also* DISCIPLINE)

Since the time John the Baptist came until now, the kingdom of heaven has been going forward in strength. People using force have been trying to take the kingdom. All the prophets and the law of Moses spoke until the time John came. They told about the things that would happen. And if you will believe the things the law and the prophets said, then you will believe that John is Elijah. The law and the prophets said he would come. You people who hear me, listen! *Matthew 11:12–15* NCV

Foreign kings order their people around, and powerful rulers call themselves everyone's friends. But don't be like them. The most important one of you should be like the least important, and your leader should be like a servant.

Luke 22:25–26 (Matthew 20:25–27) (Mark 10:42–44) CEV

COMFORT (*also* PEACE)

Blessed are those who mourn, for they shall be comforted.

Matthew 5:4 NKJV

Come to me, all of you who are tired and have heavy loads. I will give you rest. Accept my work and learn from me. I am gentle and humble in spirit. And you will find rest for your souls. The work that I ask you to accept is easy. The load I give you to carry is not heavy. *Matthew 11:28–30* NCV

But woe to you who are rich, for you are receiving your comfort in full. Woe to you who are well-fed now, for you shall be hungry. Woe to you who laugh now, for you shall mourn and weep. Woe unto you when all men speak well of you, for in the same way their fathers used to treat the false prophets. *Luke 6:24–26* NASB

Let's go to a place where we can be alone and get some rest.

Mark 6:31 CEV

Daughter, be of good comfort: thy faith hath made thee whole; go in peace.

Luke 8:48 (Matthew 9:22) (Mark 5:34, 10:52) (Luke 7:50, 18:42) KJV

I leave you peace. My peace I give you. I do not give it to you as the world does. So don't let your hearts be troubled. Don't be afraid. *John 14:27 NCV*

But when the Comforter is come, whom I will send unto you from the Father, even the Spirit of truth, which proceedeth from the Father, he shall testify of me.

John 15:26 KJV

COMMANDMENTS (*also* HOLY SPIRIT, TRADITION, VALUES)

Therefore, whoever breaks one of the least of these commandments, and teaches others to do the same, will be called least in the kingdom of heaven; but whoever does them and teaches them will be called great in the kingdom of heaven. *Matthew 5:19 NRSV*

Be ye therefore perfect, even as your Father which is in heaven is perfect. *Matthew 5:48 KJV*

Why do ye also transgress the commandment of God by your tradition? For God commanded, saying, Honour thy father and mother: and, He that curseth father or mother, let him die the death. But ye say, Whosoever shall say to his father or his mother, It is a gift, by whatsoever thou mightest be profited me; And honour not his father or his mother, he shall be free. Thus have ye made the commandment of God of none effect by your tradition.

Matthew 15:3–6 KJV

Why callest thou me good? there is none good but one, that is, God: but if thou wilt enter into life, keep the commandments. Thou shalt do no murder, Thou shalt not commit adultery, Thou shalt not steal, Thou shalt not bear false witness, Honour thy father and thy mother: and, Thou shalt love thy neighbor as thyself.

Matthew 19:17–19 (Mark 10:18–19) (Luke 18:19–20) KJV

Love the Lord your God with all your heart, soul, and mind. This is the first and most important commandment. The second most important commandment is like this one. And it is, "Love others as much as you love yourself." All the Law of Moses and the Books of the Prophets are based on these two commandments.

Matthew 22:37–40 (Mark 12:29–31) CEV

The things I taught were not from myself. The Father who sent me told me what to say and what to teach. And I know that eternal life comes from what the Father commands. So whatever I say is what the Father told me to say.

John 12:49–50 NCV

I give you a new commandment, that you love one another. Just as I have loved you, you also should love one another. By this everyone will know that you are my disciples, if you have love for one another.   *John 13:34–35* NRSV

Just as the Father has loved Me, I have also loved you; abide in My love. If you keep My commandments, you will abide in My love; just as I have kept My Father's commandments, and abide in His love. These things I have spoken to you, that My joy may be in you, and that your joy may be made full.   *John 15:9–11* NASB

This is My commandment, that you love one another, as I have loved you. Greater love has no one than this, than to lay down one's life for his friends. You are My friends if you do whatever I command you.   *John 15:12–14* NKJV

I am giving you these commands so that you may love one another.   *John 15:17* NRSV

Simon, son of Jonas, lovest thou me more than these? . . . Feed my lambs.
Simon, son of Jonas, lovest thou me? . . . Feed my sheep.
Simon, son of Jonas, lovest thou me? . . . Feed my sheep.

John 21:15–17 KJV

Follow me.

John 21:19 (Matthew 9:9) (Mark 2:14) (Luke 5:27) (John 1:43) KJV

COMMERCE (*see* BUSINESS)

COMMITMENT (*also* APATHY)

If any of you want to be my followers, you must forget about yourself. You must take up your cross and follow me. If you want to save your life you will destroy it. But if you give up your life for me, you will find it. What will you gain, if you own the whole world but destroy yourself? What would you give to get back your soul?

Matthew 16:24–26 (Mark 8:34–37) (Luke 9:23–25) CEV

I tell you the truth. Everyone who has left his house, wife, brothers, parents, or children for God's kingdom will get much more than he left. He will receive many times more in this life. And after he dies, he will live with God forever.

Luke 18:29–30 (Matthew 19:29) (Mark 10:29–30) NCV

COMMUNION (*also* WORSHIP)

Take, eat; this is My body.
Drink from it, all of you.
For this is My blood of the new covenant, which is shed for many for the remission of sins.

Matthew 26:26–28 (Mark 14:22–24) NKJV

This is my body which is given for you: this do in remembrance of me. . . . This cup is the new testament in my blood, which is shed for you.

Luke 22:19–20 (Matthew 26:26–28) (Mark 14:22–24) KJV

I tell you for certain that you won't live unless you eat the flesh and drink the blood of the Son of Man. But if you do eat my flesh and drink my blood, you will have eternal life, and I will raise you to life on the last day. My flesh is the true food, and my blood is the true drink. If you eat my flesh and drink my blood, you are one with me, and I am one with you.

John 6:53–56 CEV

COMMUNITY (*also* SOCIAL RESPONSIBILITY)

In everything do to others as you would have them do to you; for this is the law and the prophets.

Matthew 7:12 (Luke 6:31) NRSV

Any kingdom divided against itself is laid waste; and any city or house divided against itself shall not stand.

Matthew 12:25 (Mark 3:24)(Luke 16:17) NASB

Who is my mother? Who are my brothers? . . . See! These people are my mother and my brothers. My true brothers and sisters and mother are those who do the things that my Father in heaven wants.

Matthew 12:48–50 (Mark 3:33–35) (Luke 8:21) NCV

Ye know that the princes of the Gentiles exercise dominion over them, and they that are great exercise authority upon them. But it shall not be so among you: but whosoever will be great among you, let him be your minister; And whosoever will be chief among you, let him be your servant.

Matthew 20:25–27 (Mark 10:42–45) (Luke 22:25–27) KJV

You can be sure that anyone who gives up home or brothers or sisters or mother or father or children or land for me and for the good news will be rewarded. In this world they will be given a hundred times as many houses and brothers and sisters and mothers and children and pieces of land, though they will also be mistreated. And in the world to come, they will have eternal life. But many who are now first will be last, and many who are now last will be first.

Mark 10:29–31 (Matthew 19:28–30) (Luke 18:29–30) CEV

Give, and it will be given to you; good measure, pressed down, shaken together, running over, they will pour into your lap. For by your standard of measure it will be measured to you in return.

Luke 6:38 (Matthew 7:2) (Mark 4:24) NASB

And now I am no longer in the world, but they are in the world, and I am coming to you. Holy Father, protect them in your name that you have given me, so that they may be one, as we are one.   *John 17:11 NRSV*

COMPANIONSHIP (*also* FRIENDSHIP, MARRIAGE)

And remember, I am with you always, to the end of the age.   *Matthew 28:20 NRSV*

If you love me, you will do as I command. Then I will ask the Father to send you the Holy Spirit who will help you and always be with you. The Spirit will show you what is true. The people of this world cannot accept the Spirit, because they don't see or know him. But you know the Spirit, who is with you and will keep on living in you.

John 14:15–17 CEV

COMPASSION (*also* CHARITY, LOVE)

Those who are well have no need of a physician, but those who are sick. Go and learn what this means, 'I desire mercy, not sacrifice.' For I have come to call not the righteous but sinners.   *Matthew 9:12–13 (Mark 2:17) (Luke 5:31–32)* NRSV

A certain man was going down from Jerusalem to Jericho; and he fell among robbers, and they stripped him and beat him, and went off leaving him half dead. And by chance a certain priest was going down on that road, and when he saw him, he passed by on the other side. And likewise a Levite also, when he came to the place and saw him, passed by on the other side. But a certain Samaritan, who was on a journey, came upon him; and when he saw him, he felt compassion, and came to him, and bandaged up his wounds, pouring oil and wine on them; and he put him on his own beast, and brought him to an inn, and took care of him. And on the next day he took out two denarii and gave them to the innkeeper and said, "Take care of him; and whatever more you spend, when I return, I will repay you." Which of these three do you think proved to be a neighbor to the man who fell into the robbers' hands?

Go and do the same.   *Luke 10:30–36, 37* NASB

COMPETITION (*also* WORLDLINESS)

If any man desire to be first, the same shall be last of all, and servant of all.

Mark 9:35 (Matthew 20:26–27) (Mark 10:44) (Luke 22:26) KJV

You are those who justify yourselves in the sight of others; but God knows your hearts; for what is prized by human beings is an abomination in the sight of God.

Luke 16:15 NRSV

COMPLACENCY (*also* APATHY, SELF-RIGHTEOUSNESS)

So then, you will know them by their fruits. Not everyone who says to Me, "Lord, Lord," will enter the kingdom of heaven; but he who does the will of My Father who is in heaven. *Matthew 7:20–21 (Luke 6:44, 46) NASB*

But everyone who hears these sayings of Mine, and does not do them, will be like a foolish man who built his house on the sand: and the rain descended, the floods came, and the winds blew and beat on that house; and it fell. And great was its fall. *Matthew 7:26–27 (Luke 6:49) NKJV*

CONCEIT (*see* PRIDE)

CONFESSION (*also* TESTIMONY)

Whosoever therefore shall confess me before men, him will I confess also before my Father which is in heaven.

Matthew 10:32 (Luke 12:8–9) KJV

I will arise and go to my father, and will say to him, "Father, I have sinned against heaven and before you, and I am no longer worthy to be called your son. Make me like one of your hired servants." And he arose and came to his father. But when he was still a great way off, his father saw him and had compassion, and ran and fell on his neck and kissed him. *Luke 15:18–20 NKJV*

CONFLICT RESOLUTION (*also* RECONCILIATION)

Blessed are the gentle for they shall inherit the earth.
Blessed are the peacemakers, for they shall be called sons of God. *Matthew 5:5, 9 NASB*

So be careful! If you brother sins, tell him he is wrong. But if he is sorry and stops sinning, forgive him. If your brother sins against you seven times in one day, but he says that he is sorry each time, then forgive him. *Luke 17:3–4 NCV*

CONFORMITY (*also* SOCIETY)

When you pray, don't talk on and on as people do who don't know God. They think God likes to hear long prayers. Don't be like them. Your Father knows what you need before you ask.
Matthew 6:7-8 CEV

The seeds that fell among the thorn bushes are also people who hear the message. But they start worrying about the needs of this life and are fooled by the desire to get rich. So the message gets choked out, and they never produce anything.
Matthew 13:22 (Mark 4:18–19) (Luke 8:14) CEV

Go away from me, Satan! You are not helping me! You don't care about the things of God. You care only about things that men think are important.
Matthew 16:23 (Mark 8:33) (Luke 4:8) NCV

When you give a dinner or a banquet, don't invite your friends and family and relatives and rich neighbors. If you do, they will invite you in return, and you will be paid back. When you give a feast, invite the poor, the crippled, the lame, and the blind. They cannot pay you back. But God will bless you and reward you when his people rise from death.
Luke 14:12–14 CEV

You make yourselves look good in front of people. But God knows what is really in your hearts. The things that are important to people are worth nothing to God.
Luke 16:15 NCV

How can you believe when you accept glory from one another and do not seek the glory that comes from the one who alone is God?
John 5:44 NRSV

CONSCIENCE

For if you forgive men their trespasses, your heavenly Father will also forgive you. But if you do not forgive men their trespasses, neither will your Father forgive your trespasses.
Matthew 6:14 (Mark 11:25–26) NKJV

CONSCIENTIOUS OBJECTION (see PACIFISM, SOCIAL RESPONSIBILITY)

CONSTANCY (also RESPONSIBILITY)

If you continue in my word, you are truly my disciples; and you will know the truth, and the truth will make you free.

John 8:31–32 NRSV

Stay joined to me, and I will stay joined to you. Just as a branch cannot produce fruit unless it stays joined to the vine, you cannot produce fruit unless you stay joined to me. I am the vine, and you are the branches. If you stay joined to me, and I stay joined to you, then you will produce lots of fruit. But you cannot do anything without me.

John 15:4–5 CEV

Just as the Father has loved Me, I have also loved you; abide in My love. If you keep My commandments, you will abide in My love; just as I have kept My Father's commandments, and abide in His love. *John 15:9–10 NASB*

CONSUMERISM, CONSPICUOUS CONSUMPTION

Don't store up treasures on earth! Moths and rust can destroy them, and thieves can break in and steal them. Instead, store up your treasures in heaven, where moths and rust cannot destroy them, and thieves cannot break in and steal them. Your heart will always be where your treasure is. *Matthew 6:19–21 (Luke 12:33–34) CEV*

No one can serve two masters; for either he will hate the one and love the other, or else he will be loyal to the one and despise the other. You cannot serve God and mammon. *Matthew 6:24 (Luke 16:13) NKJV*

Therefore I say to you, do not worry about your life, what you will eat or what you will drink; nor about your body, what you will put on. Is not life more than food and the body more than clothing? *Matthew 6:25 (Luke 12:22–23) NKJV*

Therefore do not worry, saying, "What will we eat?" or "What will we drink?" or "What will we wear?" For it is the gentiles who strive for all these things; and indeed your heavenly Father knows that you need all these things. But strive first for the kingdom of God and his righteousness, and all these things will be given to you as well.

Matthew 6:31–33 (Luke 12:29–31) NRSV

For what will a man be profited, if he gains the whole world, and forfeits his soul? Or what will a man give in exchange for his soul?

Matthew 16:26 (Mark 8:36–37) (Luke 9:25) NASB

Take care! Be on your guard against all kinds of greed; for one's life does not consist in the abundance of possessions.

Luke 12:15 NRSV

Then I'll say to myself. 'You have stored up enough good things to last for years to come. Live it up! Eat, drink, and enjoy yourself.'" But God said to him, "You fool! Tonight you will die. Then who will get what you have stored up?" This is what happens to people who store up everything for themselves, but are poor in the sight of God.

Luke 12:19–21 CEV

You are those who justify yourselves in the sight of others; but God knows your hearts; for what is prized by human beings is an abomination in the sight of God.

Luke 16:15 NRSV

Be careful! Don't spend of your time feasting and drinking. If you do that, you will not be able to think straight. And then that day might come when you are not ready.

Luke 21:34–35 NCV

Take these things away! Do not make My Father's house a house of merchandise!   *John 2:16 NKJV*

CONTEMPLATION (*also* SPIRITUALITY)

When you pray, you should go into your room and close the door. Then pray to your Father who cannot be seen. Your Father can see what is done in secret, and he will reward you. And when you pray, don't be like those people who don't know God. They continue saying things that mean nothing. They think that God will hear them because of the many things they say. Don't be like them. Your Father knows the things you need before you ask him.

Matthew 6:6–8 NCV

Ask, and you will receive. Search, and you will find. Knock, and the door will be opened for you. Everyone who asks will receive. Everyone who searches will find. And the door will be opened for everyone who knocks.

Matthew 7:7–8 (Luke 11:9–10) CEV

But he that received seed into the good ground is he that heareth the word, and understandeth it; which also beareth fruit, and bringeth forth, some an hundredfold, some sixty, some thirty. *Matthew 13:23 (Mark 4:20) (Luke 8:15) KJV*

CONTENTION (*see* CONFLICT RESOLUTION, FIGHTING)

CONVERSION (*also* ENLIGHTENMENT)

I promise you this. If you don't change and become like this child, you will never get into the kingdom of heaven. But if you are as humble as this child, you are the greatest in the kingdom of heaven. And when you welcome one of these children because of me, you welcome me.

Matthew 18:3–5 (Mark 10:15) (Luke 18:17) CEV

Simon, Simon! Indeed, Satan has asked for you, that he may sift you as wheat. "But I have prayed for you, that your faith should not fail; and when you have returned to me, strengtyen your bretheren." *Luke 22:31–32 NKJV*

It is the Spirit who gives life; the flesh profits nothing; the words that I have spoken to you are spirit and are life.

John 6:63 NASB

If you continue in my word, you are truly my disciples; and you will know the truth, and the truth will make you free.

John 8:31-32 NRSV

COOPERATION (also COMPETITION)

And whoever shall force you to go one mile, go with him two. Give to him who asks of you, and do not turn away from him who wants to borrow from you.

Matthew 5:41–42 (Luke 6:30) NASB

Again I say unto you, That if two of you shall agree on earth as touching any thing that they shall ask, it shall be done for them of my Father which is in heaven. For where two or three are gathered together in my name, there am I in the midst of them. *Matthew 18:19–20 KJV*

COURAGE (also STRENGTH)

Do not fear those who kill the body but cannot kill the soul; rather fear him who can destroy both soul and body in hell.

Matthew 10:28 (Luke 12:4–5) NRSV

Simon, Simon, behold, Satan hath desired to have you, that he may sift you as wheat: But I have prayed for thee, that thy faith fail not: and when thou art converted, strengthen thy brethren. *Luke 22:31–32 KJV*

Peace I leave with you; my peace I give to you. I do not give to you as the world gives. Do not let your hearts be troubled, and do not let them be afraid. *John 14:27 NRSV*

These things I have spoken to you, that in Me you may have peace. In the world you have tribulation, but take courage; I have overcome the world. *John 16:33 NASB*

COURTESY (also AFFECTION)

Blessed are the meek, for they will inherit the earth.
Blessed are the peacemakers, for they will be called children of God. *Matthew 5:5, 9 NRSV*

If you greet only your friends, what's so great about that? Don't even unbelievers do that? But you must always act like your Father in heaven. *Matthew 5:47–48 (Luke 6:33) CEV*

And the King will answer and say to them, "Truly I say to you, to the extent that you did it to one of these brothers of Mine, even the least of them, you did it to Me."

Matthew 25:40 NASB

And just as you want men to do to you, you also do to them likewise. *Luke 6:31 (Matthew 7:12) NKJV*

When you welcome even a child because of me, you welcome me. And when you welcome me, you welcome the one who sent me. Whichever one of you is the most humble is the greatest.

Luke 9:48 (Matthew 18:5) (Mark 9:37) CEV

COVETOUSNESS (see GREED, SELFISHNESS)

CREATIVITY

This is why I use stories to teach the people: They see, but they don't really see. They hear, but they don't really understand. *Matthew 13:13 (Mark 4:11) (Luke 8:10) NCV*

With men this is impossible; but with God all things are possible. *Matthew 19:26 (Mark 10:27) (Luke 18:27) KJV*

"If You can!" All things are possible to him who believes.

Mark 9:23 NASB

Also, no one ever pours new wine into old leather bags for holding wine. If he does, the new wine will break the bags, and the wine will be ruined along with the bags for the wine. People always put new wine into new leather bags.

Mark 2:22 (Matthew 9:17) (Luke 5:37) NCV

So I tell you to ask and you will receive, search and you will find, knock and the door will be opened for you. Everyone who asks will receive, everyone who searches will find, and the door will be opened for everyone who knocks.

Luke 11:9–10 (Matthew 7:7–8) CEV

The wind blows where it wishes, and you hear the sound of it, but cannot tell where it comes from and where it goes. So is everyone who is born of the Spirit. *John 3:8 NKJV*

But the hour is coming, and now is, when the true worshipers will worship the Father in spirit and truth; for the Father is seeking such to worship Him. God is Spirit, and those who worship Him must worship in spirit and truth. *John 4:23–24 NKJV*

CREATOR (*also* GOD)

Surely you have read in the Scriptures. When God made the world, he made them male and female. And God said, 'So a man will leave his father and mother and be united with his wife. And the two people will become one body.'

Matthew 19:4–5 (Mark 10:6–8) NCV

In the story about the burning bush, Moses clearly shows that people will live again. He said, "The Lord is the God worshiped by Abraham, Isaac, and Jacob." So the Lord is not the God of the dead, but of the living. This means that everyone is alive as far as God is concerned.

Luke 20:37–38 (Matthew 22:31–32) (Mark 12:26–27) CEV

I tell you the truth. Before Abraham was born, I am.

John 8:58 NCV

CRIME (*also* VIOLENCE)

Before you are dragged into court, make friends with the person who has accused you of doing wrong. If you don't, you will be handed over to the judge and then to the officer who will put you in jail.   *Matthew 5:25 (Luke 12:58) CEV*

For from within, out of the heart of men, proceed evil thoughts, adulteries, fornications, murders, thefts, covetousness, wickedness, deceit, lasciviousness, an evil eye, blasphemy, pride, foolishness: All these evil things come from within, and defile the man.

Mark 7:21–23 (Matthew 15:19–20) KJV

You know the commandments. "Do not murder; do not commit adultery; do not steal; do not give false evidence; do not defraud; honour your father and mother."

Mark 10:19 (Matthew 19:18–19) (Luke 18:20) NEB

Why do you come out with swords and clubs and treat me like a criminal? I was with you everyday in the temple, and you didn't arrest me. But this is your time, and darkness is in control.

Luke 22:52–53 (Matthew 26:55–56) (Mark 14:48–49) (John 18:20–21) CEV

CRITICISM (*also* INSULTS)

Judge not, that ye be not judged. For with what judgment ye judge, ye shall be judged: and with what measure ye mete, it shall be measured to you again.

Matthew 7:1–2 (Luke 6:37–38) KJV

And why do you look at the speck that is in your brother's eye, but do not notice the log that is in your own eye? Or how can you say to your brother, "Let me take the speck out of your eye, " and behold, the log is in your own eye? You hypocrite, first take the log out of your own eye, and then you will see clearly to take the speck out of your brother's eye. *Matthew 7:3–5 (Luke 6:41–42) NASB*

Let anyone among you who is without sin be the first to throw a stone at her.

Woman, where are they? Has no one condemned you?

Neither do I condemn you. Go your way, and from now on do not sin again. *John 8:7, 10, 11 NRSV*

CRUCIFIXION (*also* RESURRECTION)

You know that after two days is the Passover, and the Son of Man will be delivered up to be crucified.

Matthew 26:2 NKJV

Eli, Eli, lama sabachthani? My God, my God, why have You forsaken me? *Matthew 27:46 (Mark 15:34) NKJV*

Father, forgive these people! They don't know what they're doing. *Luke 23:34–35 CEV*

Truly I tell you, today you will be with me in paradise.

Father, into your hands I commend my spirit.

Luke 23:43, 46 NRSV

The Father loves me because I give my life. I give my life so that I can take it back agin. No one takes it away from me. I give my own life freely. I have the right to give my life, and I have the right to take it back. This is what my Father commanded me to do. *John 10:17–18 NCV*

Woman, here is your son.

Here is your mother.

I am thirsty.
It is finished. *John 19:26, 27, 28, 30 NRSV*

CULTURAL TRANSCENDENCE (*see* REBIRTH, SELF-TRANSCENDENCE, TRADITION)

CYNICISM (*also* SPIRITUAL INSENSITIVITY)

For this people's heart is waxed gross, and their ears are dull of hearing, and their eyes they have closed; lest at any time they should see with their eyes, and hear with their ears, and should understand with their heart, and should be converted, and I should heal them.

Matthew 13:15 (Mark 4:10–12) KJV

Why are you so fearful? How is it that you have no faith?
Mark 4:40 (Luke 8:25) NKJV

And he said to him, "If they do not listen to Moses and the Prophets, neither will they be persuaded if someone rises from the dead." *Luke 16:31 NASB*

O fools, and slow of heart to believe all that the prophets have spoken. *Luke 24:25 KJV*

Truly, truly, I say to you, we speak that which we know, and bear witness of that which we have seen; and you do not receive our witness. If I told you earthly things and you do not believe, how shall you believe if I tell you heavenly things? *John 3:11–12 NASB*

And if any man hear my words, and believe not, I judge him not: for I came not to judge the world, but to save the world. *John 12:47–48 KJV*

DANCING (*also* CREATIVITY, JOY)

But to what shall I compare this generation? It is like children sitting in the market places, who call out to the other children, and say, We played the flute for you, and you did not dance; we sang a dirge, and you did not mourn.

Matthew 11:16–17 (Luke 7:31–32) NASB

For this my son was dead, and is alive again; he was lost and is found. And they began to be merry. Now his elder son was in the field: and as he came and drew nigh to the house, he heard music and dancing.   *Luke 15:24–25 KJV*

DANGER (see TEMPTATION, UNBELIEF, VIOLENCE)

DARKNESS (also DEVIL(S), LIGHT, WORLDLINESS)

Your eyes are like a window for your body. When they are good, you have all the light you need. But when your eyes are bad, everything is dark. If the light inside you is dark, you surely are in the dark.

Matthew 6:22–23 (Luke 11:34–36) CEV

So have no fear of them; for nothing is covered up that will not be uncovered, and nothing secret that will not become known. What I say to you in the dark, tell in the light; and what you hear whispered, proclaim from the housetops.

Matthew 10:26–27 (Luke 12:2–3) NRSV

Why do you come out with swords and clubs and treat me like a criminal? I was with you everyday in the temple, and you didn't arrest me. But this is your time, and darkness is in control.

Luke 22:52–53 (Matthew 26:55–56) (Mark 14:48–49) (John 18:20–21) CEV

DEATH (also LIFE)

Do not fear those who kill the body but cannot kill the soul; rather fear him who can destroy both soul and body in hell.

Matthew 10:28 (Luke 12:4–5) NRSV

Truly I say to you, there are some of those standing here who shall not taste death until they see the Son of Man coming in His kingdom.

Matthew 16:28 (Mark 9:1) (Luke 9:27) NASB

God is the God of living people, not dead people. All people are alive to God.   *Luke 20:38 (Matthew 22:32) (Mark 12:27) NCV*

Very truly, I tell you, anyone who hears my word and believes him who sent me has eternal life, and does not come under judgment, but has passed from death to life. Very truly, I tell you, the hour is coming, and is now here, when the dead will hear the voice of the Son of God, and those who hear will live. *John 5:24–25 NRSV*

Yet I do not seek my own glory; there is one who seeks it and he is the judge. Very truly, I tell you, whoever keeps my word will never see death. *John 8:50–51 NRSV*

I am the resurrection and the life. He who believes in me will have life even if he dies. And he who lives and believes in me will never die. Martha, do you believe this?

John 11:25–26 NCV

The time has come for the Son of Man to be given his glory. I tell you for certain that a grain of wheat that falls on the ground will never be more than one grain unless it dies. But if it dies, it will produce lots of wheat. If you love your life, you will lose it. If you give it up in this world, you will be given eternal life. *John 12:23–25 CEV*

DEBT (*also* LENDING)

And forgive us our debts, as we forgive our debtors.

Matthew 6:12 (Luke 11:4) KJV

DECEIT (*also* HYPOCRISY, LIES)

Beware of false prophets, who come to you in sheep's clothing, but inwardly are ravenous wolves. You will know them by their fruits. Grapes are not gathered from thorn bushes, nor figs from thistles, are they?

Matthew 7:15–16 NASB

Don't be afraid of anyone! Everything that is hidden will be found out, and every secret will be known.

Matthew 10:26 (Luke 12:2) CEV

Beware that no one leads you astray.

Matthew 24:4 (Mark 13:5) (Luke 21:8) NRSV

You know the commands: "You must not murder anyone. You must not be guilty of adultery. You must not steal., You must not tell lies about your neighbor in court. You must not cheat. Honor you father and mother."

Mark 10:19 (Matthew 19:18–19) (Luke 18:20) NCV

DECISIONS *(see* CHOICE*)*

DEEDS *(see* WORKS*)*

DEFENSE, SELF–DEFENSELESSNESS *(also* WAR*)*

You have heard that it was said, "An eye for an eye and a tooth for a tooth." But I say to you, Do not resist an evildoer. But if anyone strikes you on the right cheek, turn the other also; and if anyone wants to sue you and take your coat, give your cloak as well; and if anyone forces you to go one mile, go also the second mile.

Matthew 5:38–41 (Luke 6:29, 30) NRSV

But when someone arrests you, don't worry about what you will say or how you will say it. At that time you will be given the words to say. But you will not really be the one speaking. The Spirit from your Father will tell you what to say.

Matthew 10:19–20 (Mark 13:11) (Luke 21:12—14) CEV

DELUSION *(also* MATERIALISM*)*

You disobey God's commands in order to obey what humans have taught. You are good at rejecting God's commands so that you can follow your own teachings!

Mark 7:8–9 (Matthew 15:3–6) CEV

You are those who justify yourselves in the sight of others; but God knows your hearts; for what is prized by human beings is an abomination in the sight of God.

Luke 16:15 NRSV

DEMOCRACY *(see* POLITICS*)*

DEPENDENCE *(also* CODEPENDENCE*)*

It is written, "Man shall not live by bread alone, but by every word that proceeds from the mouth of God."

Matthew 4:4 (Luke 4:4) NKJV

Stay joined to me, and I will stay joined to you. Just as a branch cannot produce fruit unless it stays joined to the vine, you cannot produce fruit unless you stay joined to me. I am the vine, and you are the branches. If you stay joined to me, and I stay joined to you, then you will produce lots of fruit. But you cannot do anything without me.

John 15:4–5 CEV

DEPRESSION (*also* MENTAL HEALTH)

Let not your heart be troubled: you believe in God, believe also in me. In My Father's house are many mansions; if it were not so, I would have told you. I go to prepare a place for you. *John 14:1–2 NKJV*

I leave you peace. My peace I give you. I do not give it to you as the world does. So don't let your hearts be troubled. Don't be afraid. *John 14:27 NCV*

Therefore you now have sorrow; but I will see you again and your heart will rejoice, and your joy no one will take from you. *John 16:23 NKJV*

DESIRE (*also* NEED, WANTS)

And what is the seed that fell among the thorny weeds? That seed is like the person who hears the teaching but lets worries about this life and love of money stop that teaching from growing. So the teaching does not produce fruit in that person's life.

Matthew 13:22 (Mark 4:18–19) (Luke 8:14) NCV

If any of you want to be my followers, you must forget about yourself. You must take up your cross and follow me. If you want to save your life you will destroy it. But if you give up your life for me, you will find it. What will you gain if you own the whole world but destroy yourself? What would you give to get back your soul?

Matthew 16:24–26 (Mark 8:34–37) (Luke 9:23–25) CEV

You are those who justify yourselves in the sight of others; but God knows your hearts; for what is prized by human beings is an abomination in the sight of God.

Luke 16:15 NRSV

DESTRUCTION, DECAY

Don't store up treasures on earth! Moths and rust can destroy them, and thieves can break in and steal them.

Instead, store up your treasures in heaven, where moths and rust cannot destroy them, and thieves cannot break in and steal them. Your heart will always be where your treasure is. *Matthew 6:19–21 (Luke 12:33–34)* CEV

Do not fear those who kill the body but cannot kill the soul; rather fear him who can destroy both soul and body in hell.
Matthew 10:28 (Luke 12:4–5) NRSV

Every kingdom that is fighting against itself will be destroyed. And every city that is divided will fall. And every family that is divided cannot succeed.
Matthew 12:25 (Mark 3:24–25) (Luke 11:17) NCV

As for these things which you are looking at, the days will come in which there will not be left one stone upon another which will not be torn down.
Luke 21:6 (Matthew 24:2) (Mark 13:2) NASB

DEVELOPMENT (*see* GROWTH)

DEVIL(S) (*also* DARKNESS, SATAN)

Say only "Yes" if you mean "Yes," and say only "No" if you mean "No." If you must say more than "Yes" or "No," it is from the Evil One. *Matthew 5:37* NCV

The one who scattered the good seed is the Son of Man. The field is the world, and the good seeds are the people who belong to the kingdom. The weed seeds are those who belong to the evil one, and the one who scattered them is the devil. The harvest is the end of time, and angels are the ones who bring in the harvest. *Matthew 13:37–39* CEV

Then he will say to those at his left hand, "You that are accursed, depart from me into the eternal fire prepared for the devil and his angels; for I was hungry and you gave me no food, I was thirsty and you gave me nothing to drink, I was a stranger and you did not welcome me, naked and you did not give me clothing, sick and in prison and you did not visit me." *Matthew 25:41–43* NRSV

Any kingdom where people fight each other will end up ruined. And a town or family that fights will soon destroy itself. So if Satan fights against himself, how can his kingdom last? If I use the power of Beelzebub to force out demons, whose power do your own followers use to force them out? Your followers are the ones who will judge you. But when I force out demons by the power of God's Spirit, it proves that God's kingdom has already come to you.

Matthew 12:25–28 (Mark 3:23–25) (Luke 11:17–20) CEV

For this saying go thy way; the devil is gone out of thy daughter.   *Mark 7:29 (Matthew 15:28) KJV*

And these signs will accompany those who believe: by using my name they will cast out demons; they will speak in new tongues; they will pick up snakes in their hands, and if they drink any deadly thing, it will not hurt them; they will lay their hands on the sick, and they will recover.

Mark 16:17–18 NRSV

Be quiet, and come out of him!   *Luke 4:35 (Mark 1:25) NKJV*

Now the parable is this: The seed is the word of God. Those by the way side are they that hear; then cometh the devil, and taketh away the word out of their hearts, lest they should believe and be saved.

Luke 8:11–12 (Matthew 13:18–19) (Mark 4:14–15) KJV

Did I not choose you, the twelve, and one of you is a devil?

John 6:70 NKJV

Why can't you understand what I am talking about? Can't you stand to hear what I am saying? Your father is the devil, and you do exactly what he wants. He has always been a murderer and a liar. There is nothing truthful about him. He speaks on his own, and everything he says is a lie. Not only is he a liar himself, but he is also the father of all lies.

John 8:43–44 CEV

I do not have a demon; but I honor my Father, and you dishonor me. Yet I do not seek my own glory; there is one who seeks it and he is the judge.   *John 8:49–50 NRSV*

DEVOTION (also LOVE)

Blessed are those who hunger and thirst for righteousness,
For they shall be filled.   *Matthew 5:6 (Luke 6:21) NKJV*

Love the Lord your God with all your heart, soul, and
mind. This is the first and most important commandment.
The second most important commandment is like this one.
And it is, "Love others as much as you love yourself." All
the Law of Moses and the Books of the Prophets are based
on these two commandments.

Matthew 22:37–40 (Mark 12:29–31) CEV

For this reason I say to you, her sins, which are many, have
been forgiven, for she loved much; but he who is forgiven
little, loves little.   *Luke 7:47 NASB*

This is my commandment, That ye love one another, as I
have loved you. Greater love hath no man than this, that a
man lay down his life for his friends.   *John 15:12–13 KJV*

DIFFERENCES (see TOLERANCE)

DISARMAMENT (also NONRESISTANCE)

You have heard that it was said, "You shall love your
neighbor, and hate your enemy." But I say to you, love your
enemies, and pray for those who persecute you in order
that you may be sons of your Father who is in heaven; for
He causes His sun to rise on the evil and the good, and
sends rain on the righteous and the unrighteous.

Matthew 5:43–45 (Luke 6:27–28) NASB

Do not fear those who kill the body but cannot kill the soul;
rather fear him who can destroy both soul and body in hell.

Matthew 10:28 (Luke 12:4–5) NRSV

Put up again thy sword into his place: for all they that take
the sword shall perish with the sword.   *Matthew 26:52 KJV*

Salt is good. But if the salt loses its salty taste, then you
cannot make it salty again. So be full of goodness. And have
peace with each other.

Mark 9:50 (Matthew 5:13) (Luke 14:34–35) NCV

DISASTER, MISFORTUNE

Don't be worried! Have faith in God and have faith in me.

John 14:1 CEV

DISCERNMENT (*also* MYSTICISM, UNDERSTANDING)

You will know these false prophets by what they produce. Not everyone who says that I am his Lord will enter the kingdom of heaven. The only people who will enter the kingdom of heaven are those who do the things that my Father in heaven wants.   *Matthew 7:20–21 (Luke 6:44, 46) NCV*

When it is evening you say,"It will be fair weather for the sky is red"; and in the morning, "It will be foul weather today, for the sky is red and threatening." Hypocrites! You know how to discern the face of the sky, but you cannot discern the signs of the times. A wicked and adulterous generation seeks after a sign, and no sign shall be given to it except the sign of the prophet Jonah.

Matthew 16:2–4 (Mark 8:12) (Luke 12:54–56) NKJV

I thank thee, Father, Lord of heaven and earth, for hiding these things from the learned and wise, revealing them to the simple. Yes, Father, such was thy choice.

Luke 10:21 (Matthew 11:25–26) NEB

My teaching is not mine but his who sent me. Anyone who resolves to do the will of God will know whether the teaching is from God or whether I am speaking on my own. Those who speak on their own seek their own glory, but the one who seeks the glory of him who sent him is true, and there is nothing false in him.   *John 7:16–18 NRSV*

DISCIPLESHIP, DISCIPLES (also OBEDIENCE, SOCIAL ACTION)

If any of you want to be my followers, you must forget about yourself. You must take up your cross and follow me. If you want to save your life you will destroy it. But if you give up your life for me, you will find it. What will you gain if you own the whole world but destroy yourself? What would you give to get back your soul?

Matthew 16:24–26 (Mark 8:34–37) (Luke 9:23–25) CEV

Go therefore and make disciples of all nations, baptizing them in the name of the Father and of the Son and of the Holy Spirit, teaching them to obey everything that I have commanded you. And remember, I am with you always, to the end of the age. *Matthew 28:19–20 NRSV*

Whoever listens to you listens to me, and whoever rejects you rejects me, and whoever rejects me rejects the one who sent me. *Luke 10:16 (Matthew 10:40) NRSV*

So therefore, none of you can become my disciple if you do not give up all your possessions. *Luke 14:33 NRSV*

No one can come to me unless drawn by the Father who sent me; and I will raise that person up on the last day. It is written in the prophets, "And they shall all be taught by God." Everyone who has heard and learned from the Father comes to me. *John 6:44–45 NRSV*

Most assuredly, I say to you, he who receives whomever I send receives Me; and he who receives Me receives Him who sent Me. *John 13:20 (Matthew 10:40) (Luke 10:16) NKJV*

I give you a new commandment, that you love one another. Just as I have loved you, you also should love one another. By this everyone will know that you are my disciples, if you have love for one another.

John 13:34–35 (John 15:12) NRSV

Believe me that I am in the Father and the Father is in me; but if you do not, then believe me because of the works themselves. Very truly, I tell you, the one who believes in me will also do the works that I do and, in fact, will do greater works than these, because I am going to the Father.

John 14:11–12 NRSV

If ye love me, keep my commandments. *John 14:15 KJV*

I am coming to you now. But I pray these things while I am still in the world. I say these things so that these men can have all of my joy within them. I ahve given them your teaching. And the world has hated these men, because they don't belong to the world, the same as I don't belong to the world. *John 17:13–14 NCV*

I ask not only on behalf of these, but also on behalf of those who will believe in me through their word, that they may all be one. As you, Father, are in me and I am in you, may they also be in us, so that the world may believe that you have sent me. *John 17:20–21 NRSV*

I haved honored my followers in the same way that you honored me, in order that they may be one with each other, just as we are one. I am one with them, and you are one with me, so that they may become completely one. Then this world's people will know that you sent me. They will know that you love my followers as much as you love me. *John 17:22–23 CEV*

Follow me.

John 21:19 (Matthew 9:9) (Mark 2:14) (Luke 5:27) (John 1:43) KJV

DISCIPLINE (*also* COERCION)

Blessed are the meek, for they shall inherit the earth.

Matthew 5:5 NKJV

Take my yoke upon you, and learn from me; for I am gentle and humble in heart, and you will find rest for your souls. For my yoke is easy, and my burden is light.

Matthew 11:29–30 NRSV

Be careful. Don't think these little children are worth nothing. I tell you that they have angels in heaven who are always with my Father in heaven.

Matthew 18:10–11 (Luke 15:3–7) NCV

I will leave and go to my father and say to him, "Father, I have sinned against God in heaven and against you. I am no longer good enough to be called your son. Treat me like one of your workers." The younger son got up and started back to his father. But when he was still a long way off, his father saw him and felt sorry for him. He ran to his son and hugged and kissed him.   *Luke 15:18–20 CEV*

DISCRIMINATION (also PREJUDICE, SEXISM)

But I say to you that if you are angry with a brother or sister, you will be liable to judgment; and if you insult a brother or a sister, you will be liable to the council; and if you say, "You fool," you will be liable to the hell of fire.

Matthew 5:22 NRSV

Who is my mother and who are my brothers? . . . These are my mother and my brothers! Anyone who obeys my Father in heaven is my brother or sister or mother.

Matthew 12:48–50 (Mark 3:33–35) (Luke 8:21) CEV

Then those people will answer, "Lord, when did we see you hungry or thirsty? When did we see you alone and away from home? Or when did we see you without clothes or sick or in prison? When did we see these things and not help you?" Then the King will answer, "I tell you the truth. Anything you refused to do for any of my people here, you refused to do for any of my people here, you refused to do for me.   *Matthew 25:44–45 NCV*

Do to others as you would have them do to you.

Luke 6:31 (Matthew 7:12) NRSV

Judge not, and you shall not be judged. Condemn not, and you shall not be condemned. Forgive, and you will be forgiven.   *Luke 6:37 (Matthew 7:1–2) NKJV*

Do not judge according to appearance, but judge with righteous judgment.   *John 7:24 NASB*

DISEASE (see HEALING)

DISHONOR, DISRESPECT (also DISLOYALTY)

Why do you disobey God and follow your own teaching? Didn't God command you to respect your father and mother? . . . But you let people get by without helping their parents when they should. You let them say that what they have has been offered to God. Is this any way to show respect to your parents? You ignore God's commands in order to follow your own teaching.

Matthew 15:3–6 (Mark 7:11–13) CEV

You must not murder anyone. You must not be guilty of adultery. You must not steal. You must not tell lies about your neighbor in court. Honor your father and mother. Love your neighbor as you love yourself.

Matthew 19:19 (Mark 10:19) (Luke 18:20) NCV

DIVINITY (*also* AUTHORITY)

Is it not written in your law,"I said, you are gods"? If those to whom the word of God came were called"gods"—and the scripture cannot be annulled—can you say that the one whom the Father has sanctified and sent into the world is blaspheming because I said, "I am God's Son"? If I am not doing the works of my Father, then do not believe me. But if I do them, even though you do not believe me, believe the works, so that you may know and understand that the Father is in me and I am in the Father. *John 10:34–38 NRSV*

The light will be with you for only a little longer. Walk in the light while you can. Then you won't be caught walking blindly in the dark. Have faith in the light while it is with you, and you will be children of the light.

John 12:35–36 CEV

Do you not believe that I am in the Father, and the Father is in Me? The words that I say to you I do not speak on My own initiative, but the Father abiding in Me does His works. *John 14:10 NASB*

Father, I am not praying just for these followers. I am also praying for everyone else who will have faith because of what my followers will say about me. I want all of them to be one with each other, just as I am one with you and you are one with me. I also want them to be one with us. Then the people of this world will believe that you sent me.

John 17:20–21 CEV

DIVORCE (also MARRIAGE)

Furthermore it has been said, "Whoever divorces his wife, let him give her a certificate of divorce." But I say to you that whoever divorces his wife for any reason except sexual immorality causes her to commit adultery; and whoever marries a woman who is divorced commits adultery.

Matthew 5:31–32 (Matthew 19:9) (Mark 10:11–12) (Luke 16:18) NKJV

DOGMA, HUMAN DOCTRINE (also TRADITION)

And you are nothing but showoffs! Isaiah the prophet was right when he wrote that God had said,

"All of you praise me with your words,
but you never really think about me.
It is useless for you to worship me,
when you teach rules made up by humans."

Matthew 15:7–9 (Mark 7:6–8) CEV

Woe to you, scribes and Pharisees, hypocrites! for ye pay tithe of mint and anise and cumin, and have omitted the weightier matters of the law, judgment, mercy, and faith: these ought ye to have done, and not to leave the other undone. Ye blind guides, which strain at a gnat, and swallow a camel. *Matthew 23:23–24 (Luke 11:42)* KJV

You have stopped following the commands of God. Now you only follow the teachings of men. Then Jesus said to them: 'You think you are clever! You ignore the commands of God so that you can follow your own teachings!'

Mark 7:8–9 (Matthew 15:3–6) NCV

You are those who justify yourselves in the sight of others; but God knows your hearts; for what is prized by human beings is an abomination in the sight of God.

Luke 16:15 NRSV

DOUBT (also UNBELIEF)

If you have faith and don't doubt, I promise that you can do what I did to this tree. And you will be able to do even more. You can tell this mountain to get up and jump into

the sea, and it will. If you have faith when you pray, you
will be given whatever you ask for.

Matthew 21:21–22 (Mark 11:23–24) CEV

Reach hither thy finger, and behold my hands; and reach
hither thy hand, and thrust it into my side: and be not
faithless, but believing. Thomas, because thou hast seen
me, thou hast believed: blessed are they that have not seen,
and yet have believed. *John 20:27, 29 KJV*

DRUGS (see ADDICTION, ALCOHOL)

DUTY (also SOCIAL RESPONSIBILITY)

Why are you testing Me, you hypocrites?
Show me the coin used for the poll-tax.
Whose likeness and inscription is this?
Render to Caesar the things that are Caesar's; and to God
the things that are God's.

Matthew 22:18–21 (Mark 12:15–17) (Luke 20:24–25) NASB

Why did you seek Me? Did you not know that I must be
about My Father's business? *Luke 2:49 NKJV*

So you too, when you do all the things which are
commanded you, say, "We are unworthy slaves; we have
done only that which we ought to have done."

Luke 17:10 NASB

EARTH (also NATURE)

Blessed are the meek, for they will inherit the earth.

Matthew 5:5 NRSV

EASTER (see RESURRECTION)

ECONOMICS (also INVESTMENTS, MONEY, STEWARDSHIP)

And whoever compels you to go one mile, go with him two.
Give to him who asks you, and from him who wants to
borrow from you do not turn away.

Matthew 5:41–42 (Luke 6:30) NKJV

Therefore do not worry, saying, "What will we eat?" or
"What will we drink?" or "What will we wear?" For it is

the Gentiles who strive for all these things; and indeed your heavenly Father knows that you need all these things. But strive first for the kingdom of God and his righteousness and all these things will be given to you as well.

Matthew 6:31–33 (Luke 12:29–31) NRSV

And what is the seed that fell among the thorny weeds? That seed is like the person who hears the teaching but lets worries about this life and love of money stop that teaching from growing. So the teaching does not produce fruit in that person's life.

Matthew 13:22 (Mark 4:18–19) (Luke 8:14) NCV

For what will a man be profited, if he gains the whole world, and forfeits his soul? Or what will a man give in exchange for his soul?

Matthew 16:26 (Mark 8:36–37) (Luke 9:25) NASB

Then he will say to those at his left hand, "You that are accursed, depart from me into the eternal fire prepared for the devil and his angels; for I was hungry and you gave me no food, I was thirsty and you gave me nothing to drink, I was a stranger and you did not welcome me, naked and you did not give me clothing, sick and in prison and you did not visit me." *Matthew 25:41–43 NRSV*

And if you do good to those who do good to you, what credit is that to you? For even sinners do the same. And if you lend to those from whom you expect to receive, what credit is that to you? Even sinners lend to sinners, in order to receive back the same amount.

Luke 6:33–34 (Matthew 5:47) NASB

And remain in the same house, eating and drinking such things as they give, for the laborer is worthy of his wages.

Luke 10:7 (Matthew 9:10) NKJV

Take care! Be on your guard against all kinds of greed; for one's life does not consist in the abundance of possessions.

Luke 12:15 NRSV

ECUMENISM (*also* INCLUSIVENESS)

Who is my mother and who are my brothers? . . . . These are my mother and my brothers! Anyone who obeys my Father in heaven is my brother or sister or mother.

Matthew 12:48-50 (Mark 3:33-35) (Luke 8:21) CEV

Again, the kingdom of heaven is like a net that was thrown into the sea and caught fish of every kind.

Matthew 13:47 NRSV

Do not stop him; for one who does a deed of power in my name will be able soon afterward to speak evil of me. Whosoever is not against us is for us. For truly I tell you, whoever gives you a cup of water to drink because you bear the name of Christ will by no means lose the reward.

Mark 9:39-40 (Luke 9:50) NRSV

Most assuredly, I say to you, he who receives whomever I send receives Me; and he who receives Me receives Him who sent me.   *John 13:20 (Matthew 10:40) (Luke 10:16)* NKJV

Father, I pray that all people who believe in me can be one. You are in me and I am in you. I pray that these people can also be one in us, so that the world will believe that you sent me.   *John 17:21* NCV

EDUCATION (*also* LEARNING, TEACHING, WISDOM)

I use stories when I speak to them because when they look, they cannot see, and when they listen, they cannot hear or understand.   *Matthew 13:13 (Mark 4:11) (Luke 8:10)* CEV

But you must not be called 'Teacher.' You are all brothers and sisters together. You have only one Teacher.

Matthew 23:8 NCV

Can one blind man be guide to another? Will they not both fall into the ditch? A pupil is not superior to his teacher; but everyone, when his training is complete, will reaach his teacher's level.   *Luke 6:39-40 (Matthew 15:14)* NEB

I thank you, Father, Lord of heaven and earth, because you have hidden these things from the people who are wise and smart. But you have shown them to those who are like little children. Yes, Father, you did this because this is what you really wanted. *Luke 10:21 (Matthew 11:25–26)* NCV

EFFORT—SPIRITUAL (also SPIRITUAL SEARCHING)

Watch and pray, lest you enter into temptation. The spirit indeed is willing, but the flesh is weak.

Matthew 26:41 (Mark 14:38) (Luke 22:46) NKJV

Suppose one of you goes to a friend in the middle of the night and says, "Let me borrow three loaves of bread. A friend of mine has dropped in, and I don't have a thing for him to eat." And suppose your friend answers, "Don't bother me! The door is bolted, and my children and I are in bed. I cannot get up to give you something." He may not get up and give you the bread, just because you are his friend. But he will get up and give you as much as you need, simply because you are not ashamed to keep on asking. So I tell you to ask and you will receive, search and you will find, knock and the door will be opened for you. Everyone who asks will receive, everyone who searches will find, and the door will be opened for everyone who knocks.

Luke 11:5–10 CEV

EGO, EGOTISM (also BOASTING, PRIDE, SELFISH-NESS)

Beware of practicing your piety before others in order to be seen by them; for then you have no reward from your Father in heaven. So whenever you give alms, do not sound a trumpet before you, as the hypocrites do in the synagogues and in the streets, so that they may be praised by others. Truly I tell you, they have received their reward.

Matthew 6:1–2 NRSV

Don't judge other people, and you will not be judged. You will be judged in the same way that you judge others. And the forgiveness you give to others will be given to you.

Matthew 7:1–2 (Luke 6:37–38) NCV

But they do all their deeds to be noticed by men; for they broaden their phylacteries, and lengthen the tassels of their garments. And they love the place of honor at banquets, and the chief seats in the synagogues, and respectful greetings in the market places, and being called by men, Rabbi. *Matthew 23:5–7 (Luke 11:43, 46) NASB*

Many who have the highest place now will have the lowest place in the future. And those who have the lowest place now will have the highest place in the future.

Mark 10:31 (Matthew 19:30) (Matthew 20:16) (Luke 13:30) NCV

I cannot do anything on my own. The Father sent me, and he is the one who told me how to judge. I judge with fairness, because I obey him, and I don't just try to please myself. *John 5:30 CEV*

EMOTIONS (see ANGER, FEAR, HEART, JOY, LOVE)

EMPATHY (also CHARITY, LOVE, ONENESS)

Do to others as you would have them do to you.

Luke 6:31 (Matthew 7:12) NRSV

Be merciful, just as your Father is merciful. And do not judge and you will not be judged; and do not condemn, and you will not be condemned; pardon, and you will be pardoned. *Luke 6:36–37 (Matthew 7:1–2) NASB*

I give you a new commandment, that you love one another. Just as I have loved you, you also should love one another. By this everyone will know that you are my disciples, if you have love for one another. *John 13:34–35 (John 15:12) NRSV*

ENCOURAGEMENT(also ASSURANCE, FAITH)

Simon, Simon! Indeed, Satan has asked for you, that he may sift you as wheat. But I prayed for you, that your faith should not fail; and when you have returned to Me, strengthen your brethren. *Luke 22:31–32 NKJV*

I will not leave you orphans; I will come to you.

John 14:18 NKJV

Therefore you too now have sorrow; but I will see you again, and your heart will rejoice, and no one takes your joy away from you. *John 16:22 NASB*

END TIMES

For many shall come in my name, saying, I am Christ; and shall deceive many. And ye shall hear of wars and rumors of wars: see that ye be not troubled: for all these things must come to pass, but the end is not yet. For nation shall rise against nation, and kingdom against kingdom: and there shall be famines, and pestilences, and earthquakes, in divers places. All these are the beginning of sorrows. Then shall they deliver you up to be afflicted, and shall kill you: and ye shall be hated of all nations for my name's sake. And then shall many be offended, and shall betray one another, and shall hate one another. And many false prophets shall rise, and shall deceive many. And because iniquity shall abound, the love of many shall wax cold. But he that shall endure unto the end, the same shall be saved. And this gospel of the kingdom shall be preached in all the world for a witness unto all nations; and then shall the end come. When ye therefore shall see the abomination of desolation, spoken of by Daniel the prophet, stand in the holy place, (whoso readeth, let him understand:).

Matthew 24:5–15 (Mark 13:6–13) (Luke 21:8–19) KJV

If you are living in Judea at that time, run to the mountains. If you are on the roof of your house, don't go inside to get anything. If you are out in the field, don't go back for your coat. It will be a terrible time for women who are expecting babies or nursing young children. And pray that you won't have to escape in winter or on a Sabbath. This will be the worst time of suffering since the beginning of the world, and nothing this terrible will ever happen again. If God don't make the time shorter, no one will be left alive. But because of God's chosen ones, he will make the time shorter.   *Matthew 24:16–22 (Mark 13:14–20) (Luke 21:20–24) CEV*

Immediately after the tribulation of those days shall the sun be darkened, and the moon shall not give her light, and the stars shall fall from heaven, and the powers of the heavens shall be shaken: And then shall appear the sign of the Son of man in heaven: and then shall all the tribes of the earth mourn, and they shall see the Son of man coming in the clouds of heaven with power and great glory. And he shall send his angels with a great sound of a trumpet, and they shall gather together his elect from the four winds, from one end of heaven to the other. Now learn a parable of the fig tree; When his branch is yet tender, and putteth forth leaves, ye know that summer is nigh: So likewise ye, when ye shall see all these things, know that it is near, even at the doors. Verily I say unto you, This generation shall not pass, till all these things be fulfilled. Heaven and earth shall pass away, but my words shall not pass away.

Matthew 24:29–35 (Mark 13:24–31) (Luke 21:29–32) KJV

No one knows when that day or time will be. Even the Son and the angels in heaven don't know. Only the Father knows. When the Son of Man comes, it will be the same as what happened during Noah's time. In those days before the flood, people were eating and drinking. They were marrying and giving their children to be married. They were still doing those things until the day Noah entered the boat. They knew nothing about what was happening. But then the flood came, and all those people were destroyed. It will be the same when the Son of Man comes.

Matthew 24:36–39 (Mark 13:32–34) (Luke 17:26–27)NCV

Strange things will happen to the sun, moon, and stars. The nations on earth will be afraid of the roaring sea and tides, and they won't know what to do. People will be so frightened that they will faint because of what is happening to the world. Every power in the sky will be shaken. Then the Son of Man will be seen, coming in a cloud with great power and glory. When all of this starts happening, stand up straight and be brave. You will soon be set free.

Luke 21:25–28 (Matthew 24:29–31) (Mark 13:24–27) CEV

Be careful! Don't spend your time feasting and drinking. Or don't be too busy with worldly things. If you do that, you will not be able to think straight. And then that day might come when you are not ready. It will close like a trap on all people on earth.   *Luke 21:34–35 NCV*

I have much more to say to you, but right now it would be more than you could understand. The Spirit shows what is true and will come and guide you into the full truth. The Spirit does not speak on his own. He will tell you only what he has heard from me, and he will let you know what is going to happen.   *John 16:12–13* CEV

ENDURANCE (*also* PERSEVERANCE)

Brother will betray brother to death, and a father his child, and children will rise against parents and have them put to death; and you will be hated by all because of my name. But the one who endures to the end will be saved.

Matthew 10:21–22 (Matthew 24:10–13) NRSV

By your endurance you will gain your souls.

Luke 21:19 (Matthew 24:12) (Mark 13:13) NRSV

ENEMY

You have learned that they were told, "Love your neighbour, and hate your enemy." But what I tell you is this: Love your enemies and pray for your persecutors;

Matthew 5:45 (Luke 6:27–28) NEB

Behold, I give unto you power to tread on serpents and scorpions, and over all the power of the enemy: and nothing shall by any means hurt you. Notwithstanding in this rejoice not, that the spirits are subject unto you; but rather rejoice, because your names are written in heaven.

Luke 10:19–20 KJV

ENLIGHTENMENT (*also* SPIRITUALITY)

I thank you, Father, Lord of heaven and earth, because you have hidden these things from the wise and the intelligent and have revealed them to infants; yes, Father, for such was your gracious will.   *Luke 10:21 (Matthew 11:25–26)* NRSV

If then your whole body is full of light, having no part dark, the whole body will be full of light, as when the bright shining of a lamp gives you light.   *Luke 11:36* NKJV

Very truly, I tell you, no one can see the kingdom of God without being born from above.   *John 3:3* NRSV

I have come as light into the world, so that everyone who believes in me should not remain in the darkness. I do not judge anyone who hears my words and does not keep them, for I came not to judge the world, but to save the world. *John 12:46–47 NRSV*

If you love me, you will do what I have said, and my Father will love you. I will also love you and show you what I am like. . . . If anyone loves me, they will obey me. Then my Father will love them, and we will come to them and live in them. *John 14:21, 23 CEV*

I have many more things to say to you, but they are too much for you now. But when the Spirit of truth comes he will lead you into all truth. *John 16:12–13 NCV*

ENVIRONMENT (*also* NATURE, STEWARDSHIP)

Blessed are the meek, for they shall inherit the earth.
Matthew 5:5 NRSV

Your will be done
On earth as it is in heaven. *Luke 11:2 (Matthew 6:9–10) NKJV*

Gather up the leftover fragments that nothing may be lost.
John 6:11 NASB

ENVY (*see* GREED, JEALOUSY)

EQUALITY

But none of you should be called teacher. You have only one teacher, and all of you are like brothers and sisters.
Matthew 23:8 CEV

Then the King will answer, "I tell you the truth. Anything you did for any of my people here, you also did for me."
Matthew 25:40 NCV

Do to others as you would have them do to you.
Luke 6:31 (Matthew 7:12) NRSV

ETERNAL LIFE, ETERNITY (*also* IMMORTALITY)

Then the king will say to those on his right, "My father has blessed you! Come and receive the kingdom that was prepared for you before the world was created. When I was hungry, you gave me something to eat, and when I was thirsty, you gave me something to drink. When I was a stranger, you welcomed me, and when I was naked, you gave me clothes to wear. When I was sick, you took care of me, and when I was in jail, you visited me." *Matthew 25:34-36 CEV*

And as Moses lifted up the serpent in the wilderness, even so must the Son of man be lifted up: That whosoever believeth in him should not perish, but have eternal life. For God so loved the world, that he gave his only begotten Son, that whosoever believeth in him should not perish, but have everlasting life. *John 3:14-16 KJV*

Everyone who drinks of this water shall thirst again; but whoever drinks of the water that I shall give him shall never thirst; but the water that I shall give him shall become in him a well of water springing up to eternal life.

John 4:13-14 NASB

Everyone who sees the Son and believes in him has eternal life. I will raise him up on the last day. This is what my Father wants. *John 6:40 NCV*

Most assuredly, I say to you, unless a grain of wheat falls into the ground and dies, it remains alone; but if it dies, it produces much grain. He who loves his life will lose it, and he who hates his life in this world will keep it for eternal life. *John 12:24-25 NKJV*

Don't be worried! Have faith in God and have faith in me. There are many rooms in my Father's house. I wouldn't tell you this, unless it was true. I am going there to prepare a place for each of you. After I have done this, I will come back and take you with me. Then we will be together. You know the way to where I am going. *John 14:1-4 CEV*

Father, the hour is come; glorify thy Son, that thy Son also may glorify thee: As thou hast given him power over all flesh, that he should give eternal life to as many as thou hast given him. And this is life eternal, that they might know thee the only true God, and Jesus Christ, whom thou hast sent. *John 17:1-3 KJV*

EUCHARIST (*see* COMMUNION)

EVANGELISM, EVANGELISTS (*also* TESTIMONY)

The harvest is plentiful, but the workers are few.

Matthew 9:37 (Luke 10:2) NASB

And as you go, preach, saying, "The kingdom of heaven is at hand." Heal the sick, cleanse the lepers, raise the dead, cast out demons. Freely you have received, freely give.

Matthew 10:7–8 NKJV

Don't be afraid of anyone! Everything that is hidden will be found out, and every secret will be known. Whatever I say to you in the dark, you must tell in the light. And you must announce from the housetops whatever I have whispered to you.   *Matthew 10:26–27 (Luke 12:2–3) CEV*

The Good News about God's kingdom will be preached in all the world, to every nation. Then the end will come.

Matthew 24:14 (Mark 13:10) NCV

All authority in heaven and on earth has been given to me. Go therefore and make disciples of all nations, baptizing them in the name of the Father and of the Son and of the Holy Spirit, and teaching them to obey everything that I have commanded you. And remember, I am with you always, to the end of the age.   *Matthew 28:18–20 NRSV*

And the gospel must first be published among all nations.

Mark 13:10 (Matthew 24:14) KJV

Go into all the world and proclaim the good news to the whole creation.   *Mark 16:15 NRSV*

The Spirit shows what is true and will come and guide you into the full truth. The Spirit does not speak on his own. He will tell you only what he has heard from me, and he will let you know what is going to happen.   *John 16:13 CEV*

Peace be with you! As the Father sent me, I now send you. . . . Receive the Holy Spirit.   *John 20:21–22 NCV*

EVIL (*also* DEVIL(S), IMPERFECTION, INJUSTICE, SIN)

Ye have heard that it hath been said, An eye for an eye, and a tooth for a tooth: but I say unto you, that ye resist not evil: but whosoever shall smite thee on thy right cheek, turn to him the other also.   *Matthew 5:38–39 (Luke 6:29) KJV*

And lead us not into temptation, but deliver us from evil: For thine is the kingdom, and the power, and the glory, for ever. Amen.   *Matthew 6:13 (Luke 11:4) KJV*

The eye is the lamp of the body. So, if your eye is healthy, your whole body will be full of light; but if your eye is unhealthy, your whole body will be full of darkness. If then the light in you is darkness, how great is the darkness!
          Matthew 6:22–23 (Luke 11:34–36) NRSV

No one can serve two masters; for either he will hate the one and love the other, or else he will be loyal to the one and despise the other. You cannot serve God and mammon.   *Matthew 6:24 (Luke 16:13) NKJV*

What comes from your heart is what makes you unclean. Out of your heart come evil thoughts, vulgar deeds, stealing, murder, unfaithfulness in marriage, greed, meanness, deceit, indecency, envy, insults, pride, and foolishness. All of these come from your heart, and they are what make you unfit to worship God.
          Mark 7:20–23 (Matthew 15:19–20) CEV

Each tree is known by its fruit. People don't gather figs from thornbushes. And they don't get grapes from bushes. A good person has good things saved up in his heart. And so he brings good things out of his heart. But an evil person has evil things saved up in his heart. So he brings out bad things. A person speaks the things that are in his heart.
          Luke 6:44–45 (Matthew 12:35) NCV

Beware, and be on your guard against every form of greed; for not even when one has an abundance does his life consist of his possessions.   *Luke 12:15 NASB*

EXAMPLE 83

For every one that doeth evil hateth the light, neither cometh to the light, lest his deeds should be reproved.

John 3:20 KJV

EXAMPLE *(also* ROLE MODELS, WORKS)

Let your light so shine before men, that they may see your good works and glorify your Father in heaven.

Matthew 5:16 NKJV

If you love only the people who love you, then you will get no reward. Even the tax collectors do that. And if you are nice only to your friends, then you are no better than other people. Even people without God are nice to their friends. So you must be perfect, just as your Father in heaven is perfect. *Matthew 5:46–48 (Luke 6:32–33) NCV*

If you are tired from carrying heavy burdens, come to me and I will give you rest. Take the yoke I give you. Put it on your shoulders and learn from me. I am gentle and humble, and you will find rest. This yoke is easy to bear, and this burden is light. *Matthew 11:28–30 CEV*

One thing you lack: Go your way, sell whatever you have and give to the poor, and you will have treasure in heaven; and come, take up the cross, and follow Me.

Mark 10:21 (Matthew 19:21) (Luke 12:33) NKJV

Be merciful, just as your Father is merciful. Do not judge, and you will not be judged; do not condemn, and you will not be condemned. Forgive, and you will be forgiven.

Luke 6:36–37 (Matthew 7:1–2) NRSV

Do you understand what I have just done for you? You call me 'Teacher' and 'Lord.' And this is right, because that is what I am. I, your Lord and Teacher, have washed your feet. So you also should wash each other's feet. I did this as an example for you. So you should do as I have done for you. *John 13:12–15 NCV*

I am the way, and the truth, and the life. No one comes to the Father except through me. *John 14:6 NRSV*

EXTRASENSORY PERCEPTION (see FAITH, PERCEP-TION)

FAILURE (see SUCCESS)

FAIRNESS (also JUSTICE, RIGHTEOUSNESS)

Therefore, whatever you want men to do to you, do also to them, for this is the Law and the Prophets.

Matthew 7:12 (Luke 6:31) NKJV

So be careful what you do. Correct followers of mine who sin, and forgive the ones who say they are sorry. Even if one of them mistreats you seven times in one day and says, "I am sorry," you should still forgive that person.

Luke 17:3–4 CEV

So why are you angry at me for healing a person's whole body on the Sabbath day? Stop judging by the way things look! Be fair, and judge by what is really right.

John 7:23–24 NCV

FAITH (also ABILITY, BELIEF)

Ask, and it will be given to you; seek, and you will find; knock, and it will be opened to you. For everyone who asks receives, and he who seeks find, and to him who knocks it will be opened.   *Matthew 7:7–8 (Luke 11:9–10) NKJV*

You were not able to drive out the demon because your faith is too small. I tell you the truth. If your faith is as big as a mustard seed, you can say to this mountain, 'Move from here to there.' And the mountain will move. All things will be possible for you.   *Matthew 17:20-21 (Luke 17:6) NCV*

If you have faith and don't doubt, I promise that you can do what I did to this tree. And you will be able to do even more. You can tell this mountain to get up and jump into the sea, and it will. If you have faith when you pray, you will be given whatever you ask for.

Matthew 21:21–22 (Mark 11:23–24) CEV

Why are you so fearful? How is it that you have no faith?

Mark 4:40 (Luke 8:25) NKJV

If you are able!— All things can be done for the one who believes. *Mark 9:23 NRSV*

Daughter, your faith has made you well; go in peace.

Do not be afraid any longer; only believe, and she shall be made well. *Luke 8: 48, 50 (Matthew 9:22) (Mark 5:34, 36) NASB*

You people who live now have no faith. Your lives are all wrong. How long must I be with you and be patient with you? *Luke 9:41 (Matthew 17:17) (Mark 9:19) NCV*

And will not God grant justice to his chosen ones who cry to him day and night? Will he delay long in helping them? I tell you, he will quickly grant justice to them. And yet, when the Son of Man comes, will he find faith on earth? *Luke 18: 6–7 NRSV*

Let anyone who is thirsty come to me, and let the one who believes in me drink. As the scripture has said, 'Out of the believer's heart shall flow rivers of living water.' *John 7:37–38 NRSV*

Thomas, do you have faith because you have seen me? The people who have faith in me without seeing me are the ones who are really blessed! *John 20:29 CEV*

FAITHFULNESS (*also* CONSTANCY)

His lord said to him, "Well done, good and faithful servant; you have been faithful over a few things, I will make you ruler over many things. Enter into the joy of your lord." *Matthew 25:23 (Luke 19:17) NKJV*

Anyone who can be trusted in little matters can also be trusted in important matters. But anyone who is dishonest in little matters will be dishonest in important matters. *Luke 16:10 CEV*

FALSE PROPHETS (*also* HYPOCRISY, PROPHETS)

Beware of false prophets, who come to you in sheep's clothing, but inwardly they are ravenous wolves. You will know them by their fruits. Do men gather grapes from thornbushes or figs from thistles? Even so, every good tree bears good fruit, but a bad tree bears bad fruit.

Matthew 7:15–17 NKJV

You will know these false prophets by what they produce. Not everyone who says that I am his Lord will enter the kingdom of heaven. The only people who will enter the kingdom of heaven are those who do the things that my Father in heaven wants.   *Matthew 7:20–21 (Luke 6:44, 46) NCV*

You Pharisees and teachers are showoffs, and you're in for trouble! You wash the outside of your cups and dishes, while inside there is nothing but greed and selfishness. You blind Pharisee! First clean the inside of a cup, and then the outside will also be clean.   *Matthew 23:25 (Luke 11:39) CEV*

See to it that no one misleads you. For many will come in My name, saying, "I am the Christ," and will mislead many.   *Matthew 24:4–5 (Mark 13:5–6) (Luke 21:8) NASB*

For false messiahs and false prophets will appear and produce great signs and omens, to lead astray, if possible, even the elect. Take note, I have told you beforehand. So if they say to you, "Look! He is in the wilderness," do not go out. If they say, "Look! He is in the inner rooms," do not believe it. For as the lightening comes from the east and flashes as far as the west, so will be the coming of the Son of Man.   *Matthew 24:24–27 (Mark 13:21–22) (Luke 21:8) NRSV*

Take heed that you not be deceived. For many will come in My name, saying, "I am He," and, "The time has drawn near." Therefore do not go after them. But when you hear of wars and commotions do not be terrified; for these things must come to pass first, but the end will not come immediately.   *Luke 21:8–9 (Matthew 24:4–6) (Mark 13:5-7) NKJV*

Take these things away! Do not make My Father's house a house of merchandise!   *John 2:16 NKJV*

My teaching is not mine but his who sent me. Anyone who resolves to do the will of God will know whether the teaching is from God or whether I am speaking on my own. Those who speak on their own seek their own glory; but

the one who seeks the glory of him who sent him is true,
and there is nothing false in him.   *John 7:16–18 NRSV*

FAME (also WEALTH)

It is not so among you, but whoever wishes to become great
among you shall be your servant, and whoever wishes to
be first among you shall be your slave; just as the Son of
Man did not come to be served, but to serve, and to give
His life a ransom for many.

Matthew 20:26–28 (Mark 10:43–45) (Luke 22:27) NASB

For everyone who exalts himself shall be humbled, and he
who humbles himself shall be exalted.

Luke 14:11 (Matthew 23:12) (Luke 18:14) NASB

You are always making yourselves look good, but God sees
what is in your heart. The things that most people think are
important are worthless as far as God is concerned.

Luke 16:15 CEV

I don't want praise from men. But I know you—I know that
you don't have God's love in you. I have come from my
Father—I speak for him. But you don't accept me. But when
another person comes, speaking only for himself, you will
accept him. You like to have praise from each other. But
you never try to get the praise that comes from the only
God.   *John 5:41–44 NCV*

FAMILY (also AGING, CHILDREN, PARENTS)

Don't think that I came to bring peace to the earth! I came
to bring trouble, not peace. I came to turn sons against their
fathers, daughters against their mothers, and
daughters-in-law against their mothers-in-law. Your worst
enemies will be in your own family. If you love your father
or mother or even your sons and daughters more than me,
you are not fit to be my disciples. And unless you are
willing to take up your cross and come with me, you are
not fit to be my disciples. If you try to save your life, you
will lose it. But if you give it up for me, you will surely find
it.   *Matthew 10:34–39 (Luke 12:51–53, 14:26–27, 17:33) CEV*

Who is my mother and who are my brothers?

Here are my mother and my brothers! For whoever does the will of My Father in heaven is my brother and sister and mother. *Matthew 12:48–50 (Mark 3:33–35) (Luke 8:21) NKJV*

Not everyone can accept this truth about marriage. But God has made some able to accept it. There are different reasons why some men cannot marry. Some men were born without the ability to become fathers. Others were made that way later in life by other people. And other men have given up marriage because of the kingdom of heaven. But the person who can marry should accept this teaching about marriage. *Matthew 19:11–12 NCV*

But you are not to be called rabbi, for you have one teacher, and you are all students. And call no one your father on earth, for you have one Father—the one in heaven.

Matthew 23:8–9 NRSV

How can Satan force himself out? A nation whose people fight each other won't last very long. And a family that fights won't last long either. So if Satan fights against himself, that will be the end of him.

Mark 3:23–26 (Matthew 12:25–26) (Luke 11:17–18) CEV

FASHION (see CLOTHING, VANITY)

FASTING (also RENUNCIATION)

And whenever you fast, do not look dismal, like the hypocrites, for they disfigure their faces so as to show others that they are fasting. Truly I tell you, they have received their reward. But when you fast, put oil on your head and wash your face, so that your fasting may be seen not by others but by your Father who is in secret; and your Father who sees in secret will reward you.

Matthew 6:16–18 NRSV

However, this kind does not go out except by prayer and fasting. *Matthew 17:21 (Mark 9:29) NKJV*

I have food that you don't know anything about.

My food is to do what God wants! He is the one who sent me, and I must finish the work that he gave me to do.

John 4:32, 34 CEV

FATE (*see* PROVIDENCE)

FEAR (*also* ANGER, ANXIETY, GUILT, LOSS)

Why are you such cowards?...how little faith you have!

Matthew 8:26 (Mark 4:40) NEB

Don't be afraid of anyone! Everything that is hidden will be found out, and every secret will be known. Whatever I say to you in the dark, you must tell in the light. And you must announce from the housetops whatever I have whispered to you. *Matthew 10:26–27 (Luke 12:2–3) CEV*

Do not fear those who kill the body but cannot kill the soul; rather fear him who can destroy both soul and body in hell.

Matthew 10:28 (Luke 12:4–5) NRSV

Are not five sparrows sold for two copper coins? And not one of them is forgotten before God. But the very hairs of your head are all numbered. Do not fear therefore; you are of more value than many sparrows.

Luke 12:6–7 (Matthew 10:29–31) NKJV

FELLOWSHIP (*also* COMMUNITY)

This is true because if two or three people come together in my name, I am there with them. *Matthew 18:20 NCV*

FIGHTING (*also* REVENGE, WAR)

Agree with thine adversary quickly, whiles thou art in the way with him; lest at any time the adversary deliver thee to the judge, and the judge deliver thee to the officer, and thou be cast into prison. *Matthew 5:25 (Luke 12:58) KJV*

How can Satan force himself out? A nation whose people fight each other won't last very long. And a family that fights won't last long either. So if Satan fights against himself, that will be the end of him.

Mark 3:23–26 (Matthew 12:25–26) (Luke 11:17–18) CEV

Every kingdom that is fighting against itself will be destroyed. And every city that is divided will fall. And every family that is divided cannot succeed.

Matthew 12:25 (Mark 3:23) (Luke 11:17) NCV

My kingdom is not from this world. If my kingdom were from this world, my followers would be fighting to keep me from being handed over to the Jews. But as it is, my kingdom is not from here.

John 18:36 NRSV

FINAL JUDGMENT

When the Son of Man comes in his glory with all of his angels, he will sit on his royal throne. The people of all nations will be brought before him, and he will separate them, as shepherds separate their sheep from their goats. He will place the sheep on his right and the goats on his left. Then the king will say to those on his right, "My father has blessed you! Come and receive the kingdom that was prepared for you before the world was created. When I was hungry, you gave me something to eat, and when I was thirsty, you gave me something to drink. When I was a stranger you welcomed me, and when I was naked, you gave me clothes to wear. When I was sick, you took care of me, and when I was in jail, you visited me."Whenever you did it for any of my people, no matter how unimportant they seemed, you did it for me."

Matthew 25:31–36, 40 CEV

Then he will say to those at his left hand, "You that are accursed, depart from me into the eternal fire prepared for the devil and his angels; for I was hungry and you gave me no food, I was thirsty and you gave me nothing to drink, I was a stranger and you did not welcome me, naked and you did not give me clothing, sick and in prison and you did not visit me." Then they also will answer, "Lord, when was it that we saw you hungry or thirsty or a stranger or naked or sick or in prison, and did not take care of you?" Then he will answer them, "Truly I tell you, just as you did not do it to one of the least of these, you did not do it to me."

Matthew 25:41–45 NRSV

FLATTERY *(also* POPULARITY)

Woe to you when all men speak well of you,
For so did their fathers to the false prophets.   *Luke 6:26 NKJV*

FLESH *(also* WORLDLINESS)

Keep watching and praying, that you may not enter into
temptation; the spirit is willing, but the flesh is weak.

Matthew 26:41 (Mark 14:38) (Luke 22:46) NASB

What is born of the flesh is flesh, and what is born of the Spirit
is spirit.   *John 3:6 NRSV*

FOOD *(also* HUNGER)

Therefore I say to you, do not worry about your life, what
you will eat or what you will drink; nor about your body,
what you will put on. Is not life more than food and the
body more than clothing?   *Matthew 6:25 (Luke 12:22–23) NKJV*

It is written, "Man shall not live by bread alone, but by
every word of God."   *Luke 4:4 (Matthew 4:4) NKJV*

When you give a dinner or a supper, do not ask your
friends, your brothers, your relatives, nor rich neighbors,
lest they also invite you back, and you be repaid. But when
you give a feast, invite the poor, the maimed, the lame, the
blind.   *Luke 14:12–13 NKJV*

I have food that you don't know anything about.

My food is to do what God wants! He is the one who sent
me, and I must finish the work that he gave me to do.

John 4:32, 34 CEV

FOOL, FOOLISHNESS

But I say to you that if you are angry with a brother or sister,
you will be liable to judgment; and if you insult a brother
or sister, you will be liable to the council; and if you say,
"You fool," you will be liable to the hell of fire.

Matthew 5:22 NRSV

But everyone who hears these sayings of Mine, and does
not do them, will be like a foolish man who built his house
on the sand: and the rain descended, the floods came, and

the winds blew and beat on that house; and it fell. And great was its fall.   *Matthew 7:26–27 (Luke 6:49) NKJV*

Then I'll say to myself. 'You have stored up enough good things to last for years to come. Live it up! Eat, drink, and enjoy yourself.'" But God said to him, "You fool! Tonight you will die. Then who will get what you have stored up?" This is what happens to people who store up everything for themselves, but are poor in the sight of God.

Luke 12:19–21 CEV

FORGIVENESS (*also* RECONCILIATION)

And forgive us our debts, as we forgive our debtors.

Matthew 6:12 (Luke 11:4) KJV

Yes, if you forgive others for the things they do wrong, then your Father in heaven will also forgive you for the things you do wrong. But if you don't forgive the wrongs of others, then your Father in heaven will not forgive the wrong things you do.   *Matthew 6:14-15 (Mark 11:25–26) NCV*

Judge not, that you be not judged. For with what judgment you judge, you will be judged; and with the measure you use, it will be measured back to you.

Matthew 7:1–2 (Luke 6:37–38) NKJV

I do not say to you, up to seven times, but up to seventy times seven. For this reason the kingdom of heaven may be compared to a certain king who wished to settle accounts with his slaves. And when he had begun to settle them, there was brought to him one who owed him ten thousand talents. But since he did not have the means to repay, his lord commanded him to be sold, along with his wife and children and all that he had, and repayment to be made. The slave therefore falling down, prostrated himself before him, saying, "Have patience with me, and I will repay you everything." And the lord of that slave felt compassion and released him and forgave him the debt. But that slave went out and found one of his fellow slaves who owed him a hundred denarii; and he seized him and began to choke him, saying, "Pay back what you owe." So his fellow slave fell down and began to entreat him, saying, "Have patience with me and I will repay you." He was unwilling however, but went and threw him in prison until he should pay back what was owed. So when his fellow slaves saw what had happened, they were deeply grieved and came and reported to their lord all that had happened. Then summoning him, his lord said to him, "You wicked slave, I forgave you all that debt because you entreated me. Should you not also have had mercy on your fellow slave, even as I had mercy on you?" And his lord, moved with anger, handed him over to the torturers until he should repay all that was owed him. So shall My heavenly Father also do to you, if each of you does not forgive his brother from your heart.

Matthew 18:22–35 NASB

For this is My blood of the new covenant, which is shed for many for the remission of sins.

Matthew 26:28 (Mark 14:24) NKJV

Truly I say to you, all sins shall be forgiven the sons of men, and whatever blasphemies they utter; but whoever blasphemes against the Holy Spirit never has forgiveness, but is guilty of an eternal sin.

Mark 3:28–29 (Matthew 12:31–32) (Luke 12:10) NASB

And when you stand praying, if you have anything against anyone, forgive him, that your Father in heaven may also forgive you your trespasses. But if you do not forgive, neither will your Father in heaven forgive your trespasses.

Mark 11:25–26 (Matthew 6:14) NKJV

Friend, your sins are forgiven you.

Luke 5:20 (Matthew 9:2) (Mark 2:5) NRSV

Why are you thinking that? Is it easier for me to tell this crippled man that his sins are forgiven or to tell him to get up and walk? But now you will see that the Son of Man has the right to forgive sins here on earth.

Get up! Pick up your mat and walk home.

Luke 5:22–24 (Matthew 9:4–6) (Mark 2:8–11) CEV

Be merciful, just as your Father is merciful. And do not judge and you will not be judged; and do not condemn, and you will not be condemned; pardon, and you will be pardoned.   *Luke 6:36–37 (Matthew 7:1–2) NASB*

I tell you that her many sins are forgiven. This is clear because she showed great love. But the person who has only a little to be forgiven will feel only a little love...Your sins are forgiven.   *Luke 7:47–48 NCV*

So be careful what you do. Correct any followers of mine who sin, and forgive the ones who say they are sorry. Even if one of them mistreats you seven times in one day and says, "I am sorry," you should still forgive that person.

Luke 17:3–4 CEV

Thus it is written, that the Messiah is to suffer and to rise from the dead on the third day, and that repentance and forgiveness of sins is to be proclaimed in his name to all nations, beginning from Jerusalem.   *Luke 24:46–47 NRSV*

Father, forgive them; for they know not what they do.

Luke 23:34 KJV

FORNICATION (see ADULTERY, DIVORCE, LUST)

FREEDOM

Come to me, all you that are weary and are carrying heavy burdens, and I will give you rest. Take my yoke upon you, and learn from me; for I am gentle and humble in heart, and you will find rest for your souls. For my yoke is easy, and my burden is light.   *Matthew 11:28–30 NRSV*

The Spirit of the Lord is upon me, because he hath anointed me to preach the gospel to the poor; he hath sent me to heal the brokenhearted, to preach deliverance to the captives, and recovering of sight to the blind, to set at liberty them that are bruised.   *Luke 4:18 KJV*

If you continue to obey my teaching, you are truly my
followers. Then you will know the truth. And the truth will
make you free.

I tell you the truth. Everyone who lives in sin is a slave to
sin. A slave does not stay with a family forever, but a son
belongs to the family forever. So if the Son makes you free,
then you will be truly free. *John 8:31–32, 34–36 NCV*

FRIENDS, FRIENDSHIP *(also* COMMUNITY)

John the Baptist did not go around eating and drinking,
and you said, "That man has a demon in him!" But the Son
of Man goes around eating a drinking, and you say, "That
man eats and drinks too much! He is even a friend of tax
collectors and sinners." Yet Wisdom is shown to be right
by what it does. *Matthew 11:18–19 (Luke 7:33–35) CEV*

This is my commandment, that you love one another as I
have loved you. No one has greater love than this, to lay
down one's life for one's friends. You are my friends if you
do what I command you. *John 15:12–14 NRSV*

No longer do I call you servants, for a servant does not
know what his master is doing; but I have called you
friends, for all things that I have heard from My Father I
have made known to you. *John 15:15 NKJV*

GENEROSITY *(also* SERVICE)

So when you give to the poor, give very secretly. Don't let
anyone know what you are doing. Your giving should be
done in secret. Your Father can see what is done in secret,
and he will reward you. *Matthew 6:3–4 NCV*

And as you go, preach, saying, "The kingdom of heaven is
at hand." Heal the sick, raise the dead, cleanse the lepers,
cast out demons; freely you received, freely give.

Matthew 10:7–8 NASB

For whosoever shall give you a cup of water to drink in my
name, because ye belong to Christ, verily I say unto you,
he shall not lose his reward. *Mark 9:41 KJV*

Have you noticed this woman? When I came into your home, you didn't give me any water so I could wash my feet. But she has washed my feet with her tears and dried them with her hair. You didn't greet me with a kiss, but from the time I came in, she has not stopped kissing my feet. You didn't even pour olive oil on my head, but she has poured expensive perfume on my feet. So I tell you that all her sins are forgiven, and that is why she has shown great love. But anyone who has been forgiven only a little will show only a little love.   *Luke 7:44–47 CEV*

If a son asks for bread from any father among you, will he give him a stone? Or if he asks for a fish, will he give him a serpent instead of a fish? Or if he asks for an egg, will he offer him a scorpion? If you then, being evil, know how to give good gifts to your children, how much more will your heavenly Father give the Holy Spirit to those who ask him?

Luke 11:11–13 (Matthew 7:10–11) NKJV

So give for alms those things that are within; and see, everything will be clean for you.   *Luke 11:41 NRSV*

It is more blessed to give than to receive.   *Acts 20:35 NRSV*

GENTLENESS (*also* HUMILITY)

Blessed are the gentle, for they shall inherit the earth.

Matthew 5:5 NASB

Take the yoke I give you. Put it on your shoulders and learn from me. I am gentle and humble, and you will find rest. This yoke is easy to bear, and this burden is light.

Matthew 11:29–30 CEV

GLORY (*also* FAME)

And lead us not into temptation, but deliver us from evil: For thine is the kingdom, and the power, and the glory, for ever. Amen.   *Matthew 6:13 KJV*

Those who speak on their own seek their own glory; but the one who seeks the glory of him who sent him is true, and there is nothing false in him.   *John 7:18 NRSV*

If I glorify myself, my glory is nothing. It is my Father who glorifies me, he of whom you say, "He is our God," though you do not know him. But I know him; if I would say that I do not know him, I would be a liar like you. But I do know him and I keep his word. Your ancestor Abraham rejoiced that he would see my day; he saw it and was glad.

John 8:54–56 NRSV

And the glory which thou gavest me I have given them; that they may be one, even as we are one.   *John 17:22 KJV*

GOALS (*also* PRIORITIES)

But seek first the kingdom of God and His righteousness, and all these things shall be added to you. Therefore do not worry about tomorrow, for tomorrow will worry about its own things. Sufficient for the day is its own trouble.

Matthew 6:33–34 (Luke 12:31) NKJV

Ask, and you will receive. Search, and you will find. Knock, and the door will be opened for you. Everyone who asks will receive. Everyone who searches will find. And the door will be opened for everyone who knocks.

Matthew 7:7–8 (Luke 11:9–10) CEV

If anyone wants to be first, he shall be last of all, and servant of all.   *Mark 9:35 (Matthew 20:27) (Mark 10:44) NASB*

Strive to enter by the narrow door; for many, I tell you, will seek to enter and will not be able. Once the head of the house gets up and shuts the door, and you begin to stand outside and knock on the door, saying, "Lord, open up to us!" then He will answer and say to you, "I do not know where you are from."   *Luke 13:24–25 (Matthew 7:13–14) NASB*

Earthly food spoils and ruins. So don't work to get that kind of food. But work to get the food that stays good always and gives you eternal life. The Son of Man will give you that food. God the Father has shown that he is with the Son of Man.   *John 6:27 NCV*

GOD

It is written, "Man shall not live by bread alone, but by every word that proceeds from the mouth of God."

Matthew 4:4 (Luke 4:4) NKJV

Love the Lord your God with all your heart, soul and mind. This is the first and most important command.

Matthew 22:37–38 (Mark 12:29–30) NCV

Why do you call Me good? No one is good but one, that is, God. *Mark 10:18 NKJV*

With men it is impossible, but not with God; for with God all things are possible.

Mark 10:27 (Matthew 19:26) (Luke 18:27) NKJV

Have faith in God. *Mark 11:22 KJV*

Render to Caesar the things that are Caesar's, and to God the things that are God's.

Mark 12:17 (Matthew 22:21) (Luke 20:25) KJV

The most important one says: "People of Israel, you have only one Lord and God. You must love him with all your heart, soul, mind, and strength." The second most important commandment says: "Love others as much as you love yourself." No other commandment is more important than these. *Mark 12:29–30 (Matthew 22:37) CEV*

It is written, "You shall worship the Lord your God and serve Him only." *Luke 4:8 (Matthew 4:10) NASB*

It is said, "Do not put the Lord your God to the test."

Luke 4:12 (Matthew 4:7) NRSV

No servant can serve two masters. He will hate one master and love the other. Or he will follow one master and refuse to follow the other. You cannot serve both God and money.

Luke 16:13 (Matthew 6:24) NCV

You are those who justify yourselves in the sight of others; but God knows your hearts; for what is prized by human beings is an abomination in the sight of God.

Luke 16:15 NRSV

Earthly food spoils and ruins. So don't work to get that kind of food. But work to get the food that stays good always and gives you eternal life. The Son of Man will give you that food. God the Father has shown that he is with the Son of Man.   *John 6:27 NCV*

This is the work of God, that you believe in Him whom He sent.   *John 6:29 NKJV*

Most assuredly, I say to you, Moses did not give you the bread from heaven, but My Father gives you the true bread from heaven. For the bread of God is He who comes down from heaven and gives life to the world.   *John 6:33 NKJV*

One of the prophets wrote, "God will teach all of them." And so everyone who listens to the Father and learns from him will come to me. The only one who has seen the Father is the one who has come from him. No one else has ever seen the Father. I tell you for certain that everyone who has faith in me has eternal life.   *John 6:45–46 CEV*

Now the Son of Man has been glorified, and God has been glorified in him. If God has been glorified in him, God will also glorify him in himself and will glorify him at once.

John 13:31–32 NRSV

And this is life eternal, that they might know thee the only true God, and Jesus Christ, whom thou hast sent.

John 17:3 KJV

I ask not only on behalf of these, but also on behalf of those who will believe in me through their word, that they may all be one. As you, Father, are in me and I am in you, may they also be in us, so that the world may believe that you have sent me.   *John 17:20–21 NRSV*

Good Father, the people of this world don't know you. But I know you, and my followers know that you sent me. I told them what you are like, and I will tell them even more. Then the love that you have for me will become part of them, and I will be one with them.   *John 17:25–26 CEV*

Don't hold me! I have not yet gone up to the Father. But go to my brothers and tell them this: 'I am going back to my

Father and your Father. I am going back to my God and your God.' *John 20:17 NCV*

GOOD NEWS, GOSPEL (also LOVE, NEW COVENANT)

And this gospel of the kingdom will be preached in all the world as a witness to all the nations, and then the end will come. *Matthew 24:14 (Mark 13:10) NKJV*

Verily I say unto you, There is no man that hath left house, or brethren, or sisters, or father, or mother, or wife, or children, or lands, for my sake, and the gospel's, But he shall receive an hundredfold now in this time, houses, and brethren, and sisters, and mothers, and children and lands, with persecutions; and in the world to come eternal life. But many that are first shall be last; and the last first.

Mark 10:29–31 (Matthew 19:29–30) (Luke 18:29–30) KJV

Go into all the world and preach the gospel to every creature. *Mark 16:15 (Matthew 28:19) NKJV*

The Lord's Spirit has come to me,
   because he has chosen me to tell the good news to the
   poor.
The Lord has sent me
   to announce freedom for prisoners,
   to give sight to the blind,
   to free everyone who suffers *Luke 4:18 CEV*

Go and tell John the things you have seen and heard; that the blind see, the lame walk, the lepers are cleansed, the deaf hear, the dead are raised, the poor have the gospel preached to them. And blessed is he who is not offended because of Me. *Luke 7:22–23 (Matthew 11:4–6) NKJV*

GOSPEL (see GOOD NEWS, LOVE, NEW COVENANT)

GOSSIP (also SPEECH)

Why do you see the speck in your neighbor's eye, but do not notice the log in your own eye?

Matthew 7:3 (Luke 6:41) NRSV

And I tell you that people will have to explain about every careless thing they have said. This will happen on the Judgment Day. The words you have said will be used to judge you. Some of your words will prove you right, but some of your words will prove you guilty.

Matthew 12:36–37 (Luke 6:45) NCV

But what comes out of the mouth proceeds from the heart, and this is what defiles. For out of the heart come evil intentions, murder, adultery, fornication, theft, false witness, slander. These are what defile a person, but to eat with unwashed hands does not defile.

Matthew 15:18–20 (Mark 7:21–23) NRSV

A good man produces good from the store of good within himself; and an evil man from evil within produces evil. For the words that the mouth utters come from the overflowing of the heart.

Luke 6:45 (Matthew 12:34) NEB

GOVERNMENT (*also* KINGDOM OF GOD)

Why are you testing Me, you hypocrites?

Show me the coin used for the poll-tax.

Whose likeness and inscription is this? . . . .

Then render to Caesar the things that are Caesar's; and to God the things that are God's.

Matthew 22:18, 19, 20, 21 (Mark 12:15–17) (Luke 20:24–25) NASB

Yet you neglect the more important matters of the Law, such as justice, mercy, and faithfulness. These are the important things you should have done, though you should not have left the others undone either. You blind leaders! You strain out a small fly but swallow a camel.

Matthew 23:23–24 (Luke 11:42) CEV

Foreign kings order their people around, and powerful rulers call themselves everyone's friends. But don't be like them. The most important one of you should be like the least important, and your leader should be like a servant.

Luke 22:25–26 (Matthew 20:25–26) (Mark 10:42–43) CEV

GRACE (*also* BLESSING)

You have heard that it was said, "You shall love your neighbor and hate your enemy."

But I say to you, love your enemies, bless those who curse you, do good to those who hate you, and pray for those who spitefully use you and persecute you, that you may be sons of your Father in heaven; for He makes His sun rise on the evil and on the good, and sends rain on the just and on the unjust.   *Matthew 5:43–45 (Luke 6:27–28) NKJV*

Healthy people don't need a doctor, but sick people do. Go and learn what the Scriptures mean when they say, "Instead of offering sacrifices to me, I want you to be merciful to others." I did not come to invite good people to be my followers. I came to invite sinners.

Matthew 9:12–13 (Mark 2:17) (Luke 5:31–32) CEV

Saying, These last have wrought but one hour, and thou hast made them equal unto us, which have borne the burden and heat of the day. But he answered one of them, and said, Friend, I do thee no wrong: didst not thou agree with me for a penny? Take that thine is, and go thy way: I will give unto this last, even as unto thee. Is it not lawful for me to do what I will with mine own? Is thine eye evil, because I am good? So the last shall be first, and the first last: for many be called, but few chosen.

Matthew 20:12–15 KJV

Even now the harvest workers are receiving their reward by gathering a harvest that brings eternal life. Then everyone who planted the seed and everyone who harvests the crop will celebrate together. So the saying proves true, "Some plant the seed, and others harvest the crop." I am sending you to harvest crops in fields where others have done all the hard work.   *John 4:36–38 CEV*

GRATITUDE (also HUMILITY)

Were there not ten cleansed? But where are the nine? Were there not any found who returned to give glory to God except this foreigner? Arise, go your way. Your faith has made you well.   *Luke 17:17–19 NKJV*

Didn't I tell you that if you believed, you would see the glory of God? Father, I thank you that you heard me. I know that you always hear me. But I said these things because of the people here around me . I want them to believe that you sent me. Lazarus, come out!   *John 11:40, 41–42, 43 NCV*

GREATNESS (also ABILITY, STRENGTH)

What kind of man did you really go out to see? Was he someone dressed in fine clothes? People who wear expensive clothes and live in luxury are in the king's palace. What then did you go out to see? Was he a prophet? He certainly was! I tell you that he was more than a prophet. In the Scriptures, God calls John his messenger and says, "I am sending my messenger ahead of you to get things ready for you." No one ever born on this earth is greater than John. But whoever is least important in God's kingdom is greater than John.   *Luke 7:25–28 CEV*

If anyone accepts a little child like this in my name, then he accepts me. And when he accepts me, he accepts the One who sent me. He who is least among you all—he is the greatest.   *Luke 9:48 (Matthew 18:5) (Mark 9:37) NCV*

Who do people think is the greatest, a person who is served or one who serves? Isn't it the one who is served? But I have been with you as a servant.

Luke 22:27 (Matthew 20:28) (Mark 10:45) CEV

GREED (also PRIDE, USURY)

Do not lay up for yourselves treasures upon earth, where moth and rust destroy, and where thieves break in and steal. But lay up for yourselves treasures in heaven, where neither moth nor rust destroys, and where thieves do not break in or steal; for where your treasure is, there will your heart be also.   *Matthew 6:19–21 (Luke 12:33–34) NASB*

What does a man gain by winning the whole world at the cost of his true self? What can he give to buy that self back?

Mark 8:36–37 (Matthew 16:26) (Luke 9:25) NEB

Beware, and be on your guard against every form of greed; for not even when one has an abundance does his life consist of his possessions. *Luke 12:15 NASB*

GRIEF (*also* LOSS)

Those who are sad now are happy. God will comfort them.
Matthew 5:4 NCV

The Spirit of the Lord is upon me, because he hath anointed me to preach the gospel to the poor; he hath sent me to heal the brokenhearted, to preach deliverance to the captives, and recovering of sight to the blind, to set at liberty them that are bruised. *Luke 4:18 KJV*

Blessed are you who hunger now, for you shall be filled. Blessed are you who weep now, for you shall laugh.
Luke 6:21 NKJV

I will ask the Father, and he will give you another Helper. He will give you this Helper to be with you forever.
John 14:16 NCV

GROWTH (*see* PROCESS)

GUIDANCE (*also* HOLY SPIRIT, MYSTICISM)

Take the yoke I give you. Put it on your shoulders and learn from me. I am gentle and humble, and you will find rest. This yoke is easy to bear, and this burden is light.
Matthew 11:29–30 CEV

Let them alone; they are blind guides of the blind. And if a blind man guides a blind man, both will fall into a pit.
Matthew 15:14 (Luke 6:39) NASB

When the Advocate comes, whom I will send to you from the Father, the Spirit of truth who comes from the Father, he will testify on my behalf. You also are to testify because you have been with me from the beginning. I have said these things to you to keep you from stumbling.
John 15:26 - 16:1 NRSV

I have many more things to say to you, but they are too much for you now. But when the Spirit of truth comes he will lead you into all truth. *John 16:12 NCV*

GUILT (*also* ANGER, FEAR, REPENTANCE)

If you forgive others for the wrongs they do to you, your Father in heaven will forgive you. But if you don't forgive others, your Father will not forgive your sins.

Matthew 6:14-15 (Mark 11:25-26) CEV

Go your way; and as you have believed, so let it be done for you.
Matthew 8:13 NKJV

If I had not come and spoken to them, they would not be guilty of sin. But now they have no excuse for their sin. Everyone who hates me also hates my Father. I have done things no one else has ever done. If they had not seen me do these things, they would not be guilty. But they did see me do these things, and they still hate me and my Father too.
John 15:22-24 CEV

HARMLESSNESS (*also* INNOCENCE)

Blessed are the poor in spirit, for theirs is the kingdom of
heaven.
Blessed are the gentle, for they shall inherit the earth.
Blessed are the peacemakers, for they shall be called sons
of God.
Matthew 5:3, 5, 9 NASB

Do not fear those who kill the body but cannot kill the soul; rather fear him who can destroy both soul and body in hell.
Matthew 10:28 (Luke 12:4-5) NRSV

This is what I say to all who will listen to me: Love your enemies, and be good to everyone who hates you. Ask God to bless anyone who curses you, and pray for everyone who is cruel to you. If someone slaps you on one cheek, don't stop that person from slapping you on the other cheek. If someone wants to take your coat, don't try to keep back your shirt. Give to everyone who asks and don't ask people to return what they have taken from you. Treat others just as you want to be treated.
Luke 6:27-31 (Matthew 5:39-42, 44) CEV

HARMONY (also COMMUNITY, PEACE, PEACE OF MIND)

Therefore if you bring your gift to the altar, and there remember that your brother has something against you, leave your gift there before the altar, and go your way. First be reconciled to your brother, and then come and offer your gift.

Matthew 5:23–24 NKJV

A new commandment I give to you, that you love one another, even as I have loved you, that you also love one another. *John 13:34 (John 15:12, 17) NASB*

HASTE (also PATIENCE)

So do not worry about tomorrow, for tomorrow will bring worries of its own. Today's trouble is enough for today.

Matthew 6:34 (Luke 12:31) NRSV

And the cares of this world, and the deceitfulness of riches, and the lusts of other things entering in, choke the word, and it becometh unfruitful.

Mark 4:19 (Matthew 13:22) (Luke 8:14) KJV

HATRED (also JUDGMENT)

No one can serve two masters; for either he will hate the one and love the other, or else he will be loyal to the one and despise the other. You cannot serve God and mammon. *Matthew 6:24 (Luke 16:13) NKJV*

Brother will betray brother to death, and a father his child, and children will rise against parents and have them put to death; and you will be hated by all because of my name. But the one who endures to the end will be saved.

Matthew 10:21–22 (Matthew 24:10–13) (Mark 13:13) (Luke 21:17,19) NRSV

I say to you who are listening to me, love your enemies. Do good to those who hate you. Ask God to bless those who say bad things to you. Pray for those who are cruel to you. If anyone slaps you on your cheek, let him slap the other cheek too. If someone takes your coat, do not stop him from taking your shirt. *Luke 6:27–29 (Matthew 5:43–45) NCV*

He that heareth you heareth me; and he that despiseth you despiseth me; and he that despiseth me despiseth him that sent me. *Luke 10:16 (Matthew 10:40) KJV*

The world cannot hate you, but it hates Me because I testify of it that its works are evil. *John 7:7 NKJV*

If the people of this world hate you, just remember that they hated me first. If you belonged to the world, its people would love you. But you don't belong to the world. I have chosen you to leave the world behind, and that is why its people hate you. *John 15:18–19 CEV*

He who hates me also hates my Father. *John 15:23 NCV*

HEALING (*also* FAITH)

I will come and heal him. *Matthew 8:7 NKJV*

Go your way; and as you have believed, so let it be done for you. *Matthew 8:13 NKJV*

Healthy people don't need a doctor. Only the sick need a doctor. Go and learn what this means: 'I want faithful love more than I want animal sacrifices.' I did not come to invite good people. I came to invite sinners.

Matthew 9:12–13 (Mark 2:17) (Luke 5:31–32) NCV

And as you go, preach, saying, "The kingdom of heaven is at hand." Heal the sick, cleanse the lepers, raise the dead, cast out demons. Freely you have received, freely give.

Matthew 10:7–8 NKJV

Stretch forth thine hand.

Matthew 12:13 (Mark 3:5) (Luke 6:10) KJV

So God's promise came true just as the prophet Isaiah had said,

"These people will listen and listen,
  but never understand. They will look and look,
  but never see.

All of them have stubborn minds!
  Their ears are stopped up,
  and their eyes are covered.

They cannot see or hear or understand.
 If they could, they would turn to me,
   and I would heal them."   *Matthew 13:14–15 CEV*

Because of this answer go your way; the demon has gone out of your daughter.

Ephphatha! . . . Be opened!

Mark 7:29, 34 (Matthew 15:28) NASB

Thou dumb and deaf spirit, I charge thee, come out of him, and enter no more into him. This kind can come forth by nothing, but prayer and fasting.   *Mark 9:25, 29 KJV*

And these signs will accompany those who believe: by using my name they will cast out demons; they will speak in new tongues; they will pick up snakes in their hands, and if they drink any deadly thing, it will not hurt them; they will lay their hands on the sick, and they will recover.

Mark 16:17–18 NRSV

Why are you thinking that? Is it easier for me to tell this crippled man that his sins are forgiven or to tell him to get up and walk? But now you will see that the Son of Man has the right to forgive sins here on earth. . . Get up! Pick up your mat and walk home.

Luke 5:22–24 (Matthew 9:4–6) (Mark 2:8–11) CEV

Go and tell John the things you have seen and heard; that the blind see, the lame walk, the lepers are cleansed, the deaf hear, the dead are raised, the poor have the gospel preached to them. And blessed is he who is not offended because of Me.   *Luke 7:22–23 (Matthew 11:4–6) NKJV*

Who is the one who touched Me?

Someone did touch Me, for I was aware that power had gone out of Me.

Daughter, your faith has made you well; go in peace.

Do not be afraid any longer; only believe, and she shall be made well.

Luke 8:45, 46, 48, 50 (Matthew 9:22) (Mark 5:30, 34, 36) NASB

Weren't ten men healed? Where are the other nine? Why was this foreigner the only one who came back to thank God? You may get up and go. Your faith has made you well.   *Luke 17:17–19 CEV*

Go your way; your son lives.   *John 4:50 NKJV*

Do you want to be healed?

Pick up your mat and walk!

You are now well. But don't sin anymore or something worse might happen to you.   *John 5:6, 8, 14 CEV*

This sickness is not unto death, but for the glory of God, that the Son of God might be glorified thereby.

John 11:4 KJV

Where have you put his body?

Didn't I tell you that if you had faith, you would see the glory of God?

Father, I thank you for answering my prayer. I know that you always answer my prayers. But I said this, so that the people here would believe that you sent me.

Lazarus, come out!

Untie him and let him go.   *John 11:34, 40, 41–42, 43, 44 CEV*

HEALTH (*also* MENTAL HEALTH, WHOLENESS)

But strive first for the kingdom of God and his righteousness, and all these things will be given to you as well.   *Matthew 6:33 (Luke 12:31) NRSV*

Daughter, be of good comfort; thy faith hath made thee whole.

Matthew 9:22 (Mark 5:34, 10:52) (Luke 7:50, 8:48, 18:42) KJV

The eye is the lamp of the body. So, if your eye is healthy, your whole body will be full of light; but if your eye is unhealthy, your whole body will be full of darkness. If then the light in you is darkness, how great is the darkness!

Matthew 6:22–23 (Luke 11:34–36) NRSV

If then your whole body is full of light, having no part dark, the whole body will be full of light, as when the bright shining of a lamp gives you light.   *Luke 11:36 NKJV*

HEART (*also* SPIRITUALITY)

Blessed are the pure in heart: for they shall see God.

Matthew 5:8 KJV

You have heard that it was said, "You shall not commit adultery." But I say to you that everyone who looks at a woman with lust has already committed adultery with her in his heart. *Matthew 5:27–28 NRSV*

For where your treasure is, there your heart will be also.

Matthew 6:21 (Luke 12:34) NRSV

Come to me, all you that are weary and are carrying heavy burdens, and I will give you rest. Take my yoke upon me, and learn from me; for I am gentle and humble in heart, and you will find rest for your souls. For my yoke is easy, and my burden is light. *Matthew 11:28–30 NRSV*

Don't you know that the food you put into your mouth goes into your stomach and then out of your body? But the words that come out of your mouth come from your heart. And they are what make you unfit to worship God. Out of your heart come evil thoughts, murder, unfaithfulness in marriage, vulgar deeds, stealing, telling lies, and insulting others. These are what make you unclean.

Matthew 15:17–20 (Mark 7:18–23) CEV

Why do you reason because you have no bread? Do you not yet perceive nor understand? Is your heart still hardened? Having eyes, do you not see? And having ears, do you not hear? And do you not remember?

Mark 8:17–18 (Matthew 16:8–9) NKJV

A good person has good things saved up in his heart. And so he brings good things out of his heart. But an evil person has evil things saved up in his heart. So he brings out bad things. A person speaks the things that are in his heart.

Luke 6:45 (Matthew 12:35) NCV

Let not your heart be troubled: you believe in God, believe also in me. *John 14:1 NKJV*

HEAVEN (*also* KINGDOM OF GOD)

Blessed are the poor in spirit: for theirs is the kingdom of heaven.   *Matthew 5:3 (Luke 6:20)* KJV

Store up treasure in heaven, where there is no moth and no rust to spoil it, no thieves to break in and steal. For where your treasure is, there will your heart be also.

Matthew 6:20–21 (Luke 12:33–34) NEB

Then they will see the Son of Man coming in the clouds with great power and glory. And then He will send his angels, and gather together His elect from the four winds, from the farthest part of earth to the farthest part of heaven.

Mark 13:26–27 (Matthew 24:30–31) (Luke 21:27) NKJV

Verily, verily, I say unto you, Hereafter ye shall see heaven open, and the angels of God ascending and descending upon the Son of man.   *John 1:51* KJV

No one has ascended into heaven except the one who descended from heaven, the Son of Man. And just as Moses lifted up the serpent in the wilderness, so must the Son of Man be lifted up, that whoever believes in him may have eternal life.   *John 3:13–15* NRSV

Where I am going, you cannot follow me now; but you will follow afterward.   *John 13:36* NRSV

Don't be worried! Have faith in God and have faith in me. There are many rooms in my Father's house. I wouldn't tell you this, unless it was true. I am going there to prepare a place for each of you. After I have done this, I will come back and take you with me. Then we will be together. You know the way to where I am going.   *John 14:1–4* CEV

HEBREW SCRIPTURES, OLD TESTAMENT (*also* LAW, NEW COVENANT)

Do not think that I have come to abolish the law or the prophets; I have come not to abolish but to fulfill. For truly I tell you, until heaven and earth pass away, not one letter, not one stroke of a letter, will pass from the law until all is accomplished.   *Matthew 5:17–18* NRSV

You are mistaken, not understanding the Scriptures, or the power of God. For in the resurrction they neither marry, nor are given in marriage, but are like angels in heaven. But regarding the resurrection of the dead, have you not read that which was spoken to you by God, saying, "I am the God of Abraham, and the God of Isaac, and the God of Jacob?" He is not the God of the dead but of the living.

Matthew 22:29 (Mark 1:4–27) (Luke 20:34–38) NASB

Put your sword away. Anyone who lives by fighting will die by fighting. Don't you know that I could ask my Father, and right away he would send me more than twelve armies of angels? But then, how could the words of the Scriptures come true, which say that this must happen?

Matthew 26:52–54 CEV

But the rich man said, "Abraham, then please send Lazarus to my father's home. Let him warn my five brothers, so they won't come to this horrible place," Abraham answered, "Your brothers can read what Moses and the prophets wrote. They should pay attention to that." Then the rich man said, "No, that's not enough! If only someone from the dead would go to them, they would listen and turn to God." So Abraham said, "If they won't pay attention to Moses and the prophets, they won't listen even to someone who comes back from the dead."   *Luke 16:27–31 CEV*

The law and the prophets were until John. Since that time the kingdom of God has been preached, and everyone is presssing into it. And it is easier for heaven and earth to pass away than or one tittle of the law to fail.

Luke 16:16–17 (Matthew 11:12–13) NKJV

You search the scriptures because you think that in them you have eternal life; and it is they that testify on my behalf. Yet you refuse to come to me to have life.

John 5:39–43 NRSV

Do not think that I will accuse you before the Father; the one who accuses you is Moses, in whom you have set your hope. For if you believed Moses, you would believe Me; for he wrote of Me. But if you do not believe his writings, how will you believe My words?   *John 5:45–47 NASB*

In your Scriptures doesn't God say, "You are gods?" The Scriptures cannot be destroyed, and God spoke to those people and called them gods. So why do you accuse me of a terrible sin for saying that I am the Son of God? After all, it is the Father who prepared me for this work. He is also the one who sent me into the world.   *John 10:34–36 CEV*

HELP (*also* SERVICE)

Give to everyone who asks you; when a man takes what is yours, do not demand it back. Treat others as you would like them to treat you.   *Luke 6:30–31 (Matthew 5:42, 7:12) NEB*

HERESY (*see* BLASPHEMY)

HEROISM (*see* GREATNESS)

HOARDING (*also* INVESTMENTS)

Then I'll say to myself. "You have stored up enough good things to last for years to come. Live it up! Eat, drink, and enjoy yourself." But God said to him, "You fool! Tonight you will die. Then who will get what you have stored up?" This is what happens to people who store up everything for themselves, but are poor in the sight of God.   *Luke 12:19–21 CEV*

HOLY (*also* DIVINITY, PURIFICATION, RIGHTEOUSNESS)

You hypocrite, first take the log out of your own eye, and then you will see clearly to take the speck out of your neighbor's eye. Do not give what is holy to dogs; and do not throw your pearls before swine, or they will trample them under foot and turn and maul you.

Matthew 7:5–6 NRSV

HOLY SPIRIT (*also* BAPTISM, GUIDANCE, MYSTICISM, POWER, REBIRTH, SPEECH, SPIRITUALITY)

If I cast out demons by the Spirit of God, surely the kingdom of God has come upon you.

Matthew 12:28 (Mark 3:25) (Luke 11:20) NKJV

I tell you that any sinful thing you do or say can be forgiven. Even if you speak against the Son of Man, you can be forgiven. But if you speak against the Holy Spirit, you can never be forgiven, either in this life or in the life to come.

Matthew 12:31–32 (Mark 3:28–29) (Luke 12:10) CEV

I tell you for certain that before you can get into God's kingdom, you must be born not only by water, but by the Spirit. Humans give life to their children. Yet only God's Spirit can change you into a child of God. Don't be surprised when I say that you must be born from above. Only God's Spirit gives new life. The Spirit is like the wind that blows wherever it wants to. You can hear the wind, but you don't know where it comes from or where it is going.   *John 3:5–8 CEV*

It is the Spirit who gives life; the flesh profits nothing. The words that I speak to you are spirit, and they are life.

John 6:63 NKJV

If you love me, you will do as I command. Then I will ask the Father to send you the Holy Spirit who will help you and always be with you. The Spirit will show you what is true. The people of this world cannot accept the Spirit, because they don't see or know him. But you know the Spirit, who is with you and will keep on living in you.

John 14:15–17 CEV

But the Helper will teach you everything. He will cause you to remember all the things I told you. This Helper is the Holy Spirit whom the Father will send in my name.

John 14:26 NCV

I still have many things to say to you, but you cannot bear them now. When the Spirit of truth comes, he will guide you into all the truth; for he will not speak on his own, but will speak whatever he hears, and he will declare to yout he things that are to come.   *John 16:12–13 NRSV*

I am sending you just as the Father has sent me. Receive the Holy Spirit.   *John 20:21–22 CEV*

HOMELESSNESS

Give to him that asketh thee, and from him that would
borrow of thee turn not thou away.   *Matthew 5:42 KJV*

Then the king will say to those on his right, "My father has
blessed you! Come and receive the kingdom that was
prepared for you before the world was created. When I was
hungry, you gave me something to eat, and when I was
thirsty, you gave me something to drink. When I was a
stranger, you welcomed me, and when I was naked, you
gave me clothes to wear. When I was sick, you took care of
me, and when I was in jail, you visited me."
                                              Matthew 25:34–36 CEV

God will bless you people who are poor.
His kingdom belongs to you!
God will bless you hungry people.
You will have plenty to eat!
God will bless you people who are crying.
You will laugh!   *Luke 6:20–21 CEV*

Give to everyone who asks you. When a person takes
something that is yours, don't ask for it back. Do for other
people what you want them to do for you.
                                Luke 6:30–31 (Matthew 5:42, 7:12) NCV

Foxes have holes, and birds of the air have nests; but the
Son of Man has nowhere to lay his head.
                                         Luke 9:58 (Matthew 9:20) NRSV

If you would only give what you have to the poor,
everything you do would please God.   *Luke 11:41 CEV*

Sell your possessions and give to charity; make yourselves
purses which do not wear out, an unfailing treasure in
heaven, where no thief comes near, nor moth destroys. For
where your treasure is, there will your heart be also.
          Luke 12:33–34 (Matthew 19:21) (Mark 10:21) (Luke 18:22) NASB

When you give a dinner or a supper, do not ask your
friends, your brothers, your relatives, nor rich neighbors,
lest they also invite you back, and you be repaid. But when

you give a feast, invite the poor, the maimed, the lame, the blind. And you will be blessed, because they cannot repay you; for you shall be repaid at the resurrection of the just.

Luke 14:12–14 NKJV

HOMOSEXUALITY (see SEX)

HONESTY (also CHARACTER)

When you make a promise, say only "Yes" or "No." Anything else comes from the devil.   *Matthew 5:37 CEV*

You know the commandments. "Do not murder. Be faithful in marriage. Do not steal. Do not tell lies about others. Do not cheat. Respect your father and mother."

Mark 10:19 (Matthew 19:17–19) (Luke 18:20) CEV

Beware of the yeast of the Pharisees, that is, their hypocrisy. Nothing is covered up that will not be uncovered, and nothing secret that will not become known. Therefore whatever you have said in the dark will be heard in the light, and what you have whispered behind closed doors will be proclaimed from the housetops.

Luke 12:1–3 (Matthew 10:26–27) (Mark 4:22) (Luke 8:17) NRSV

Whoever is faithful in a very little is faithful also in much; and whoever is dishonest in a very little is dishonest also in much.   *Luke 16:10 NRSV*

For everyone who does evil hates the light, and does not come to the light, lest his deeds should be exposed. But he who practices the truth comes to the light, that his deeds may be manifested as having been wrought in God.

John 3:20–21 NASB

HONOR (also LOVE, PRAISE)

Whoever is the greatest should be the servant of others. If you put yourself above others, you will be put down. But if you humble yourself, you will be honored.

Matthew 23:11–12 (Luke 14:11) (Luke 18:14) CEV

A prophet is not without honor, except in his own country, among his own relatives, and in his own house.

Mark 6:4 (Matthew 13:57) NKJV

HOPE (*also* FAITH)

He may not get up and give you the bread, just because you are his friend. But he will get up and give you as much as you need, simply because you are not ashamed to keep on asking. So I tell you to ask and you will receive, search and you will find, knock and the door will be opened for you. Everyone who asks will receive, everyone who searches will find, and the door will be opened for everyone who knocks.   *Luke 11:8–10* CEV

For God so loved the world, that he gave his only begotten Son, that whosoever believeth in him should not perish, but have everlasting life. For God sent not his Son into the world to condemn the world; but that the world through him might be saved.   *John 3:16–17* KJV

If you keep on obeying what I have said, you truly are my disciples. You will know the truth, and the truth will set you free.   *John 8:31–32* CEV

So if the Son makes you free, you will be free indeed.

John 8:36 NRSV

However when He, the Spirit of truth, has come, He will guide you into all truth; for He will not speak on His own authority, but whatever He hears He will speak; and He will tell you things to come.   *John 16:13* NKJV

HOSPITALITY (*also* COURTESY)

He that receiveth you receiveth me, and he that receiveth me receiveth him that sent me. He that receiveth a prophet in the name of a prophet shall receive a prophet's reward; and he that receiveth a righteous man in the name of a righteous man shall receive a righteous man's reward. And whosoever shall give to drink unto one of these little ones a cup of cold water only in the name of a disciple, verily I say unto you, he shall in no wise lose his reward.

Matthew 10:40–42 (Mark 9:41) KJV

"When I was hungry, you gave me something to eat, and when I was thirsty, you gave me something to drink. When I was a stranger you welcomed me, and when I was naked, you gave me clothes to wear. When I was sick, you took care of me, and when I was in jail, you visited me."

"Whenever you did it for any of my people, no matter how unimportant they seemed, you did it for me."

Matthew 25:35–36, 40 CEV

Have you noticed this woman? When I came into your home, you didn't give me any water so I could wash my feet. But she has washed my feet with her tears and dried them with her hair. You didn't greet me with a kiss, but from the time I came in, she has not stopped kissing my feet.

Luke 7:44–45 CEV

When you give a dinner or a banquet, don't invite your friends and family and relatives and rich neighbors. If you do, they will invite you in return, and you will be paid back. When you give a feast, invite the poor, the crippled, the lame, and the blind. They cannot pay you back. But God will bless you and reward you when his people rise from death.

Luke 14:12–14 CEV

HUMANITY, HUMANKIND (*also* SELF-ACTUALIZATION)

Watch and pray, lest you enter into temptation. The spirit indeed is willing, but the flesh is weak.

Matthew 26:41 (Mark 14:38) (Luke 22:46) NKJV

The Sabbath was made for man, and not man for the Sabbath. Consequently, the Son of Man is Lord even of the Sabbath.

Mark 2:27–28 (Matthew 12:8) (Luke 6:5) NASB

Most assuredly, I say to you, unless one is born of water and the Spirit, he cannot enter the kingdom of God. That which is born of the flesh is flesh, and that which is born of the Spirit is spirit. Do not marvel that I said to you, "You must be born again."

John 3:5–7 NKJV

It is the spirit that gives life; the flesh is useless. The words that I have spoken to you are spirit and life.

John 6:63 NRSV

In your Scriptures doesn't God say, "You are gods?" The Scriptures cannot be destroyed, and God spoke to those people and called them gods. *John 10:34–35 CEV*

HUMILITY (also GENTLENESS)

Blessed are the poor in spirit, for theirs is the kingdom of heaven.

Blessed are the meek, for they shall inherit the earth.

Blessed are the peacemakers, for they shall be called sons of God. *Matthew 5:3, 5, 9 NKJV*

But I tell you not to try to get even with a person who has done something to you. When someone slaps your right cheek, turn and let that person slap your other cheek. If someone sues you for your shirt, give up you coat as well. If a soldier forces you to carry his pack one mile, carry it two miles. *Matthew 5:39–40 (Luke 6:29) CEV*

Take my yoke upon you, and learn from me; for I am gentle and humble in heart, and you will find rest for your souls. For my yoke is easy, and my burden is light.
Matthew 11:29–30 NRSV

I promise you this. If you don't change and become like this child, you will never get into the kingdom of heaven. But if you are as humble as this child, you are the greatest in the kingdom of heaven.

Matthew 18:3–4 (Mark 10:15) (Luke 18:17)) CEV

Why callest thou me good? there is none good but one, that is, God: but if thou wilt enter into life, keep the commandments. *Matthew 19:17 (Mark 10:18) (Luke 18:19) KJV*

It is not so among you, but whoever wishes to become great among you shall be your servant, and whoever wishes to be first among you shall be your slave; just as the Son of Man did not come to be served, but to serve, and to give His life a ransom for many.

Matthew 20:26–28 (Mark 10:43–45) (Luke 22:27) NASB

Neither be ye called masters: for one is your Master, even Christ. But he that is greatest among you shall be your servant. And whosoever shall exalt himself shall be abased; and he that shall humble himself shall be exalted.

Matthew 23:10–12 (Mark 9:35) (Luke 14:11, 18:14) KJV

My Father, Lord of heaven and earth, I am grateful that you hid all this from the wise and educated people and showed it to ordinary people. Yes, Father, that is what pleased you.

Luke 10:21 (Matthew 11:25–26) CEV

So likewise you, when you have done all those things which you are commanded, say, "We are unprofitable servants. We have done what was our duty to do."

Luke 17:10 NKJV

It was this man, I tell you, and not the other, who went home acquitted of his sins. For everyone who exalts himself will be humbled; and whoever humbles himself will be exalted.

Luke 18:14 NEB

I cannot do anything on my own. The Father sent me, and he is the one who told me how to judge. I judge with fairness, because I obey him, and I don't just try to please myself.

John 5:30 CEV

But I do not seek My glory; there is One who seeks and judges.

John 8:50 NASB

If I glorify myself, my glory is nothing. It is my Father who glorifies me, he of whom you say, "He is our God," though you do not know him. But I know him; if I would say that I do not know him, I would be a liar like you. But I do know him and I keep his word.

John 8:54–55 NRSV

I don't speak on my own. I say only what the Father who sent me has told me to say.

John 12:49 CEV

HUNGER (*also* NEED, THIRST)

Give us this day our daily bread.

Matthew 6:11 (Luke 11:3) KJV

Then the righteous will answer Him, saying, "Lord, when did we see You hungry and feed You, or thirsty and give You drink? When did we see You a stranger and take You in, or naked and clothe You? Or when did we see You sick, or in prison, and come to You?" And the King will answer and say to them, "Assuredly I say to you, inasmuch as you did it to one of the least of these My brethren, you did it to Me."   *Matthew 25:37–40 NKJV*

Then the people will ask, "Lord, when did we fail to help you when you were hungry or thirsty or a stranger or naked or sick or in jail?" The king will say to them, "Whenever you failed to help any of my people, no matter how unimportant they seemed, you failed to do it for me."
Matthew 25:44–45 CEV

You surely have read what David did when he and his followers were hungry. He went into the house of God and took the sacred loaves of bread that only priests were supposed to eat. He not only ate some himself, but even gave some to his followers.
Luke 6:3–4 (Matthew 12:3–4) (Mark 2:25–26) CEV

But woe to you who are rich, for you have received your consolation. Woe to you who are full now, for you will be hungry. Woe to you who are laughing now, for you will mourn and weep.   *Luke 6:24–25 NRSV*

Simon, son of Jonas, lovest thou me more than these?
Feed my lambs.
Simon, son of Jonas, lovest thou me?
Feed my sheep.
Simon, son of Jonas, lovest thou me?
Feed my sheep.   *John 21:15–17 KJV*

HYPOCRISY, HYPOCRITES *(also* RELIGIOSITY)

And why do you look at the speck that is in your brother's eye, but do not notice the log that is in your own eye? Or how can you say to your brother, "Let me take the speck out of your eye," and behold, the log is in your own eye? You hypocrite, first take the log out of your own eye, and then you will see clearly to take the speck out of your brother's eye.   *Matthew 7:3–5 (Luke 6:41–42) NASB*

Why do you disobey God and follow your own teaching? Didn't God command you to respect your father and mother?...But you let people get by without helping their parents when they should. You let them say that what they have has been offered to God. Is this any way to show respect to your parents? You ignore God's commands in order to follow your own teaching. And you are nothing but showoffs! Isaiah the prophet was right when he wrote that God had said,

"All of you praise me with your words
     but you never really think about me.
It is useless for you to worship me,
     when you teach rules made up by humans."

Matthew 15:3–9 (Mark 7:6–13) CEV

The scribes and Pharisees have seated themselves in the chair of Moses; therefore all that they tell you, do and observe, but do not do according to their deeds; for they say things, and do not do them. And they tie up heavy loads, and lay them on men's shoulders; but they themselves are unwilling to move them with so much as a finger. But they do all their deeds to be noticed by men; for they broaden their phylacteries, and lengthen the tassels of their garments. And they love the place of honor at banquets, and the chief seats in the synagogues, and respectful greetings in the market places, and being called by men, Rabbi.   *Matthew 23:2–7 (Luke 11:43, 46) NASB*

You are in for trouble! You are supposed to lead others, but you are blind. You teach that it doesn't matter if a person swears by the temple. But you say that it does matter if someone swears by the gold in the temple. You blind fools! Which is greater, the gold or the temple that makes the gold sacred? You also teach that it doesn't matter if a person swears by the altar. But you say that it does matter if someone swears by the gift on the altar. Are you blind? Which is more important, the gift or the altar that makes the gift sacred?

Matthew 23:16–19 (Mark 12:40) (Luke 20:47) CEV

Why do you call me 'Lord, Lord,' but do not do what I say?

Luke 6:46 (Matthew 7:21) NCV

Now you Pharisees clean the outside of the cup and of the dish, but inside you are full of greed and wickedness. You fools! Did not the one who made the outside make the inside also? So give for alms those things that are within; and see, everything will be clean for you.

Luke 11:39–41 (Matthew 23:25–26) NRSV

You Pharisees are in for trouble! You love the front seats in the meeting places, and you like to be greeted with honor in the market. But you are in for trouble! You are like unmarked graves that people walk on without even knowing it.

Luke 11:43–44 (Matthew 23:2, 6–7, 27) (Mark 12:38–39) CEV

Beware of the yeast of the Pharisees, that is, their hypocrisy. Nothing is covered up that will not be uncovered, and nothing secret that will not become known. Therefore whatever you have said in the dark will be heard in the light, and what you have whispered behind closed doors will be proclaimed from the housetops.

Luke 12:1–3 (Matthew 10:26–27) (Mark 4:22) (Luke 8:17) NRSV

Ye hypocrites, ye can discern the face of the sky and of the earth; but how is it that ye do not discern this time? Yea, and why even of yourselves judge ye not what is right?

Luke 12:56–57 (Matthew 16:3) KJV

You hypocrites, does not each of you on the Sabbath untie his ox or his donkey from the stall, and lead him away to water him? And this woman, a daughter of Abraham as she is, whom Satan has bound for eighteen long years, should she not have been released from this bond on the Sabbath day?

Luke 13:15–16 (Matthew 12:11–12) (Luke 14:5) NASB

If ye love me, keep my commandments.   *John 14:15 KJV*

IDEALISM (*also* ALTRUISM, SPIRITUALITY)

Because of your little faith. For truly I tell you, if you have faith the size of a mustard seed, you will say to this mountain, "Move from here to there," and it will move; and nothing will be impossible for you.

Matthew 17:20 (Luke 17:6) NRSV

Why do you say, "If you can"? Anything is possible for someone who has faith. *Mark 9:23 CEV*

With men it is impossible, but not with God; for with God all things are possible.

Mark 10:27 (Matthew 19:26) (Luke 18:27) NKJV

IDOLATRY (*also* MATERIALISM)

No man can serve two masters: for either he will hate the one, and love the other; or else he will hold to the one, and despise the other. Ye cannot serve God and mammon.

Matthew 6:24 (Luke 16:13) KJV

You hypocrites, rightly did Isaiah prophesy of you, saying,
  "This people honors Me with their lips,
  but their heart is far away from Me.
  But in vain do they worship Me,
  teaching as doctrines the precepts of men."

Matthew 15:7–9 (Mark 7:6–7) NASB

You disobey God's commands in order to obey what humans have taught. You are good at rejecting God's commands so that you can follow your own teachings!

Mark 7:8–9 (Matthew 15:3–6) CEV

You are those who justify yourselves in the sight of others; but God knows your hearts; for what is prized by human beings is an abomination in the sight of God.

Luke 16:15 NRSV

God's kingdom is coming, but not in a way that you will be able to see with your eyes. People will not say, "Look! God's kingdom is here!" or "There it is!" No, God's kingdom is within you.

Luke 17:20–21 (Matthew 24:23) (Mark 13:21) NCV

ILLUSION (*also* DELUSION, WORLDLINESS)

Don't be greedy! Owning a lot of things won't make your life safe. *Luke 12:15 CEV*

The Kingdom of God cometh not with observation: Neither shall they say, Lo here! or, lo there! for, behold the kingdom of God is within you.

Luke 17:20–21 (Matthew 24:23) (Mark 13:21) KJV

IMITATION (*see* CONFORMITY)

IMMORALITY (*also* VALUES)

You have heard that it was said, "You shall not commit adultery." But I say to you that everyone who looks at a woman with lust has already committed adultery with her in his heart. *Matthew 5:27–28* NRSV

The seeds that fell among the thorn bushes are also people who hear the message. But they start worrying about the needs of this life and are fooled by the desire to get rich. So the message gets choked out, and they never produce anything. *Matthew 13:22 (Mark 4:18–19) (Luke 8:14)* CEV

That which proceeds out of the man, that is what defiles the man. For from within, out of the heart of men, proceed the evil thoughts, fornications, thefts, murders, adulteries, deeds of coveting and wickedness, as well as deceit, sensuality, envy, slander, pride and foolishness. All these evil things proceed from within and defile the man.

Mark 7:20–23 (Matthew 15:19–20) NASB

You cannot be the slave of two masters. You will like one more than the other or be more loyal to one than to the other. You cannot serve God and money.

Luke 16:13 (Matthew 6:24) CEV

You are those who justify yourselves in the sight of others; but God knows your hearts; for what is prized by human beings is an abomination in the sight of God.

Luke 16:15 NRSV

IMMORTALITY (*also* ETERNAL LIFE, RESURRECTION)

And fear not them which kill the body, but are not able to kill the soul: but rather fear him which is able to destroy both soul and body in hell. *Matthew 10:28 (Luke 12:4–5)* KJV

Assuredly, I say to you, there are some standing here who shall not taste death till they see the Son of Man coming in His kingdom. *Matthew 16:28 (Mark 9:1) (Luke 9:27)* NKJV

You can be sure that anyone who gives up home or wife or brothers or family or children because of God's kingdom will be given much more in this life. And in the future world they will have eternal life.

Luke 18:29–30 (Matthew 19:29) (Mark 10:29–30) CEV

The people in this world get married. But in the future world no one who is worthy to rise from death will either marry or die. They will be like the angels and will be God's children, because they have been raised to life. In the story about the burning bush, Moses clearly shows that people will live again. He said, "The Lord is the God worshiped by Abraham, Isaac, and Jacob." So the Lord is not the God of the dead, but of the living. This means that everyone is alive as far as God is concerned.

Luke 20:34–38 (Matthew 22:30–32) (Mark 12:25–27) CEV

I am the bread of life! Your fathers ate the manna in the wilderness, and are dead. This is the bread which comes down from heaven, that one may eat of it and not die. I am the living bread which came down from heaven. If anyone eats of this bread, he will live forever; and the bread that I shall give is my flesh, which I shall give for the life of the world. *John 6:48–51* NKJV

INCLUSIVENESS (*also* ECUMENISM)

Don't condemn others, and God will not condemn you. God will be as hard on you as you are on others! He will treat you exactly as you treat them.

Matthew 7:1–2 (Luke 6:37–38) CEV

But the Son of Man goes around eating and drinking, and you say, 'That man eats and drinks too much! He is even a friend of tax collectors and sinners." Yet Wisdom is shown to be right by what it does. *Matthew 11:19 (Luke 7:34–35)* CEV

Who is my mother? Who are my brothers?
Here are my mother and my brothers. Whoever does the

will of my heavenly Father is my brother, my sister, my mother.   *Matthew 12:48–50 (Mark 3:33–35) (Luke 8:21) NEB*

The Scriptures say, 'My house should be called a place of worship for all nations." But you have made it a place where robbers hide!"

Mark 11:17 (Matthew 21:13) (Luke 19:46) CEV

Go into all the world and proclaim the good news to the whole creation.   *Mark 16:15 NRSV*

The servant told his master what happened, and the master became so angry that he said, "Go as fast a you can to every street and alley in town! Bring in everyone who is poor or crippled or blind or lame." When the servant returned, he said, "Master, I've done what you told me, and there is still plenty room for more people." His master then told him, "Go out along the back roads and fence rows and make people come in, so that my house will be full."

Luke 14:21–23 CEV

It is written in the prophets, 'God will teach all the people.' Everyone who listens to the Father and learns from him comes to me. No one has seen the Father except the One who is from God. Only he has seen the Father. I tell you the truth. He who believes has eternal life.   *John 6:45–46 NCV*

A thief comes only to rob, kill, and destroy. I came so that everyone would have life, and have it in its fullest.

John 10:10 CEV

This voice has come for your sake, not for mine. Now is the judgment of this world; now the ruler of this world will be driven out. And I, when I am lifted up from the earth, will draw all people to myself.   *John 12:30–32 NRSV*

INDECISION, UNCERTAINTY (see CHOICE)

INJUSTICE (also JUSTICE, OPPRESSION)

Don't judge other people, and you will not be judged. You will be judged in the same way that you judge others. And the forgiveness you give to others will be given to you.

Matthew 7:1–2 (Luke 6:37–38) NCV

You have heard that is was said, 'Love your neighbor and hate your enemies.' But I tell you, love your enemies. Pray for those who hurt you. If you do this, then you will be true sons of your Father in heaven. Your Father causes the sun to rise on good people and on bad people. Your Father sends rain to those who do good and to those who do wrong.   *Matthew 5:43–45 (Luke 6:27–28) NCV*

Then he will say to those at his left hand, "You that are accursed, depart from me into the eternal fire prepared for the devil and his angels; for I was hungry and you gave me no food, I was thirsty and you gave me nothing to drink, I was a stranger and you did not welcome me, naked and you did not give me clothing, sick and in prison and you did not visit me." Then they also will answer, "Lord, when was it that we saw you hungry or thirsty or a stranger or naked or sick or in prison, and did not take care of you?" Then he will answer them, "Truly I tell you, just as you did not do it to one of the least of these, you did not do it to me."   *Matthew 25:41–45 NRSV*

Woe to you lawyers! For you have taken away the key of knowledge. You did not enter in yourselves, and those who were entering in you hindered.

Luke 11:52 (Matthew 23:13) NKJV

INNOCENCE (*also* HARMLESSNESS)

Blessed are the pure in heart: for they shall see God.

Matthew 5:8 KJV

I am sending you like lambs into a pack of wolves. So be as wise a snakes and as innocent as doves.

Matthew 10:16 CEV

Yea; have ye never read, Out of the mouth of babes and sucklings thou hast perfected praise?   *Matthew 21:16 KJV*

I thank you, Father, Lord of heaven and earth, because you have hidden these things from the wise and the intelligent and have revealed them to infants; yes, Father, for such was your gracious will.   *Luke 10:21 (Matthew 11:25–26) NRSV*

Suffer little children to come unto me, and forbid them not: for of such is the kingdom of God. Verily I say unto you, Whosoever shall not receive the kingdom of God as a little child shall in no wise enter therein.

Luke 18:16–17 (Matthew 19:14, 18:3) (Mark 10:14–15) KJV

INSECURITY, LOW SELF-ESTEEM (*also* SECURITY, SELF-RESPECT)

Go your way; let it be done to you as you have believed.

Matthew 8:13 NASB

Do you believe that I can make you see again?
You believe that I can make you see again. So this will happen. *Matthew 9:28, 29 NCV*

It is because you don't have enough faith! But I can promise you this. If you had faith no larger than a mustard seed, you could tell this mountain to move from here to there. And it would. Everything would be possible for you.

Matthew 17:20-21 (Luke 17:6) CEV

And I say unto you, Ask, and it shall be given you; seek, and ye shall find; knock, and it shall be opened unto you. For every one that asketh receiveth; and he that seeketh findeth; and to him that knocketh it shall be opened.

Luke 11:9–10 (Matthew 7:7–8) KJV

If then your whole body is full of light, having no part dark, the whole body will be full of light, as when the bright shining of a lamp gives you light. *Luke 11:36 NKJV*

INSINCERITY (*see* HYPOCRISY)

INSULTS (*also* CRITICISM, GOSSIP)

God will bless you when people insult you, mistreat you, and tell all kinds of evil lies about you because of me. Be happy and excited! You will have a great reward in heaven. People did these same things to the prophets who lived long ago. *Matthew 5:11–12 (Luke 6:22–23) CEV*

But I say to you that if you are angry with a brother or sister, you will be liable to judgment; and if you insult a brother or sister, you will be liable to the council; and if you say, "You fool," you will be liable to the hell of fire.

Matthew 5:22 NRSV

INTEGRITY (*also* VIRTUE)

But I say to you, do not swear at all: neither by heaven, for it is God's throne; nor by the earth; for it is His footstool; nor by Jerusalem, for it is the city of the great King. Nor shall you swear by your head, because you cannot make one hair white or black. But let your "Yes" be "Yes," and your "No," "No." For whatever is more than these is from the evil one. *Matthew 5:34–37 NKJV*

Whoever can be trusted with small things can also be trusted with large things. Whoever is dishonest in little things will be dishonest in large things too.

Luke 16:10 NCV

INTELLECTUALISM (*also* REASON)

Verily I say unto you, Except ye be converted, and become as little children, ye shall not enter into the kingdom of heaven. Whosoever therefore shall humble himself as this little child, the same is greatest in the kingdom of heaven.

Matthew 18:3–4 (Mark 10:15) (Luke 18:17) KJV

My Father, Lord of heaven and earth, I am grateful that you hid all this from the wise and educated people and showed it to ordinary people. Yes, Father, that is what pleased you.

Luke 10:21 (Matthew 11:25–26) CEV

INTROSPECTION, SELF-KNOWLEDGE (*also* SOLITUDE)

And why do you look at the speck that is in your brother's eye, but do not notice the log that is in your own eye? Or how can you say to your brother, "Let me take the speck out of your eye," and behold, the log is in your own eye? You hypocrite, first take the log out of your own eye, and then you wil see clearly to take the speck out of your brother's eye. *Matthew 7:3–5 NASB*

Ask, and you will receive. Search, and you will find. Knock, and the door will be opened for you. Everyone who asks will receive. Everyone who searches will find. And the door will be opened for everyone who knocks.

Matthew 7:7–8 (Luke 11:9–10) CEV

For from within, out of the heart of men, proceed evil thoughts, adulteries, fornications, murders, thefts, covetousness, wickedness, deceit, lewdness, an evil eye, blasphemy, pride, foolishness. All these evil things come from within and defile a man.

Mark 7:21–23 (Matthew 15:19–20) NKJV

The kingdom of God cometh not with observation: Neither shall they say, Lo here! or, lo there! for, behold, the kingdom of God is within you.

Luke 17:20–21 (Matthew 24:23) (Mark 13:21) KJV

INTUITION (also HOLY SPIRIT, MYSTICISM)

I thank you, Father, Lord of heaven and earth, because you have hidden these things from the wise and the intelligent and have revealed them to infants; yes, Father, for such was your gracious will.   *Luke 10:21 (Matthew 11:25–26) NRSV*

There is still much that I could say to you, but the burden would be too great for you now. However, when he comes who is the Spirit of truth, he will guide you into all the truth;

John 16:12 NEB

INVESTMENTS (also ECONOMICS, RICHES)

Don't store up treasures on earth! Moths and rust can destroy them, and thieves can break in and steal them. Instead, store up your treasures in heaven, where moths and rust cannot destroy them, and thieves cannot break in and steal them. Your heart will always be where your treasure is.   *Matthew 6:19–21 (Luke 12:33–34) CEV*

Some time later the master of those servants returned. He called them in and asked what they had done with his money. The servant who had been given five thousand coins brought them in with the five thousand he had earned. He said, "Sir, you gave me five thousand coins, and I have earned five thousand more." "Wonderful!" his master replied, "You are a good and faithful servant. I left you in charge of only a little, but now I will put you in charge of much more. Come and share in my happiness!"

Matthew 25:19–21 (Luke 19:12–17) CEV

For what will it profit a man if he gains the whole world, and loses his own soul? Or what will a man give in exchange for his soul?

Mark 8:36–37 (Matthew 16:26) (Luke 9:25) NKJV

If you cannot be trusted with this wicked wealth, who will trust you with true wealth? And if you cannot be trusted with what belongs to someone else, who will give you something that will be your own? You cannot be the slave of two masters. You will like one more than the other or be more loyal to one than to the other. You cannot serve God and money.

Luke 16:11–13 CEV

JEALOUSY (*also* GREED)

Now his elder son was in the field: and as he came and drew nigh to the house, he heard musick and dancing. And he called one of the servants, and asked what these things meant. And he said unto him, Thy brother is come; and thy father hath killed the fatted calf, because he hath received him safe and sound. And he was angry, and would not go in: therefore came his father out, and intreated him. And he answering said to his father, Lo, these many years do I serve thee, neither transgressed I at any time thy commandment: and yet thou never gavest me a kid, that I might make merry with my friends: But as soon as this thy son was come, which hath devoured thy living with harlots, thou hast killed for him the fatted calf. And he said unto him, Son, thou art ever with me, and all that I have is thine. It was meet that we should make merry, and be glad: for this thy brother was dead, and is alive again; and was lost, and is found.

Luke 15:25–32 KJV

JOY (*also* LIGHT)

His lord said to him, "Well done, good and faithful servant;
you have been faithful over a few things, I will make you
ruler over many things. Enter into the joy of your lord."

Matthew 25:23 (Luke 19:17) NKJV

Blessed are ye, when men shall hate you, and when they
shall separate you from their company, and shall reproach
you, and cast out your name as evil, for the Son of man's
sake. Rejoice ye in that day, and leap for joy: for, behold,
your reward is great in heaven: for in the like manner did
their fathers unto the prophets.

Luke 6:22–23 (Matthew 5:11–12) KJV

If then your whole body is full of light, having no part dark,
the whole body will be full of light, as when the bright
shining of a lamp gives you light.   *Luke 11:36 NKJV*

What man among you, if he has a hundred sheep and has
lost one of them, does not leave the ninety-nine in the open
pasture, and go after the one which is lost, until he finds it?
And when he has found it, he lays it on his shoulders,
rejoicing. And when he comes home, he calls together his
friends and his neighbors, saying to them, "Rejoice with
me, for I have found my sheep which was lost!" I tell you
that in the same way, there will be more joy in heaven over
one sinner who repents, than over ninety-nine righteous
persons who need no repentance.

Luke 15:4–7 (Matthew 18:12–13) NASB

Just as the Father has loved Me, I have also loved you; abide
in My love. If you keep My commandments, you will abide
in My love; just as I have kept My Father's commandments,
and abide in His love. These things I have spoken to you,
that My joy may be in you, and that your joy may be made
full.   *John 15:9–11 NASB*

Most assuredly, I say to you that you will weep and lament,
but the world will rejoice; and you will be sorrowful, but
your sorrow will be turned into joy. A woman, when she
is in labor, has sorrow because her hour has come; but as

soon as she has given birth to the child, she no longer remembers the anguish, for joy that a human being has been born into the world. Therefore you now have sorrow; but I will see you again and your heart will rejoice, and your joy no one will take from you.   *John 16:20–22 NKJV*

Father, I am on my way to you. But I say these things while I am still in the world, so that my followers will have the same complete joy that I do. I have told them your message. But the people of this world hate them, because they don't belong to this world, just as I don't.   *John 17:13–14 CEV*

JUDGMENT (*also* ACCUSATIONS, SELF-RIGHTEOUSNESS)

You have heard that it was said to our people long ago, 'You must not murder anyone. Anyone who murders another will be judged. But I tell you, if you are angry with your brother, you will be judged. And if you say bad things to your brother, you will be judged by the Jewish council. And if you call your brother a fool, then you will be in danger of the fire of hell.   *Matthew 5:21–22 NCV*

Judge not, that you be not judged. For with what judgment you judge, you will be judged; and with the measure you use, it will be measured back to you. And why do you look at the speck in your brother's eye, but do not consider the plank in your own eye? Hypocrite! First remove the plank from your own eye; and then you will see clearly to remove the speck from your brother's eye.

Matthew 7:1–3, 5 (Luke 6:37–38, 41–42) NKJV

I promise you that on the day of judgment, everyone will have to account for every careless word they have spoken. On that day they will be told that they are either innocent or guilty because of the things they have said.

Matthew 12:36–37 (Luke 6:45) CEV

Judge not according to appearance, but judge with righteous judgment.   *John 7:24 NASB*

Is there anyone here who has never sinned? The person without sin can throw the first stone at this woman.

Woman, all of those people have gone. Has no one judged you guilty?

So I also don't judge you. You may go now, but don't sin again. *John 8:7, 10, 11 NCV*

Ye judge after the flesh; I judge no man. *John 8:15 KJV*

For judgment I have come into this world, that those who do not see may see, and that those who see may be made blind. *John 9:39 NKJV*

This voice has come for your sake, not for mine. Now is the judgment of this world; now the ruler of this world will be driven out. And I, when I am lifted up from the earth, will draw all people to myself. *John 12:30–32 NRSV*

I am not the one who will judge those who refuse to obey my teachings. I came to save the people of this world, not to be their judge. But everyone who rejects me and my teachings will be judged on the last day by what I have said.
John 12:47–48 CEV

JUSTICE (also EQUALITY, INJUSTICE)

Therefore, however you want people to treat you, so treat them, for this is the Law and the Prophets.

Matthew 7:12 (Luke 6:31) NASB

How terrible for you, teachers of the law and Pharisees! You are hypocrites! You give to God one-tenth of everything you earn—even your mint, dill, and cummin. But you don't obey the really important teachings of the law—being fair, showing mercy, and being loyal. These are the things you should do, as well as those other things. You guide the people, but you are blind! You are like a person who picks a fly out of his drink and then swallows a camel!
Matthew 23:23–24 (Luke 11:42) NCV

Then the king will say to those on his right, "My father has blessed you! Come and receive the kingdom that was prepared for you before the world was created. When I was

hungry, you gave me something to eat, and when I was
thirsty, you gave me something to drink. When I was a
stranger, you welcomed me, and when I was naked, you
gave me clothes to wear. When I was sick, you took care of
me, and when I was in jail, you visited me."

Matthew 25:34–37 CEV

In a certain city there was a judge who neither feared God
nor had respect for people. In that city there was a widow
who kept coming to him and saying, "Grant me justice
against my opponent." For a while he refused; but later he
said to himself, "Though I have no fear of God and no
respect for anyone, yet because this widow keeps bothering
me, I will grant her justice, so that she may not wear me out
by continually coming."
Listen to what the unjust judge says. And will not God
grant justice to his chosen ones who cry to him day and
night? Will he delay long in helping them? I tell you, he
will quickly grant justice to them. And yet, when the Son
of Man comes, will he find faith on earth?

Luke 18:2–5, 6–7 NRSV

Don't judge others, and God will not judge you. Don't be
hard on others, and God will not be hard on you. Forgive
others, and God will forgive you. If you give to others, you
will be given a full amount in return. It will be packed
down, shaken together, and spilling over into your lap. The
way you treat others is the way you will be treated.

Luke 6:37–38 (Matthew 7:1–2) CEV

KARMA (*see* JUSTICE)

KINDNESS (*also* SERVICE)

Do to others as you would have them do to you.

Luke 6:31 (Matthew 7:12) NRSV

But love your enemies, do good, and lend, hoping for
nothing in return; and your reward will be great, and you
will be sons of the Most High. For He is kind to the
unthankful and evil. Therefore be merciful, just as your
Father also is merciful. *Luke 6:35–36 (Matthew 5:44–45) NKJV*

KINGDOM OF GOD, KINGDOM OF HEAVEN
(*also* HEAVEN)

Repent: for the kingdom of heaven is at hand.

Matthew 4:17 (Mark 1:15) KJV

Blessed are those who are persecuted for righteousness' sake,
For theirs is the kingdom of heaven.   *Matthew 5:10 NKJV*

Do not go into the way of the Gentiles, and do not enter a
city of the Samaritans. But go rather to the lost sheep of the
house of Israel. And as you go, preach, saying "The
kingdom of heaven is at hand."

Matthew 10:5–7 (Luke 10:9) NKJV

Any kingdom where people fight each other will end up
ruined. And a town or family that fights will soon destroy
itself. So if Satan fights against himself, how can his
kingdom last? If I use the power of Beelzebul to force out
demons, whose power do your own followers use to force
them out? Your followers are the ones who will judge you.
But when I force out demons by the power of God's Spirit,
it proves that God's kingdom has already come to you.

Matthew 12:25–28 (Mark 3:23–25) (Luke 11:17–20) CEV

The kingdom of heaven may be compared to someone who
sowed good seed in his field; but while everybody was
asleep, an enemy came and sowed weeds among the
wheat, and then went away . So when the plants came up
and bore grain, then the weeds appeared as well. And the
slaves of the householder came and said to him, "Master,
did you not sow good seed in your field? Where, then, did
these weeds come from?" He answered, "An enemy has
done this." The slaves said to him, "Then do you want us
to go and gather them?" But he replied. "No; for in
gathering the weeds you would uproot the wheat along
with them. Let both of them grow together until the
harvest; and at harvest time I will tell the reapers, "Collect
the weeds first and bind them in bundles to be burned, but
gather the wheat into my barn.' "   *Matthew 13:24–30 NRSV*

The kingdom of heaven is like a mustard seed, which a man took and sowed in his field; and this is smaller than all other seeds; but when it is full grown, it is larger than the garden plants, and becomes a tree, so that the birds of the air come and nest in its branches.

Matthew 13:31–32 (Mark 4:30-32) (Luke 13:18–19) NASB

The kingdom of heaven is like yeast that a woman took and mixed in with three measures of flour until all of it was leavened. *Matthew 13:33 (Luke 13:20–21)* NRSV

The one who scattered the good seed is the Son of Man. The field is the world, and the good seeds are the people who belong to the kingdom. The weed seeds are those who belong to the evil one, and the one who scattered them is the devil. The harvest is the end of time, and angels are the ones who bring in the harvest. Weeds are gathered and burned. That's how it will be at the end of time. The Son of Man will send out his angels, and they will gather from his kingdom everyone who does wrong or causes others to sin. Then he will throw them into a flaming furnace, where people will cry and grit their teeth in pain. But everyone who has done right will shine like the sun in their Father's kingdom. If you have ears, pay attention!

Matthew 13:37–43 CEV

Again, the kingdom of heaven is like treasure hidden in a field, which a man found and hid; and for joy over it he goes and sells all that he has and buys that field.

Matthew 13:44 NKJV

Again, the kingdom of heaven is like a merchant seeking fine pearls, and upon finding one pearl of great value, he went and sold all that he had, and bought it.

Matthew 13:45–46 NASB

Therefore every scribe who has been trained for the kingdom of heaven is like the master of a household who brings out of his treasure what is new and what is old.

Matthew 13:52 NRSV

Assuredly I say to you that it is hard for a rich man to enter the kingdom of heaven. And again I say to you, it is easier for a camel to go through the eye of a needle than for a rich man to enter the kingdom of God.

Matthew 19:23–24 (Mark 10:23–25) (Luke 18:24–25) NKJV

For the kingdom of heaven is like a landowner who went out early in the morning to hire laborers for his vineyard. Now when he had agreed with the laborers for a denarius a day, he sent them into his vineyard. And he went out about the third hour and saw others standing idle in the marketplace, and said to them, "You also go into the vineyard, and whatever is right I will give you." So they went. Again he went out about the sixth and the ninth hour, and did likewise. And about the eleventh hour he went out and found others standing idle, and said to them, "Why have you been here standing idle all day?" They said to him, "Because no one hired us." He said to them, "You also go into the vineyard, and whatever is right you will receive." So when evening had come, the owner of the vineyard said to his steward, "Call the laborers and give them their wages, beginning with the last to the first." And when those came who were hired about the eleventh hour, they each received a denarius. But when the first came, they supposed that they would receive more; and they likewise received each a denarius. And when they had received it, they complained against the landowner, saying, "These last men have worked only one hour, and you made them equal to us who have borne the burden and the heat of the day." But he answered one of them and said, "Friend, I am doing you no wrong. Did you not agree with me for a denarius? Take what is yours and go your way. I wish to give to this last man the same as to you. Is it not lawful for me to do what I wish with my own things? Or is your eye evil because I am good?" So the last will be first, and the first last. For many are called, but few chosen.

Matthew 20:1–16 NKJV

Have you never read in the scriptures:
The stone that the builders rejected
has become the cornerstone;
this was the Lord's doing,
and it is amazing in our eyes?
Therefore I tell you, the kingdom of God will be taken away
from you and given to a people that produces the fruits of
the kingdom. The one who falls on this stone will be broken
to pieces; and it will crush anyone on whom it falls.

Matthew 21:42–44 NRSV

The kingdom of God is like a man who casts seed upon the
soil; and goes to bed at night and gets up by day, and the
seed sprouts up and grows—how, he himself does not
know. The soil produces crops by itself; first the blade, then
the head, then the mature grain in the head. But when the
crop permits, he immediately puts in the sickle, because the
harvest has come.   *Mark 4:26–29 NASB*

Blessed are you poor,
For yours is the kingdom of God.   *Luke 6:20 NKJV*

There will be weeping and gnashing of teeth there when
you see Abraham and Isaac and Jacob and all the prophets
in the kingdom of God, but yourselves being cast out. And
they will come from east and west, and from north and
south, and will recline at the table in the kingdom of God.
And behold, some are last who will be first and some are
first who will be last.   *Luke 13:28–30 (Matthew 8:11–12) NASB*

The kingdom of God cometh not with observation: Neither
shall they say, Lo here! or, Lo there! for, behold, the
kingdom of God is within you.

Luke 17:20-21 (Matthew 24:23) (Mark 13:21) KJV

Let the little children come to Me, and do not forbid them;
for of such is the kingdom of God. Assuredly, I say to you,
whoever does not receive the kingdom of God as a little
child will by no means enter it.

Luke 18:16–17 (Matthew 19:14) (Mark 10:14) NKJV

I tell you for certain that you must be born from above before you can see God's kingdom! *John 3:3 CEV*

Most assuredly, I say to you, unless one is born of water and the Spirit, he cannot enter the kingdom of God. That which is born of the flesh is flesh, and that which is born of the Spirit is spirit. Do not marvel that I said to you, "You must be born again." The wind blows where it wishes, and you hear the sound of it, but cannot tell where it comes from and where it goes. So is everyone who is born of the Spirit.

John 3:5–8 NKJV

My kingdom does not belong to this world. If it did, my followers would have fought to keep the Jewish leaders from handing me over to you. No, my kingdom does not belong to this world. *John 18:36 CEV*

KNOWLEDGE (*also* UNDERSTANDING)

Continue to ask, and God will give to you. Continue to search, and you will find. Continue to knock, and the door will open for you. Yes, everyone who continues asking will receive. He who continues searching will find. And he who continues knocking will have the door opened for him.

Matthew 7:7–8 (Luke 11:9–10) NCV

My teaching is not Mine, but His who sent me. If any man is willing to do His will, he shall know of the teaching, whether it is of God, or whether I speak from Myself. He who speaks from himself seeks his own glory; but He who is seeking the glory of the one who sent Him, He is true, and there is no unrighteousness in Him.

John 7:16–18 NASB

If you continue in my word, you are truly my disciples; and you will know the truth, and the truth will make you free.

John 8:31-32 NRSV

LABOR (*also* BUSINESS)

And can any of you by worrying add a single hour to your span of life? And why do you worry about clothing? Consider the lilies of the field, how they grow; they neither

toil nor spin, yet I tell you, even Solomon in all his glory
was not clothed like one of these.

Matthew 6:27–29 (Luke 12:25–27) NRSV

Come to me, all you that are weary and are carrying heavy
burdens, and I will give you rest. Take my yoke upon you,
and learn from me; for I am gentle and humble in heart,
and you will find rest for your souls. For my yoke is easy,
and my burden is light.   *Matthew 11:28–30* NRSV

Don't work for food that spoils. Work for food that gives
eternal life. The Son of Man will give you this food, because
God the Father has given him the right to do so.

John 6:27 CEV

LANGUAGE (*also* SPEECH)

And these signs shall follow them that believe; In my name
shall they cast out devils; they shall speak with new
tongues.   *Mark 16:17* KJV

LAUGHTER (*also* JOY)

Blessed are you who hunger now for you shall be satisfied.
Blessed are you who weep now, for you shall laugh.

Luke 6:21 NASB

Woe unto you that are full! for ye shall hunger. Woe unto
you that laugh now! for ye shall mourn and weep. Woe
unto you when all men shall speak well of you! for so did
their fathers to the false prophets.   *Luke 6:25–26* KJV

LAW (*also* COMMANDMENTS, HEBREW SCRIPTURES)

Treat others as you want them to treat you. This is what the
Law and the Prophets are all about.

Matthew 7:12 (Luke 6:31) CEV

Have you not read what David did when he was hungry,
he and those who were with him: how he entered the house
of God and ate the shewbread which was not lawful for
him to eat, nor for those who were with him, but only for
the priests? Or have you not read in the law that on the
Sabbath the priests in the temple profane the Sabbath, and

are blameless? Yet I say to you that in this place there is One greater than the temple. But if you had known what this means, "I desire mercy and not sacrifice," you would not have condemned the guiltless. For the Son of Man is Lord even of the Sabbath.

Matthew 12:3–8 (Mark 2:25–28) (Luke 6:3–5) NKJV

Love the Lord your God with all your heart, soul, and mind. This is the first and most important commandment. The second most important commandment is like this one. And it is, "Love others as much as you love yourself." All the Law of Moses and the Books of the Prophets are based on these two commandments.

Matthew 22:37–40 (Mark 12:29–31) CEV

And it is easier for heaven and earth to pass away than for one tittle of the law to fail.   *Luke 16:17 (Matthew 5:18) NKJV*

If a man receives circumcision on the Sabbath that the Law of Moses may not be broken, are you angry with Me because I made an entire man well on the Sabbath? Do not judge according to appearance, but judge with righteous judgement.   *John 7:23–24 NASB*

LEADERSHIP (*also* AUTHORITY)

Blessed are you, Simon Bar-Jonah, for flesh and blood has not revealed this to you, but My Father who is in heaven. And I also say to you that you are Peter, and on this rock I will build My church, and the gates of Hades shall not prevail against it.   *Matthew 16:17–18 NKJV*

But he who is greatest among you shall be your servant. And whoever exalts himself will be humbled, and he who humbles himself will be exalted.

Matthew 23:11–12 (Luke 14:11) (Luke 18:14) NKJV

Can a blind man lead another blind man? No! Both of them will fall into a ditch. A student is not better than his teacher. But when the student has fully learned all that he has been taught, then he will be like his teacher.

Luke 6:39–40 (Matthew 15:14) NCV

Foreign kings order their people around, and powerful rulers call themselves everyone's friends. But don't be like them. The most important one of you should be like the least important, and your leader should be like a servant.

Luke 22:25–26 (Matthew 20:25–27) (Mark 10:42–44) CEV

LEARNING (*also* EDUCATION)

Come to Me, all you who labor and are heavy laden, and I will give you rest. Take My yoke upon you and learn from Me, for I am gentle and lowly in heart, and you will find rest for your souls. For My yoke is easy and My burden is light. *Matthew 11:28–30 NKJV*

It is written in the prophets, And they shall be all taught of God. Every man therefore that hath heard, and hath learned of the Father, cometh unto me. *John 6:45 KJV*

LEGALISM (*also* MORALITY, SELF-RIGHTEOUSNESS)

You ignore God's commands in order to follow your own teaching. And you are nothing but showoffs! Isaiah the prophet was right when he wrote that God had said,

"All of you praise me with your words
but you never really think about me.

It is useless for you to worship me,
when you teach rules made up by humans."

Matthew 15:6–9 (Mark 7:6–9) CEV

You search the Scriptures, because you think you will find eternal life in them. The Scriptures tell about me, but you refuse to come to me for eternal life. *John 5:39 CEV*

LENDING (*also* MONEY)

Give to him that asketh thee, and from him that would borrow of thee turn not thou away. *Matthew 5:42 KJV*

Give to everyone who asks you. When a person takes something that is yours, don't ask for it back. Do for other people what you want them to do for you.

Luke 6:30–31 (Matthew 5:42, 7:12) NCV

And if you lend to those from whom you hope to receive back, what credit is that to you? for even sinners lend to sinners to receive as much back. But love your enemies, do good, and lend, hoping for nothing in return; and your reward will be great, and you will be sons of the Most High. For He is kind to the unthankful and evil.   *Luke 6:34–35 NKJV*

LIBERATION   (*also* ADDICTIONS, CODEPENDENCE)

Take My yoke upon you and learn from Me, for I am gentle and lowly in heart, and you will find rest for your souls. For My yoke is easy and My burden is light.

Matthew 11:29–30 NKJV

But don't act like them. If you want to be great, you must be the servant of all the others. And if you want to be first, you must be everyone's slave. The Son of Man did not come to be a slave master, but a slave who will give his life to rescue many people.

Mark 10:43–44 (Matthew 20:26–27) (Luke 22:26) CEV

The Spirit of the Lord is upon me, because he hath anointed me to preach the gospel to the poor; he hath sent me to heal the broken hearted, to preach deliverance to the captives, and recovering of sight to the blind, to set at liberty them that are bruised.   *Luke 4:18 KJV*

LIES (*also* DECEIT)

But the words that come out of your mouth come from your heart. And they are what make you unfit to worship God. Out of your heart come evil thoughts, murder, unfaithfulness in marriage, vulgar deeds, stealing, telling lies, and insulting others.   *Matthew 15:18–20 (Mark 7:20–23) CEV*

You don't understand what I say because you cannot accept my teaching. Your father is the devil. You belong to him and want to do what he wants. He was a murderer from the beginning. He was against the truth, because there is no truth in him. He is a liar, and he is like the lies he tells. He is the father of lies.   *John 8:43–44 NCV*

LIFE (*also* DEATH, ETERNAL LIFE, SOUL)

Therefore I say to you, do not worry about your life, what you will eat or what you will drink; nor about your body, what you will put on. Is not life more than food and the body more than clothing?   *Matthew 6:25 (Luke 12:22–23) NKJV*

For what will it profit them if they gain the whole world but forfeit their life? Or what will they give in return for their life?   *Matthew 16:26 (Mark 8:36–37) (Luke 9:25) NRSV*

Why do you ask me about what is good? There is only one who is good. If you wish to enter into life, keep the commandments.   *Matthew 19:17 (Mark 10:18) (Luke 18:19) NRSV*

If you want to save your life, you will destroy it. But if you give up your life for me and for the good news, you will save it. What will you gain , if you own the whole world but destroy yourself? What could you give to get back your soul?   *Mark 8:35–37 (Matthew 16:25–26) (Luke 9:24–25) CEV*

In the story about the burning bush, Moses clearly shows that people will live again. He said, "The Lord is the God worshiped by Abraham, Isaac, and Jacob." So the Lord is not the God of the dead, but of the living. This means that everyone is alive as far as God is concerned.
     Luke 20:37–38 (Matthew 22:31–32) (Mark 12:26–27) CEV

For as the Father raises the dead and gives life to them, even so the Son gives life to whom He will.   *John 5:21 NKJV*

I am the bread that gives life! Your ancestors ate manna in the desert, and later they died. But the bread from heaven has come down, so that no one who eats it will ever die. I am that bread from heaven! Everyone who eats it will live forever. My flesh is the life-giving bread that I give to the people of this world.   *John 6:48–51 CEV*

It is the spirit that gives life; the flesh is useless. The words that I have spoken to you are spirit and life.
     John 6:63 NRSV

I am the resurrection and the life; he who believes in Me shall live even if he dies, and everyone who lives and believes in Me shall never die. Do you believe this?

John 11:25–26 NASB

I am the way, the truth, and the life. No one comes to the Father, except through Me. If you had known Me, you would have known My Father also; and from now on you know Him and have seen Him.   *John 14:6 NKJV*

In a little while the world will no longer see me, but you will see me; because I live, you also will live. On that day you will know that I am in my Father, and you in me, and I in you.   *John 14:19–20 NRSV*

LIGHT (*also* MYSTICISM)

You are the light of the world. A city set on a hill cannot be hidden. Nor do men light a lamp, and put it under the peck-measure, but on the lampstand; and it gives light to all who are in the house. Let your light shine before men in such a way that they may see your good works, and glorify your Father who is in heaven.

Matthew 5:14–16 (Mark 4:21) (Luke 8:16) (Luke 11:33) NASB

Your eye is the lamp of your body. If your eye is healthy, your whole body is full of light; but if it is not healthy, your body is full of darkness. Therefore consider whether the light in you is not darkness. If then your whole body is full of light, with no part of it in darkness, it will be as full of light as when a lamp gives you light with its rays.

Luke 11:34–36 (Matthew 6:22–23) NRSV

And this is the judgment, that the light is come into the world, and men loved the darkness rather than the light; for their deeds were evil. For everyone who does evil hates the light, and does not come to the light, lest his deeds should be exposed. But he who practices the truth comes to the light, that his deeds may be manifested as having been wrought in God.   *John 3:19–21 NASB*

I am the light of the world. Whoever follows me will never walk in darkness but will have the light of life.

John 8:12 NRSV

The light will be with you for only a little longer. Walk in the light while you can. Then you won't be caught walking blindly in the dark. Have faith in the light while it is with you, and you will be children of the light.

John 12:35–36 CEV

I have come as light into the world, so that everyone who believes in me should not remain in the darkness. I do not judge anyone who hears my words and does not keep them, for I came not to judge the world, but to save the world.

John 12:46–47 NRSV

LISTENING (*also* MEDITATION)

He that hath ears to hear, let him hear.

Matthew 11:15 (Matthew 13:9) KJV

The seeds that fell among the thorn bushes are also people who hear the message. But they start worrying about the needs of this life and are fooled by the desire to get rich. So the message gets choked out, and they never produce anything. *Matthew 13:22 (Mark 4:18–19) (Luke 8:14) CEV*

More than that, blessed are those who hear the word of God and keep it! *Luke 11:28 NKJV*

So therefore, none of you can become my disciple if you do not give up all your possessions. Salt is good; but if salt has lost its taste, how can its saltiness be restored? It is fit neither for the soil nor for the manure pile; they throw it away. Let anyone with ears to hear listen! *Luke 14:33–35 NRSV*

My sheep hear my voice. I know them, and they follow me. I give them eternal life, and they will never perish. No one will snatch them out of my hand. *John 10:27–28 NRSV*

LONELINESS (*also* COMMUNITY)

And remember, I am with you always, to the end of the age. *Matthew 28:20 NRSV*

I will not leave you comfortless: I will come to you.

John 14:18 KJV

If you love me, you will do as I command. Then I will ask the Father to send you the Holy Spirit who will help you and always be with you. *John 14:15–16 CEV*

Indeed the hour is coming, yes, has now come, that you will be scattered, each to his own, and will leave Me alone. And yet I am not alone, because the Father is with Me.

John 16:32 NKJV

LOOKS *(see* APPEARANCE, WORLDLINESS)
LOSS *(also* ATTACHMENT)

Whoever tries to hold on to his life will give up true life. Whoever gives up his life for me will hold on to true life.

Matthew 10:39 (Luke 17:33) NCV

Don't store up treasures on earth! Moths and rust can destroy them, and thieves can break in and steal them. Instead, store up your treasures in heaven, where moths and rust cannot destroy them, and thieves cannot break in and steal them. Your heart will always be where your treasure is. *Matthew 6:19–21 (Luke 12:33–34) CEV*

No one can serve two masters; for either he will hate the one and love the other, or else he will be loyal to the one and despise the other. You cannot serve God and mammon. *Matthew 6:24 (Luke 16:13) NKJV*

For what will it profit them if they gain the whole world but forfeit their life? Or what will they give in return for their life? *Matthew 16:26 (Mark 8:36) (Luke 9:25) NRSV*

LOVE *(also* AFFECTION, FORGIVENESS, ONENESS)

This is what I say to all who will listen to me: Love your enemies, and be good to everyone who hates you. Ask God to bless anyone who curses you, and pray for everyone who is cruel to you. If someone slaps you on one cheek, don't stop that person from slapping you on the other cheek. If someone wants to take your coat, don't try to keep back your shirt. Give to everyone who asks and don't ask people

to return what they have taken from you. Treat others just
as you want to be treated.

Luke 6:27–31 (Matthew 5:39–42, 44) CEV

For if ye love them which love you, what thank have ye?
for sinners also love those that love them.

Luke 6:32 (Matthew 5:46) KJV

I give you a new commandment, that you love one another.
Just as I have loved you, you also should love one another.
By this everyone will know that you are my disciples, if you
have love for one another.   *John 13:34–35 (John 15:12) NRSV*

If you love me, you will do what I have said, and my Father
will love you. I will also love you and show you what I am
like.   *John 14:21 CEV*

If anyone loves Me, he will keep My word; and My Father
will love him, and We will come to him and make Our
home with him. He who does not love Me does not keep
My words; and the word which you hear is not Mine but
the Father's who sent Me.   *John 14:23–24 NKJV*

Just as the Father has loved Me, I have also loved you; abide
in My love. If you keep My commandments, you will abide
in My love; just as I have kept My Father's commandments,
and abide in His love. These things I have spoken to you,
that My joy may be in you, and that your joy may be made
full.   *John 15:9–11 NASB*

This is my commandment, that you love one another as I
have loved you. No one has greater love than this, to lay
down one's life for one's friends. You are my friends if you
do what I command you.   *John 15:12–14 NRSV*

For the Father himself loveth you, because ye have loved
me, and have believed that I came out from God.

John 16:27 KJV

I have honored my followers in the same way that you
honored me, in order that they may be one with each other,
just as we are one. I am one with them, and you are one
with me, so that they may be completely one. Then this
world's people will know that you sent me. They will know

that you love my followers as much as you love me. Father, I want everyone you have given me to be with me, wherever I am. Then they will see the glory that you have given me, because you loved me before the world was created. Good Father, the people of this world don't know you. But I know you, and my followers know that you sent me. I told them what you are like, and I will tell them even more. Then the love that you have for me will become part of them, and I will be one with them.   *John 17:22–26 CEV*

LOYALTY (see DUTY, TRUST)

LUST (also DESIRE)

You have heard that it was said, "You shall not commit adultery." But I say to you that everyone who looks at a woman with lust has already committed adultery with her in his heart.   *Matthew 5:27–28 NRSV*

Now these are the ones sown among thorns; they are the ones who hear the word, and the cares of this world, the deceitfulness of riches, and the desires for other things entering in choke the word, and it becomes unfruitful.

Mark 4:18–19 (Matthew 13:22) (Luke 8:14) NKJV

LUXURY (see MATERIALISM)

MAN, MANKIND (see HUMANITY)

MARRIAGE (also CELIBACY, DIVORCE)

But from the beginning of the creation God made them male and female. For this cause shall a man leave his father and mother, and cleave to his wife; And they twain shall be one flesh: so then they are no more twain, but one flesh. What therefore God hath joined together, let not man put asunder.   *Mark 10:6–9 (Matthew 19:4–6) KJV*

The people in this world get married. But in the future world no one who is worthy to rise from death will either marry or die. They will be like the angels and will be God's children, because they have been raised to life.

Luke 20:34–36 (Matthew 22:30) (Mark 12:25) CEV

MARTYRDOM (also PERSECUTION, SACRIFICE)

And brother will deliver up brother to death, and a father his child; and children will rise up against parents, and cause them to be put to death. And you will be hated by all on account of My name, but it is the one who has endured to the end who will be saved.

Matthew 10:21–22 (Matthew 24:10–13) (Mark 13:12–13)
(Luke 21:16–19) NASB

This is my commandment, that you love one another as I have loved you. No one has greater love than this, to lay down one's life for one's friends. You are my friends if you do what I command you. *John 15:12–14 NRSV*

MASCULINITY, MACHO, MANLINESS (also CONFORMITY)

You know that you have been taught, "An eye for an eye and a tooth for a tooth." But I tell you not to try to get even with a person who has done something to you. When someone slaps your right cheek, turn and let that person slap your other cheek. *Matthew 5:38–39 (Luke 6:29) CEV*

I promise you this. If you don't change and become like this child, you will never get into the kingdom of heaven. But if you are as humble as this child, you are the greatest in the kingdom of heaven. And when you welcome one of these children because of me, you welcome me.

Matthew 18:3–5 (Mark 10:15) (Luke 18:17) CEV

Not all men can accept this statement, but only those to whom it has been given. For there are eunuchs who were born that way from their mother's womb; and there are eunuchs who were made eunuchs by men; and there are also eunuchs who made themselves eunuchs for the sake of the kingdom of heaven. He who is able to accept this, let him accept it. *Matthew 19:11–12 NASB*

Have you noticed this woman? When I came into your home, you didn't give me any water so I could wash my feet. But she has washed my feet with her tears and dried them with her hair. You didn't greet me with a kiss, but from the time I came in, she has not stopped kissing my feet.　　　　　　　　　　　　　*Luke 7:44–45 CEV*

Whoever receives this child in my name receives me; and whoever receives me receives the One who sent me. For the least among you all—he is the greatest.

Luke 9:48 (Matthew 18:5) (Mark 9:37) NEB

You make yourselves look good in front of people. But God knows what is really in your hearts. The things that are important to people are worth nothing to God.

Luke 16:15 NCV

The Spirit is the one who gives life! Human strength can do nothing. The words that I have spoken to you are from the life-giving Spirit.　　　　　　　　　　*John 6:63 CEV*

MATERIALISM (*also* ANXIETY, APPEARANCE, STRESS, WORLDLINESS)

It is written, "Man shall not live by bread alone, but by every word that proceeds from the mouth of God."

Matthew 4:4 (Luke 4:4) NKJV

Don't store up treasures on earth! Moths and rust can destroy them, and thieves can break in and steal them. Instead, store up your treasures in heaven, where moths and rust cannot destroy them, and thieves cannot break in and steal them. Your heart will always be where your treasure is.　　　　*Matthew 6:19–21 (Luke 12:33–34) CEV*

No one can serve two masters; for either he will hate the one and love the other, or else he will be loyal to the one and despise the other. You cannot serve God and mammon.　　　　　　　　*Matthew 6:24 (Luke 16:13) NKJV*

And what is the seed that fell among the thorny weeds? That seed is like the person who hears the teaching but lets worries about this life and love of money stop that teaching from growing. So the teaching does not produce fruit in that person's life.　　*Matthew 13:22 (Mark 4:18–19) (Luke 8:14) NCV*

If any of you want to be my followers, you must forget about yourself. You must take up your cross and follow me. If you want to save your life, you will destroy it. But if you give up your life for me, you will find it. What will you gain, if you own the whole world but destroy yourself? What would you give to get back your soul?

Matthew 16:24–26 (Mark 8:34–37) (Luke 9:23–25) CEV

Assuredly I say to you that it is hard for a rich man to enter the kingdom of heaven. And again I say to you, it is easier for a camel to go through the eye of a needle than for a rich man to enter the kingdom of God.

Matthew 19:23–24 (Mark 10:23–25) (Luke 18:24–25) NKJV

Beware, and be on your guard against every form of greed; for not even when one has an abundance does his life consist of his possessions. *Luke 12:15* NASB

A rich man's farm produced a big crop, and he said to himself, "What can I do? I don't have a place large enough to store everything." Later, he said, "Now I know what I'll do. I'll tear down my barns and build bigger ones, where I can store all my grain and other goods. Then I'll say to myself. 'You have stored up enough good things to last for years to come. Live it up! Eat, drink, and enjoy yourself.' " But God said to him, "You fool! Tonight you will die. Then who will get what you have stored up?" This is what happens to people who store up everything for themselves, but are poor in the sight of God. *Luke 12:16–21* CEV

So therefore, none of you can become my disciple if you do not give up all your possessions. *Luke 14:33* NRSV

You still lack one thing. Sell all that you have and distribute to the poor, and you will have treasure in heaven; and come, follow Me. *Luke 18:22 (Matthew 19:21) (Mark 10:21)* NKJV

Take these things away! Do not make My Father's house a house of merchandise! *John 2:16* NKJV

It is the spirit that gives life; the flesh is useless. The words that I have spoken to you are spirit and life. But among you there are some who do not believe. . . . *John 6:63–64* NRSV

Why can't you understand what I am talking about? Can't you stand to hear what I am saying? Your father is the devil, and you do exactly what he wants. He has always been a murderer and a liar. There is nothing truthful about him. He speaks on his own, and everything he says is a lie. Not only is he a liar himself, but he is also the father of all lies.

John 8:43–44 CEV

MEDITATION (*also* PRAYER)

Blessed are the pure in heart: for they shall see God.

Matthew 5:8 KJV

He who has ears to hear, let him hear!　　*Matthew 11:15 NKJV*

To you it has been granted to know the mysteries of the kingdom of heaven, but to them it has not been granted. For whoever has, to him shall more be given, and he shall have an abundance; but whoever does not have, even what he has shall be taken away from him.

Matthew 13:11–12 (Mark 14:11–12) (Luke 8:10) NASB

Therefore I speak to them in parables; because while seeing they do not see, and while hearing they do not hear, nor do they understand. And in their case the prophecy of Isaiah is being fulfilled, which says,

> "You will keep on hearing, but will not
> understand;
> and will keep on seeing, but will not perceive;
> for the heart of this people has become dull,
> and with their ears they scarcely hear,
> and they have closed their eyes
> lest they should see with their eyes,
> and hear with their ears,
> and understand with their
> heart and return,
> and I should heal them."

But blessed are your eyes, because they see; and your ears, because they hear. For truly I say to you, that many prophets and righteous men desired to see what you see, and did not see it; and to hear what you hear, and did not hear it.　　*Matthew 13:13–17 NASB*

Blessed are the eyes which see the things you see; for I tell you that many prophets and kings have desired to see what you see, and have not seen it, and to hear what you hear, and have not heard it.   *Luke 10:23–24 (Matthew 13:17) NKJV*

God's kingdom is not something you can see. There is no use saying, "Look! Here it is" or "Look! There it is." God's kingdom is here with you.

Luke 17:20–21 (Matthew 24:23) (Mark 13:21) CEV

I can of Myself do nothing. As I hear, I judge; and My judgment is righteous, because I do not seek My own will but the will of the Father who sent Me.

John 5:30 (John 5:19) (John 6:38) NKJV

He that is of God heareth God's words: ye therefore hear them not, because ye are not of God.   *John 8:47 KJV*

'King' is your word. My task is to bear witness to the truth. For this was I born; for this I came into the world, and all who are not deaf to truth listen to my voice.   *John 18:37 NEB*

MEEKNESS (see GENTLENESS)

MENTAL HEALTH (also WHOLENESS)

If you forgive others for the wrongs they do to you, your Father in heaven will forgive you. But if you don't forgive others, your Father will not forgive your sins.

Matthew 6:14-15 (Mark 11:25–26) CEV

Which of you by taking thought can add one cubit unto his stature?   *Matthew 6:27 (Luke 12:25) KJV*

Therefore do not worry, saying, "What will we eat?" or "What will we drink?" or "What will we wear?" For it is the gentiles who strive for all these things; and indeed your heavenly Father knows that you need all these things. But strive first for the kingdom of God and his righteousness, and all these things will be given to you as well.

Matthew 6:31–33 (Luke 12:29–31) NRSV

Go your way; let it be done to you as you have believed.

Matthew 8:13 NASB

In your patience possess ye your souls.

Luke 21:19 (Matthew 24:12) (Mark 13:13) KJV

Don't let your hearts be troubled. Trust in God and trust in me.   *John 14:1 NCV*

Peace I leave with you; my peace I give to you. I do not give to you as the world gives. Do not let your hearts be troubled, and do not let them be afraid.   *John 14:27 NRSV*

MERCY (*also* FORGIVENESS)

Blessed are the merciful,
For they shall obtain mercy.   *Matthew 5:7 NKJV*

Healthy people don't need a doctor, but sick people do. Go and learn what the Scriptures mean when they say, "Instead of offering sacrifices to me, I want you to be merciful to others." I did not come to invite good people to be my followers. I came to invite sinners.

Matthew 9:12–13 (Mark 2:17) (Luke 5:31–32) CEV

Then summoning him, his lord said to him, "You wicked slave, I forgave you all that debt because you entreated me. Should you not also have had mercy on your fellow slave, even as I had mercy on you?"   *Matthew 18:32–33 NASB*

You give God a tenth of the spices from your garden, such as mint, dill, and cumin. Yet you neglect the more important matters of the Law, such as justice, mercy, and faithfulness. These are the important things you should have done, though you should not have left the others undone either. You blind leaders! You strain out a small fly but swallow a camel.   *Matthew 23:23–24 (Luke 11:42) CEV*

Be merciful, just as your Father is merciful. And do not judge and you will not be judged; and do not condemn, and you will not be condemned; pardon, and you will be pardoned.   *Luke 6:36–37 (Matthew 7:1–2) NASB*

METAPHYSICS (also BELIEF, FAITH, KINGDOM OF GOD, HOLY SPIRIT, INTUITION, LOVE, MIRACLES, SIGNS)

Blessed are the pure in heart,
For they shall see God. *Matthew 5:8 NKJV*

But you will not really be the one speaking. The Spirit from your Father will tell you what to say.

Matthew 10:20 (Luke 12:12) CEV

I thank you, Father, Lord of heaven and earth, because you have hidden these things from the people who are wise and smart. But you have shown them to those who are like little children. Yes, Father, you did this because this is what you really wanted. *Luke 10:21 (Matthew 11:25–26) NCV*

If I have told you earthly things and you do not believe, how will you believe if I tell you heavenly things? *John 3:12 NKJV*

MIND (also REASON)

Ask, and it will be given you; search, and you will find; knock, and the door will be opened for you: For everyone who asks receives, and everyone who searches finds, and for everyone who knocks, the door will be opened.

Matthew 7:7–8 (Luke 11:9–10) NRSV

Go your way; and as you have believed, so let it be done for you. *Matthew 8:13 NKJV*

Love the Lord your God with all your heart, soul, and mind. This is the first and most important commandment.

Matthew 22:37–38 (Mark 12:29–30) CEV

MINISTRY (also HEALING, LIBERATION)

Follow Me, and I will make you fishers of men.

Matthew 4:19 (Mark 1:17) NKJV

You are the light of the world. A city set on an hill cannot be hidden. Nor do men light a lamp, and put it under the peck-measure, but on the lampstand; and it gives light to all who are in the house. Let your light shine before men in such a way that they may see your good works, and glorify your Father who is in heaven.

Matthew 5:14–16 (Mark 4:21) (Luke 8:16) (Luke 11:33) NASB

It is not so among you, but whoever wishes to become great among you shall be your servant, and whoever wishes to be first among you shall be your slave; just as the Son of Man did not come to be served, but to serve, and to give His life a ransom for many.

Matthew 20:26–28 (Mark 10:43–45) (Luke 22:27) NASB

When I was hungry, you gave me something to eat, and when I was thirsty, you gave me something to drink. When I was a stranger you welcomed me, and when I was naked, you gave me clothes to wear. When I was sick, you took care of me, and when I was in jail, you visited me."

"Whenever you did it for any of my people, no matter how unimportant they seemed, you did it for me."

Matthew 25:35–36, 40 CEV

The Spirit of the Lord is upon me,
    because he has anointed me to bring good news to
    the poor.

He has sent me to proclaim release to the captives
    and recovery of sight to the blind,
    to let the oppressed go free,
    to proclaim the year of the Lord's favor.

Luke 4:18–19 NRSV

The harvest truly is great, but the labourers are few: pray ye therefore the Lord of the harvest, that he would send forth labourers into his harvest. Go your ways: behold, I send you forth as lambs among wolves.

Luke 10:2–3 (Matthew 9:37–38) KJV

But when you give a feast, invite the poor, the maimed, the lame, the blind. And you will be blessed, because they cannot repay you; for you shall be repaid at the resurrection of the just. *Luke 14:13–14* NKJV

Peace be with you. As the Father has sent me, so I send you.

John 20:21 NRSV

Simon, son of Jonah, do you love Me?

Do you love Me?

Feed My sheep.

John 21:17 NKJV

MINORITIES (*see* SOCIAL RESPONSIBILITY)

MIRACLES (*also* SPIRITUALITY)

And as you go, preach, saying, "The kingdom of heaven is at hand." Heal the sick, cleanse the lepers, raise the dead, cast out demons. Freely you have received, freely give.

Matthew 10:7–8 NKJV

Why doth this generation seek after a sign? verily I say unto you, There shall no sign be given unto this generation.

Mark 8:12 (Matthew 16:4) (Matthew 12:39) (Luke 11:29) KJV

Do not stop him; for no one who does a deed of power in my name will be able soon afterward to speak evil of me. Whoever is not against us is for us. For truly I tell you, whoever gives you a cup of water to drink because you bear the name of Christ will by no means lose the reward.

Mark 9:39–41 (Luke 9:50) NRSV

And these signs will accompany those who have believed: in My name they will cast out demons, they will speak with new tongues; they will pick up serpents, and if they drink any deadly poison, it shall not hurt them; they will lay hands on the sick, and they will recover.

Mark 16:17–18 NASB

Go and tell John the things you have seen and heard; that the blind see, the lame walk, the lepers are cleansed, the deaf hear, the dead are raised, the poor have the gospel preached to them. And blessed is he who is not offended because of Me.

Luke 7:22–23 (Matthew 11:4–6) NKJV

Very truly, I tell you, the Son can do nothing on his own, but only what he sees the Father doing; for whatever the Father does, the Son does likewise. The Father loves the Son and shows him all that he himself is doing; and he will show him greater works than these, so that you will be astonished. Indeed, just as the Father raises the dead and gives them life, so also the Son gives life to whomever he wishes.   *John 5:19–21 NRSV*

Believe me that I am in the Father and the Father is in me; but if you do not, then believe me because of the works themselves. Very truly, I tell you, the one who believes in me will also do the works that I do and, in fact, will do greater works than these, because I am going to the Father.
John 14:11–12 NRSV

MISSION, MISSIONARIES (*also* SOCIAL ACTION)

The harvest truly is plentiful, but the laborers are few. Therefore pray the Lord of the harvest to send out laborers into His harvest.   *Matthew 9:37–38 (Luke 10:2) NKJV*

Go not into the way of the Gentiles, and into any city of the Samaritans enter ye not: But go rather to the lost sheep of the house of Israel. And as ye go, preach, saying, The kingdom of heaven is at hand. Heal the sick, cleanse the lepers, raise the dead, cast out devils: freely ye have received, freely give. Provide neither gold, nor silver, nor brass in your purses, Nor scrip for your journey, neither two coats, neither shoes, nor yet staves: for the workman is worthy of his meat. And into whatsoever city or town ye shall enter, enquire who in it is worthy; and there abide till ye go hence. And when ye come into an house, salute it. And if the house be worthy, let your peace come upon it: but if it be not worthy, let your peace return to you. And whosoever shall not receive you, nor hear your words, when ye depart out of that house or city, shake off the dust of your feet.

Matthew 10:5–14 (Mark 6:8–11) (Luke 9:3–5; 10:3–11) KJV

I am the good shepherd. I know my sheep, and they know me. Just as the Father knows me, I know the Father, and I give up my life for my sheep. I have other sheep that are not in this sheep pen. I must bring them together too, when they hear my voice. Then there will be one flock of sheep and one shepherd. *John 10:14–16 CEV*

As thou hast sent me into the world, even so have I also sent them into the world. And for their sakes I sanctify myself, that they also might be sanctified through the truth. Neither pray I for these alone, but for them also which shall believe on me through their word; That they all may be one; as thou, Father, art in me, and I in thee, that they also may be one in us: that the world may believe that thou hast sent me. *John 17:18–21 KJV*

Simon, Son of John, do you love me? Feed my sheep.

John 21:17 CEV

MISTAKES (see IMPERFECTION, SIN)
MONEY (also MATERIALISM)

No one can be a slave to two masters. He will hate one master and love the other. Or he will follow one master and refuse to follow the other. So you cannot serve God and money at the same time.

Matthew 6:24 (Luke 16:13) NCV

Show me the coin used for the poll-tax.

Whose likeness and inscription is this?

Then render to Caesar the things that are Caesar's; and to God the things that are God's.

Matthew 22:19–21 (Mark 12:15–17) (Luke 20:24–25) NASB

So therefore, none of you can become my disciple if you do not give up all your possessions. *Luke 14:33 NRSV*

MORALITY (also LEGALISM)

Therefore, whoever breaks one of the least of these commandments, and teaches others to do the same, will be called least in the kingdom of heaven; but whoever does them and teaches them will be called great in the kingdom of heaven. *Matthew 5:19 NRSV*

Why callest thou me good? there is none good but one, that is, God: but if thou wilt enter into life, keep the commandments. Thou shalt do no murder, Thou shalt not commit adultery, Thou shalt not steal, Thou shalt not bear false witness, Honour thy father and thy mother: and, Thou shalt love thy neighbour as thyself.

Matthew 19:17–19 (Mark 10:18–19) (Luke 18:19–20) KJV

Love the Lord your God with all your heart, soul, and mind. This is the first and most important commandment. The second most important commandment is like this one. And it is, "Love others as much as you love yourself." All the Law of Moses and the Books of the Prophets are based on these two commandments.

Matthew 22:37–40 (Mark 12:29–31) CEV

My mother and my brothers are those who hear the word of God, and do it. *Luke 8:21 (Matthew 12:50) (Mark 3:35)* NRSV

A new commandment I give unto you, That ye love one another; as I have loved you, that ye also love one another. By this shall all men know that ye are my disciples, if ye have love one to another. *John 13:34–35* KJV

They who have my commandments and keep them are those who love me; and those who love me will be loved by my Father, and I will love them and reveal myself to them. . . . Those who love me will keep my word, and my Father will love them, and we will come to them and make our home with them. *John 14:21, 23* NRSV

MORTALITY (*see* DEATH, IMMORTALITY)

MOTIVATION (*also* PURPOSE)

Do not lay up for yourselves treasures upon earth, where moth and rust destroy, and where thieves break in and steal. But lay up for yourselves treasures in heaven, where neither moth nor rust destroys, and where thieves do not break in or steal; for where your treasure is, there will your heart be also. *Matthew 6:19–21 (Luke 12:33–34)* NASB

But seek first the kingdom of God and His righteousness, and all these things shall be added to you. Therefore do not worry about tomorrow, for tomorrow will worry about its own things. Sufficient for the day is its own trouble.

Matthew 6:33–34 (Luke 12:31) NKJV

But don't act like them. If you want to be great, you must be the servant of all the others. And if you want to be first, you must be everyone's slave. The Son of Man did not come to be a slave master, but a slave who will give his life to rescue many people.

Mark 10:43–44 (Matthew 20:26–27) (Luke 22:26) CEV

If you love your life, you will lose it. If you give it up in this world, you will be given eternal life. If you serve me, you must go with me. My servants will be with me wherever I am. If you serve me, my Father will honor you.

John 12:25–26 CEV

If you love me, you will do the things I command. I will ask the Father, and he will give you another Helper. He will give you this Helper to be with you forever.

John 14:15–16 NCV

MOURNING (see GRIEF)

MURDER (also VIOLENCE)

You know that our ancestors were told, "Do not murder" and "A murderer must be brought to trial." But I promise you that if you are angry with someone, you will have to stand trial. If you call someone a fool, you will be taken to court. And if you say that someone is worthless, you will be in danger of the fires of hell. *Matthew 5:21–22 CEV*

But what comes out of the mouth proceeds from the heart, and this is what defiles. For out of the heart come evil intentions, murder, adultery, fornication, theft, false witness, slander. These are what defile a person, but to eat with unwashed hands does not defile.

Matthew 15:18–20 (Mark 7:21–23) NRSV

You know the commandments. "Do not murder. Be faithful in marriage. Do not steal. Do not tell lies about others. Do not cheat. Respect your father and mother."

Mark 10:19 (Matthew 19:17–19) (Luke 18:20) CEV

MUSIC (*also* CREATIVITY, JOY)

But to what shall I compare this generation? It is like children sitting in the market places, who call out to the other children, and say, We played the flute for you, and you did not dance; we sang a dirge, and you did not mourn.
Matthew 11:16–17 (Luke 7:31–32) NASB

For this my son was dead, and is alive again; he was lost and is found. And they began to be merry. Now his elder son was in the field: and as he came and drew nigh to the house, he heard musick and dancing.   *Luke 15:24–25* KJV

MYSTERY

I thank You, Father, Lord of heaven and earth, that You have hidden these things from the wise and prudent and have revealed them to babes. Even so, Father, for so it seemed good in Your sight.   *Matthew 11:25–26 (Luke 10:21)* NKJV

Who hath ears to hear, let him hear. Because it is given unto you to know the mysteries of the kingdom of heaven, but to them it is not given.
Matthew 13:9, 11 (Mark 4:9, 11) (Luke 8:8, 10) KJV

This is why I use stories to teach people: They see, but they don't really see. They hear, but they don't really understand.   *Matthew 13:13 (Mark 4:11–12) (Luke 8:10)* NCV

Do not marvel that I said to you, "You must be born again." The wind blows where it wishes, and you hear the sound of it, but cannot tell where it comes from and where it goes. So is everyone who is born of the Spirit.   *John 3:7–8* NKJV

If you disbelieve me when I talk to you about things on earth, how are you to believe if I should talk about the things of heaven?   *John 3:12* NEB

I have much more to say to you, but right now it would be more than you could understand. The Spirit shows what is true and will come and guide you into the full truth. The Spirit does not speak on his own. He will tell you only what he has heard from me, and he will let you know what is going to happen.   *John 16:12–13* CEV

MYSTICISM, SPIRITUAL PERCEPTION

It is written, "Man shall not live by bread alone, but by every word that proceeds from the mouth of God."

Matthew 4:4 (Luke 4:4) NKJV

Blessed are the pure in heart: for they shall see God.

Matthew 5:8 KJV

But when they deliver you up, do not worry about how or what you should speak. For it will be given to you in that hour what you should speak; for it is not you who speak, but the Spirit of your Father who speaks in you.

Matthew 10:19–20 NKJV

Because it is given unto you to know the mysteries of the kingdom of heaven, but to them it is not given. For whosoever hath, to him shall be given, and he shall have more abundance: but whosoever hath not, from him shall be taken away even that he hath. Therefore speak I to them in parables: because they seeing see not; and hearing they hear not, neither do they understand. And in them is fulfilled the prophecy of Esaias, which saith, By hearing ye shall hear, and shall not understand; and seeing ye shall see, and shall not perceive: For this people's heart is waxed gross, and their ears are dull of hearing, and their eyes they have closed; lest at any time they should see with their eyes, and hear with their ears, and should understand with their heart, and should be converted, and I should heal them. But blessed are your eyes, for they see: and your ears, for they hear. For verily I say unto you, That many prophets and righteous men have desired to see those things which ye see, and have not seen them; and to hear those things which ye hear, and have not heard them.

Matthew 13:11–17 KJV

So I say to you, ask, and it will be given to you; seek, and you will find; knock, and it will be opened to you. For everyone who asks receives, and he who seeks finds, and to him who knocks it will be opened.

Luke 11:9–10 (Matthew 7:7–8) NKJV

The kingdom of God cometh not with observation: Neither shall they say, Lo here! or, Lo there! for, behold, the kingdom of God is within you.

Luke 17:20–21 (Matthew 24:23) (Mark 13:21) KJV

It is the spirit that gives life; the flesh is useless. The words that I have spoken to you are spirit and life. But among you there are some who do not believe. *John 6:63–64 NRSV*

My sheep hear my voice. I know them, and they follow me. I give them eternal life, and they will never perish. No one will snatch them out of my hand. *John 10:27–28 NRSV*

If you love me, you will do what I have said, and my Father will love you. I will also love you and show you what I am like. . . . If anyone loves me, they will obey me. Then my Father will love them, and we will come to them and live in them. *John 14:21, 23 CEV*

Thou sayest that I am a king. To this end was I born, and for this cause came I into the world, that I should bear witness unto the truth. Every one that is of the truth heareth my voice. *John 18:37 KJV*

NATIONALISM (*see* PATRIOTISM)

NATURE (*also* PROCESS)

But I say to you, love your enemies, and pray for those who persecute you in order that you may be sons of your Father who is in heaven; for He causes His sun to rise on the evil and the good, and sends rain on the righteous and the unrighteous. *Matthew 5:44–45 (Luke 6:35–36) NASB*

Look at the birds of the air, for they neither sow nor reap nor gather into barns; yet your heavenly Father feeds them. Are you not of more value than they? Which of you by worrying can add one cubit to his stature?

Matthew 6:26–27 (Luke 12:24–25) NKJV

The kingdom of God is as if someone would scatter seed on the ground, and would sleep and rise night and day, and the seed would sprout and grow, he does not know how. The earth produces of itself, first the stalk, then the head, then the full grain in the head. But when the grain is ripe, at once he goes in with his sickle, because the harvest has come. *Mark 4:26–29 NRSV*

Whereunto shall we liken the kingdom of God? or with what comparison shall we compare it? It is like a grain of mustard seed, which, when it is sown in the earth, is less than all the seeds that be in the earth: But when it is sown, it groweth up, and becometh greater than all herbs, and shooteth out great branches; so that the fowls of the air may lodge under the shadow of it.

Mark 4:30–32 (Matthew 13:31–32) (Luke 13:18–19) KJV

Foxes have holes, and birds of the air have nests; but the Son of Man has nowhere to lay his head.

Luke 9 :58 (Matthew 9:20) NRSV

Five sparrows are sold for just two pennies, but God does not forget a one of them. *Luke 12:6 (Matthew 10:29) CEV*

Look how the wild flowers grow! They don't work hard to make their clothes. But I tell you that Solomon with all his wealth was not as well clothed as one of these flowers. God gives such beauty to everything that grows in the fields, even though it is here today and thrown into a fire tomorrow. Won't he do even more for you? You have such little faith! *Luke 12:27–28 (Matthew 6:28–30) CEV*

A certain man had a fig tree planted in his vineyard, and he came seeking fruit on it and found none. Then he said to the keeper of his vineyard, "Look, for three years I have come seeking fruit on this fig tree and find none. Cut it down; why does it use up the ground?" But he answered and said to him, "Sir, let it alone this year also, until I dig around it and fertilize it. And if it bears fruit, well. But if not, after that you can cut it down." *Luke 13:6–9 NKJV*

I tell you for certain that a grain of wheat that falls on the ground will never be more than one grain unless it dies. But if it dies, it will produce lots of wheat. If you love your life, you will lose it. If you give it up in this world, you will be given eternal life. *John 12:23–25 CEV*

NEED (also DESIRE, WANTS)

It is written, "Man shall not live by bread alone, but by every word that proceeds from the mouth of God."

Matthew 4:4 (Luke 4:4) NKJV

In your prayers do not go babbling on like the heathen, who imagine that the more they say the more likely they are to be heard. Do not imitate them. Your Father knows what your needs are before you ask him.   *Matthew 6:7–8 NEB*

I tell you not to worry about your life! Don't worry about having something to eat or wear.

Life is more than food or clothing. Look at the crows! They don't plant or harvest, and they don't have storehouses or barns. But God takes care of them. You are much more important than any birds. Can worry make you live longer? If you don't have power over small things, why worry about everything else?   *Luke 12:22–26 (Matthew 6:25–27) CEV*

NEGLIGENCE (see CARELESSNESS)

NEIGHBOR (see COMMUNITY, SOCIAL RESPONSIBILITY)

NEW AGE (also SPIRITUAL, SEARCHING)

You can tell who the false prophets are by their deeds. Not everyone who calls me their Lord will get into the kingdom of heaven. Only the ones who obey my Father in heaven will get in.   *Matthew 7:20–21 (Luke 6:44, 46) CEV*

Do not stop him; for no one who does a deed of power in my name will be able soon afterward to speak evil of me. Whoever is not against us is for us. For truly I tell you, whoever gives you a cup of water to drink because you bear the name of Christ will by no means lose the reward.

Mark 9:39–40 (Luke 9:50) NRSV

Be careful that no one fools you. Many people will come and use my name. They will say, 'I am the One.' And they will fool many.   *Mark 13:5–6 (Matthew 24:4–5) (Luke 21:8) NCV*

Take heed that you not be deceived. For many will come in My name, saying, "I am He," and,"The time has drawn near." Therefore do not go after them. But when you hear of wars and commotions, do not be terrified; for these things must come to pass first, but the end will not come immediately. *Luke 21:8–9 (Matthew 24:4–6) (Mark 13:5–7) NKJV*

But the Holy Spirit will come and help you, because the Father will send the Spirit to take my place. The Spirit will teach you everything and will remind you of what I said while I was with you. I give you peace, the kind of peace that only I can give. It is not like the peace that this world can give. So don't be worried or afraid. *John 14:26–27 CEV*

NEW COVENANT, NEW TESTAMENT, NEW PARADIGM

You have heard that it was said to our people long ago, 'You must not murder anyone. Anyone who murders another will be judged.' But I tell you, if you are angry with your brother, you will be judged. And if you say bad things to your brother, you will be judged by the Jewish council. And if you call your brother a fool, then you will be in danger of the fire of hell. *Matthew 5:21–22 NCV*

You have heard that it was said, "You shall not commit adultery." But I say to you that everyone who looks at a woman with lust has already committed adultery with her in his heart. *Matthew 5:27–28 NRSV*

You know that our ancestors were told, "Don't use the Lord's name to make a promise unless you are going to keep it." But I tell you not to swear by anything when you make a promise! Heaven is God's throne, so don't swear by heaven. The earth is God's footstool, so don't swear by the earth. Jerusalem is the city of the great king, so don't swear by your own head. You cannot make one hair white or black. When you make a promise, say only "Yes" or "No." Anything else comes from the devil.

Matthew 5:33–37 CEV

You have heard that it was said, "An eye for an eye, and a tooth for a tooth." But I tell you, don't stand up against an evil person. If someone slaps you on the right cheek, then turn and let him slap the other cheek too. If someone wants to sue you in court and take your shirt, then let him have your coat too. If a soldier forces you to go with him one mile, then go with him two miles. If a person asks you for something, then give it to him. Don't refuse to give to a person who wants to borrow from you.

Matthew 5:38–42 (Luke 6:29, 30) NCV

Take, eat; this is My body.

Drink from it, all of you.

For this is My blood of the new covenant, which is shed for many for the remission of sins.

Matthew 26:26–28 (Mark 14:22–24) NKJV

No one patches old clothes by sewing on a piece of new cloth. The new piece would shrink and tear a bigger hole. No one pours new wine into old wineskins. The wine would swell and burst the old skins. Then the wine would be lost, and the skins would be ruined. New wine must be put into new wineskins.

Mark 2:21–22 (Matthew 9:16–17) (Luke 5:36–37) CEV

NONRESISTANCE, NONVIOLENCE
(also DISARMAMENT)

Blessed are the peacemakers, for they will be called children of God.

Blessed are those who are persecuted for righteousness' sake, for theirs is the kingdom of heaven.

Matthew 5:9–10 NRSV

You have heard that it was said, "An eye for an eye and a tooth for a tooth." But I say to you, Do not resist an evildoer.

Matthew 5:38–39 NRSV

This is what I say to all who will listen to me: Love your enemies, and be good to everyone who hates you. Ask God to bless anyone who curses you, and pray for everyone who is cruel to you. If someone slaps you on one cheek, don't stop that person from slapping you on the other cheek. If someone wants to take your coat, don't try to keep back your shirt. Give to everyone who asks and don't ask people to return what they have taken from you. Treat others just as you want to be treated.

Luke 6:27–31 (Matthew 5:39–42, 44) CEV

OATHS, SWEARING (also BLASPHEMY, SPEECH)

Again you have that heard it was said to those of old, "You shall not swear falsely, but shall perform your oaths to the Lord." But I say to you, do not swear at all: neither by heaven, for it is God's throne; nor by the earth; for it is His footstool; nor by Jerusalem, for it is the city of the great King. Nor shall you swear by your head, because you cannot make one hair white or black. But let your "Yes" be "Yes, " and your "No," "No." For whatever is more than these is from the evil one.   *Matthew 5:33–37* NKJV

I promise you that on the day of judgment, everyone will have to account for every careless word they have spoken. On that day they will be told that they are either innocent or guilty because of the things they have said.

Matthew 12:36–37 (Luke 6:45) CEV

You are in for trouble! You are supposed to lead others, but you are blind. You teach that it doesn't matter if a person swears by the temple. But you say that it does matter if someone swears by the gold in the temple. You blind fools! Which is greater, the gold or the temple that makes the gold sacred? You also teach that it doesn't matter if a person swears by the altar. But you say that it does matter if someone swears by the gift on the altar. Are you blind? Which is more important, the gift or the altar that makes the gift sacred?

Matthew 23:16–19 (Mark 12:40) (Luke 20:47) CEV

OBEDIENCE (also DISCIPLESHIP, SOCIAL ACTION)

You will know these false prophets by what they produce. Not everyone who says that I am his Lord will enter the kingdom of heaven. The only people who will enter the kingdom of heaven are those who do the things that my Father in heaven wants.   *Matthew 7:20–21 (Luke 6:44, 46)* NCV

Therefore whosoever heareth these sayings of mine, and doeth them, I will liken him unto a wise man, which built his house upon a rock: And the rain descended, and the floods came, and the winds blew, and beat upon that house; and it fell not: for it was founded upon rock. And every one that heareth these sayings of mine, and doeth them not, shall be likened unto a foolish man, which built his house upon sand: And the rain descended, and the floods came, and the winds blew, and beat upon that house; and it fell: and great was the fall of it.   *Matthew 7:24–27 (Luke 6:47–49) KJV*

What do you think? A man had two sons; he went to the first and said, "Son, go and work in the vineyard today." He answered, "I will not"; but later he changed his mind and went. The father went to the second and said the same; and he answered, "I go, sir"; but he did not go. Which of the two did the will of his father?   *Matthew 21:28–31 NRSV*

Why do you keep on saying that I am your Lord, when you refuse to do what I say?   *Luke 6:46 (Matthew 7:21) CEV*

> When you pray, say:
>   Our Father in heaven,
>   Hallowed be Your name.
>   Your kingdom come.
>   Your will be done
>   On earth as it is in heaven.
>
>   *Luke 11:2 (Matthew 6:9–10) NKJV*

More than that, blessed are those who hear the word of God and keep it!   *Luke 11:28 NKJV*

If you love me, you will do as I command. Then I will ask the Father to send you the Holy Spirit who will help you and always be with you. The Spirit will show you what is true. The people of this world cannot accept the Spirit, because they don't see or know him. But you know the Spirit, who is with you and will keep on living in you.

                    John 14:15–17 CEV

They who have my commandments and keep them are those who love me; and those who love me will be loved by my Father, and I will love them and reveal myself to them.

John 14:21 NRSV

Just as the Father has loved Me, I have also loved you; abide in My love. If you keep My commandments, you will abide in My love; just as I have kept My Father's commandments, and abide in His love. These things I have spoken to you, that My joy may be in you, and that your joy may be made full.

John 15:9–11 NASB

OLD TESTAMENT (*see* HEBREW SCRIPTURES)

OMNIPOTENCE (*also* POWER)

All authority in heaven and on earth has been given to me.

Matthew 28:18 NRSV

With men it is impossible, but not with God; for with God all things are possible.

Mark 10:27 (Matthew 19:26) (Luke 18:27) NKJV

Abba! Father! All things are possible for Thee; remove this cup from Me: yet not what I will, but what Thou wilt.

Mark 14:36 (Matthew 26:39) (Luke 22:42) NASB

The things which are impossible with men are possible with God.

Luke 18:27 KJV

ONENESS—WITH CHRIST (*also* UNITY)

Then they will also answer Him, saying, 'Lord, when did we see You hungry or thirsty or a stranger or naked or sick or in prison, and did not minister to You? Then He will answer them, saying, 'Assuredly, I say to you, inasmuch as you did not do it to one of the least of these, you did not do it to Me.'

Matthew 25:44–45 NKJV

Do not stop him; for no one who does a deed of power in my name will be able soon afterward to speak evil of me. Whoever is not against us is for us.

Mark 9:39-40 (Luke 9:50) NRSV

When you welcome even a child because of me, you welcome me. And when you welcome me, you welcome the one who sent me. Whichever one of you is the most humble is the greatest.

Luke 9:48 (Matthew 18:5) (Mark 9:37) CEV

But I do not seek My glory; there is One who seeks and judges. *John 8:50 NASB*

My sheep know my voice, and I know them. They follow me, and I give them eternal life, so that they will never be lost. No one can snatch them out of my hand. My Father gave them to me, and he is greater than all others. No one can snatch them from his hands, and I am one with the Father. *John 10:27–30 CEV*

If I don't do what my Father does, then don't believe me. But if I do what my Father does, even though you don't believe in me, believe what I do. Then you will know and understand that the Father is in me and I am in the Father.

John 10:37–38 NCV

Whoever believes in me believes not in me but in him who sent me. And whoever sees me sees him who sent me. I have come as light into the world, so that everyone who believes in me should not remain in the darkness.

John 12:44–46 NRSV

Most assuredly, I say to you, he who receives whomever I send receives Me; and he who receives Me receives Him who sent Me. *John 13:20 (Matthew 10:40) (Luke 10:16) NKJV*

Have I been with you all this time, Philip, and you still do not know me? Whoever has seen me has seen the Father. How can you say, "Show us the Father"? Do you not believe that I am in the Father and the Father is in me? The words that I say to you I do not speak on my own; but the Father who dwells in me does his works. Believe me that I am in the Father and the Father is in me; but if you do not, then believe me because of the works themselves.

John 14:9–11 NRSV

In a little while the world will no longer see me, but you will see me; because I live, you also will live. On that day you will know that I am in my Father, and you in me, and I in you.

John 14:19–20 NRSV

Abide in Me, and I in you. As the branch cannot bear fruit of itself, unless it abides in the vine; neither can you, unless you abide in Me. I am the vine, you are the branches. He who abides in Me, and I in him, bears much fruit; for without Me you can do nothing. *John 15:4–5 NKJV*

I ask not only on behalf of these, but also on behalf of those who will believe in me through their word, that they may all be one. As you, Father, are in me and I am in you, may they also be in us, so that the world may believe that you have sent me. *John 17:20–21 NRSV*

OPENMINDEDNESS (*also* LISTENING)

Judge not, that you be not judged. For with what judgment you judge, you will be judged; and with the measure you use, it will be measured back to you.

Matthew 7:2 (Luke 6:37–38) NKJV

Ask, and you will receive. Search, and you will find. Knock, and the door will be opened for you. Everyone who asks will receive. Everyone who searches will find. And the door will be opened for everyone who knocks.

Matthew 7:7–8 (Luke 11:9–10) CEV

For this people's heart is waxed gross, and their ears are dull of hearing, and their eyes they have closed; lest at any time they should see with their eyes, and hear with their ears, and should understand with their heart, and should be converted, and I should heal them. *Matthew 13:15 KJV*

Why do you talk about having no bread? Have you no inkling yet? Do you still not understand? Are your minds closed? *Mark 8:17 (Matthew 16:8–9) NEB*

Very truly, I tell you, we speak of what we know and testify to what we have seen; yet you do not receive our testimony. If I have told you about earthly things and you do not

believe, how can you believe if I tell you about heavenly
things?   *John 3:11–12 NRSV*

OPINIONS (see BELIEF, ENLIGHTENMENT)

OPPORTUNITY

Jerusalem, Jerusalem, the city that kills the prophets and
stones those who are sent to it! How often have I desired to
gather your children together as a hen gathers her brood
under her wings, and you were not willing!

Matthew 23:37 (Luke 13:34) NRSV

My time has not yet come, but your time is always here.

John 7:6 (John 2:4) CEV

OPPRESSION (also INJUSTICE)

Come to me, all you that are weary and are carrying heavy
burdens, and I will give you rest. Take my yoke upon you,
and learn from me; for I am gentle and humble in heart,
and you will find rest for your souls. For my yoke is easy,
and my burden is light.   *Matthew 11:28–30 NRSV*

Elijah certainly will come and get everything ready. In fact,
he has already come. But the people did not recognize him
and treated him just as they wanted to. They will soon
make the Son of Man suffer in the same way.

Matthew 17:11-12 (Mark 9:12–13) CEV

The Spirit of the Lord is upon me, because he hath anointed
me to preach the gospel to the poor; he hath sent me to heal
the broken hearted, to preach deliverance to the captives,
and recovering of sight to the blind, to set at liberty them
that are bruised.   *Luke 4:18 KJV*

Foreign kings order their people around, and powerful
rulers call themselves everyone's friends. But don't be like
them. The most important one of you should be like the
least important, and your leader should be like a servant.
Who do people think is the greatest, a person who is served
or one who serves? Isn't it the one who is served? But I have
been with you as a servant.

Luke 22:25–27 (Matthew 20:25–28) (Mark 10:42–45) CEV

ORDER (see LAW)

ORDINATION

Follow Me, and I will make you fishers of men.

Matthew 4:19 (Mark 1:17) NKJV

Ye have not chosen me, but I have chosen you, and ordained you, that ye should go and bring forth fruit, and that your fruit should remain: that whatsoever ye shall ask of the Father in my name, he may give it to you.

John 15:16 KJV

PACIFISM (also PEACE)

Blessed are the meek, for they will inherit the earth.
Blessed are the peacemakers, for they will be called
   children of God.
Blessed are those who are persecuted for righteousness'
   sake, for theirs is the kingdom of heaven.

Matthew 5:5, 9–10 NRSV

You know that you have been taught, "An eye for an eye and a tooth for a tooth." But I tell you not to try to get even with a person who has done something to you. When someone slaps your right cheek, turn and let that person slap your other cheek. If someone sues you for your shirt, give up you coat as well. If a soldier forces you to carry his pack one mile, carry it two miles.

Matthew 5:38–40 (Luke 6:29) CEV

Do not fear those who kill the body but cannot kill the soul; rather fear him who can destroy both soul and body in hell.

Matthew 10:28 (Luke 12:4–5) NRSV

Put up your sword. All who take the sword die by the sword.

Matthew 26:52 NEB

PAIN (also HEALING)

Go your way; let it be done to you as you have believed.

Matthew 8:13 NASB

The Lord's Spirit has come to me,
  because he has chosen me to tell the good news to
  the poor.

The Lord has sent me
  to announce freedom for prisoners,
  to give sight to the blind,
  to free everyone who suffers   *Luke 4:18 CEV*

When a woman gives birth to a baby, she has pain, because
her time has come. But when her baby is born, she forgets
the pain. She forgets because she is so happy that a child
has been born into the world. It is the same with you. Now
you are sad. But I will see you again and you will be happy.
And no one will take away your joy.

John 16:21-22 NCV

These things I have spoken to you, that in Me you may have
peace. In the world you will have tribulation; but be of good
cheer; I have overcome the world.   *John 16:33 NKJV*

PARADOX

If any want to become my followers, let them deny
themselves and take up their cross and follow me. For those
who want to save their life will lose it, and those who lose
their life for my sake, and for the sake of the gospel, will
save it.   *Mark 8:34–35 (Matthew 16:24–25) (Luke 9:23–24) NRSV*

For everyone who exalts himself will be humbeld, and
everyone who humbles himself will be exalted.

Luke 14:11 (Matthew 23:12) (Luke 18:14) NASB

PARENTS (also CHILDREN)

Why do you disobey God and follow your own teaching?
Didn't God command you to respect your father and
mother?... But you let people get by without helping their
parents when they should. You let them say that what they
have has been offered to God. Is this any way to show
respect to your parents? You ignore God's commands in
order to follow your own teaching.

Matthew 15:3–6 (Mark 7:8–13) CEV

If a son asks for bread from any father among you, will he give him a stone? Or if he asks for a fish, will he give him a serpent instead of a fish? Or if he asks for an egg, will he offer him a scorpion? If you then, being evil, know how to give good gifts to your children, how much more will your heavenly Father give the Holy Spirit to those who ask Him?

Luke 11:11–13 (Matthew 7:10–11) NKJV

You will be betrayed even by parents and brothers, by relatives and friends; and they will put some of you to death. *Luke 21:16 (Matthew 24:21) (Mark 13:12) NRSV*

Dear woman, why come to me? My time has not yet come.

John 2:4 NCV

PAST, THE (*also* FORGIVENESS, TIME)

If you forgive others for the wrongs they do to you, your Father in heaven will forgive you. But if you don't forgive others, your Father will not forgive your sins.

Matthew 6:14 (Mark 11:25–26) CEV

No one, after putting his hand to the plough and looking back, is fit for the kingdom of God.

Luke 21:19 (Matthew 24:12) (Mark 13:13) KJV

Suffer little children to come unto me, and forbid them not: for of such is the kingdom of God. Verily I say unto you, Whosoever shall not receive the kingdom of God as a little child shall in no wise enter therein. *Luke 18:16–17 KJV*

PATIENCE (*also* CONSTANCY)

But if you keep on being faithful right to the end, you will be saved.

Matthew 24:13 (Matthew 10:22) (Mark 13:13) (Luke 21:19) CEV

But the ones that fell on the good ground are those who, having heard the word with a noble and good heart, keep it and bear fruit with patience.

Luke 8:15 (Matthew 13:23) (Mark 4:20) NKJV

A certain man had a fig tree planted in his vineyard, and he came seeking fruit on it and found none. Then he said to the keeper of his vineyard, "Look, for three years I have come seeking fruit on this fig tree and find none. Cut it down; why does it use up the ground?" But he answered and said to him, "Sir, let it alone this year also, until I dig around it and fertilize it. And if it bears fruit, well. But if not, after that you can cut it down." *Luke 13:6–9 NKJV*

In your patience possess ye your souls.

Luke 21:19 (Matthew 24:12) (Mark 13:13) KJV

PATRIOTISM

You have heard people say, "Love your neighbors and hate your enemies." But I tell you to love your enemies and pray for anyone who mistreats you. Then you will be acting like your Father in heaven. He makes the sun rise on both good and bad people. And he sends rain for the ones who do right and for the ones who do wrong.

Matthew 5:43–45 (Luke 6:27–28) CEV

For if ye love them which love you, what reward have ye? do not even the publicans the same?

Matthew 5:46 (Luke 6:32) KJV

Why are you testing Me, you hypocrites?

Show me the coin used for the poll-tax.

Whose likeness and inscription is this?

Then render to Caesar the things that are Caesar's; and to God the things that are God's.

Matthew 22:18, 19, 20, 21 (Mark 12:15–17) (Luke 20:24–25) NASB

A prophet is not without honor except in his own country, among his own relatives, and in his own house.

Mark 6:4 (Matthew 13:57) NKJV

PEACE, PEACE OF MIND (*also* PACIFISM)

Blessed are the meek, for they shall inherit the earth.

Matthew 5:5 NKJV

Blessed are the peacemakers, for they will be called children of God. Blessed are those who are persecuted for righteousness' sake, for theirs is the kingdom of heaven.

Matthew 5:9–10 NRSV

Therefore if you bring your gift to the altar, and there remember that your brother has something against you, leave your gift there before the altar, and go your way. First be reconciled to your brother, and then come and offer your gift. Agree with your adversary quickly, while you are on the way with him, lest your adversary deliver you to the judge, the judge hand you over to the officer, and you be thrown into prison. *Matthew 5:23–25 (Luke 12:58) NKJV*

If you forgive others for the wrongs they do to you, your Father in heaven will forgive you. But if you don't forgive other, your Father will not forgive your sins.

Matthew 6:14-15 (Mark 11:25-26)CEV

Which of you by worrying can add one cubit to his stature?
Matthew 6:27 (Luke 12:25) NKJV

But more than anything else, put God's work first and do what He wants. Then all the other things will be yours as well. Don't worry about tomorrow. It will take care of itself. You have enough to worry about today.

Matthew 6:33-34 (Luke 12:31) CEV

Don't condemn others, and God will not condemn you. God will be as hard on you as you are on others! He will treat you exactly as you treat them. *Matthew 7:1-2 (Luke 6:37-38) CEV*

When you enter that home, say, "Peace be with you." If the people there welcome you, let your peace stay there. But if they don't welcome you, take back the peace you wished for them. *Matthew 10:12–13(Luke 10:5–6) NCV*

But I say to you that listen, Love your enemies, do good to those who hate you, bless those who curse you, pray for those who abuse you. If anyone strikes you on the cheek, offer the other also; and from anyone who takes away your coat do not withhold even your shirt. Give to everyone who begs from you; and if anyone takes away your goods, do not ask for them again. Do to others as you would have them do to you. *Luke 6:27–31 (Matthew 5:39–42, 44) NRSV*

Martha, Martha, you are worried and bothered about so many things; but only a few things are necessary, really

only one, for Mary has chosen the good part, which shall
not be taken away from her.   *Luke 10:41-42 NASB*

Peace I leave with you; my peace I give to you. I do not give
to you as the world gives. Do not let your hearts be
troubled, and do not let them be afraid.   *John 14:27 NRSV*

These things I have spoken to you, that in Me you may have
peace. In the world you will have tribulation; but be of good
cheer; I have overcome the world.   *John 16:33 NKJV*

PERCEPTION (*also* REVELATION, VISION(S))

Your eyes are like a window for your body. When they are
good, you have all the light you need. But when your eyes
are bad, everything is dark. If the light inside you is dark,
you surely are in the dark.

Matthew 6:22–23 (Luke 11:34–36) CEV

Go your way; let it be done to you as you have believed.

Matthew 8:13 NASB

I use stories when I speak to them because when they look,
they cannot see, and when they listen, they cannot hear or
understand. So God's promise came true, just as the
prophet Isaiah had said,

> "These people will listen and listen, but never
>   understand.
> They will look and look, but never see.
> All of them have stubborn minds! Their ears are
>   stopped up, and their eyes are covered.
> They cannot see or hear or understand.
> If they could, they would turn to me,
>   and I would heal them."

Matthew 13:13–15 (Mark 4:11–12) (Luke 8:10) CEV

Why do you reason because you have no bread? Do you
not yet perceive nor understand? Is your heart still
hardened? Having eyes, do you not see? And having ears,
do you not hear? Is your heart still hardened?

Mark 8:17–18 (Matthew 16:8–9) NKJV

The kingdom of God cometh not with observation: Neither shall they say, Lo here! or, Lo there! for, behold, the kingdom of God is within you.

Luke 17:20–21 (Matthew 24:23) (Mark 13:21) KJV

Only God's Spirit gives new life. The Spirit is like the wind that blows wherever it wants to. You can hear the wind, but you don't know where it comes from or where it is going. *John 3:8* CEV

And the Father himself, which hath sent me, hath borne witness of me. Ye have neither heard his voice at any time, nor seen his shape. And ye have not his word abiding in you: for whom he hath sent, him ye believe not.

John 5:37–38 KJV

My sheep hear my voice. I know them, and they follow me.
John 10:27 NRSV

And I will pray the Father, and he shall give you another Comforter, that he may abide with you for ever; Even the Spirit of truth; whom the world cannot receive, because it seeth him not, neither knoweth him: but ye know him; for he dwelleth with you, and shall be in you.

John 14:16–17 KJV

PERFECTION (*also* DIVINITY)

Be perfect, therefore, as your heavenly Father is perfect.
Matthew 5:48 NRSV

If thou wilt be perfect, go and sell that thou hast, and give to the poor, and thou shalt have treasure in heaven: and come and follow me.

Matthew 19:21 (Mark 10:21) (Luke 18:22) KJV

PERSECUTION (*also* OPPRESSION)

Blessed are those who are persecuted for righteousness' sake,
For theirs is the kingdom of heaven.
Blessed are you when they revile and persecute you, and say all kinds of evil against you for My sake. Rejoice and

be exceedingly glad, for great is your reward in heaven, for so they persecuted the prophets who were before you.

Matthew 5:10–12 (Luke 6:22–23) NKJV

You have heard that it was said, "You shall love your neighbor, and hate your enemy." But I say to you, love your enemies, and pray for those who persecute you in order that you may be sons of your Father who is in heaven; for He causes His sun to rise on the evil and the good, and sends rain on the righteous and the unrighteous.

Matthew 5:43–45 (Luke 6:27–28) NASB

Behold, I send out as sheep in the midst of wolves. Therefore be wise as serpents and harmless as doves. But beware of men, for they will deliver you up to councils and scourge you in their synagogues. You will be brought before governors and kings for My sake, as a testimony to them and to the Gentiles.   *Matthew 10:16–18 NKJV*

Brother will betray brother to death, and a father his child, and children will rise against parents and have them put to death; and you will be hated by all because of my name. But the one who endures to the end will be saved.

Matthew 10:21–22 (Matthew 24:10–13) (Mark 13:12–13)
(Luke 21:16–19) NRSV

And fear not them which kill the body, but are not able to kill the soul: but rather fear him which is able to destroy both soul and body in hell.   *Matthew 10:28 (Luke 12:4) KJV*

But before all these things, they will lay their hands on you and will persecute you, delivering you to the synagogues and prisons, bringing you before kings and governors for My name's sake. It will lead to an opportunity for your testimony. So make up your minds not to prepare beforehand to defend yourselves; for I will give you utterance and wisdom which none of your opponents will be able to resist or refute.

Luke 21:12–15 (Matthew 10:17–21) (Mark 13:9–11) NASB

If the people of this world hate you, just remember that they hated me first. If you belonged to the world, its people would love you. But you don't belong to the world. I have chosen you to leave the world behind, and that is why its people hate you. *John 15:18–19 CEV*

PERSEVERANCE (*also* EFFORT, ENDURANCE)

But the one who endures to the end will be saved.

Matthew 10:22 (Matthew 24:13) (Mark 13:13) (Luke 21:19) NRSV

But that on the good ground are they, which in an honest and good heart, having heard the word, keep it, and bring forth fruit with patience.

Luke 8:15 (Matthew 13:23) (Mark 4:20) KJV

In a certain city there was a judge who neither feared God nor had respect for people. In that city there was a widow who kept coming to him and saying, "Grant me justice against my opponent." For a while he refused; but later he said to himself, "Though I have no fear of God and no respect for anyone, yet because this widow keeps bothering me, I will grant her justice, so that she may not wear me out by continually coming."

Listen to what the unjust judge says. And will not God grant justice to his chosen ones who cry to him day and night? Will he delay long in helping them? I tell you, he will quickly grant justice to them. And yet, when the Son of Man comes, will he find faith on earth? *Luke 18:2–5, 6–7 NRSV*

If you keep on obeying what I have said, you truly are my disciples. You will know the truth, and the truth will set you free. *John 8:31–32 CEV*

PESSIMISM (*also* HOPE)

Let not your heart be troubled; you believe in God, believe also in Me. *John 14:1 NKJV*

Peace I leave with you; my peace I give to you. I do not give to you as the world gives. Do not let your hearts be troubled, and do not let them be afraid. *John 14:27 NRSV*

I told you these things so that you can have peace in me. In this world you will have trouble. But be brave! I have defeated the world! *John 16:33 NCV*

PETTINESS (see SUPERFICIALITY)

PHILOSOPHY (see METAPHYSICS)

PIETY (also RELIGIOSITY)

Beware of practicing your piety before others in order to be seen by them; for then you have no reward from your Father in heaven.   *Matthew 6:1 NRSV*

Why do you keep on saying that I am your Lord, when you refuse to do what I say?   *Luke 6:46 (Matthew 7:21) CEV*

PLEASURE (also CELEBRATION)

But woe to you who are rich, for you are receiving your comfort in full. Woe to you who are well-fed now, for you shall be hungry. Woe to you who laugh now, for you shall mourn and weep. Woe to you when all men speak well of you, for in the same way their fathers used to treat the false prophets.   *Luke 6:24–26 NASB*

And that which fell among thorns are they, which, when they have heard, go forth, and are choked with cares and riches and pleasures of this life, and bring no fruit to perfection.   *Luke 8:14 (Matthew 13:22) (Mark 4:18–19) KJV*

Then I'll say to myself, "You have stored up enough good things to last for years to come. Live it up! Eat, drink, and enjoy yourself." But God said to him, "You fool! Tonight you will die. Then who will get what you have stored up?" This is what happens to people who store up everything for themselves, but are poor in the sight of God."
                                    Luke 12:18–21 CEV

Therefore I say to you, do not worry about your life, what you will eat; nor about the body, what you will put on. Life is more than food, and the body is more than clothing.
                          Luke 12:22–23 (Matthew 6:25) NKJV

Be careful! Don't spend your time feasting and drinking. Or don't be too busy with worldly things. If you do that, you will not be able to think straight. And then that day might come when you are not ready. It will close like a trap on all people on earth.   *Luke 21:34–35 NCV*

POLITICS (*see* GOVERNMENT, KINGDOM OF GOD)

POPULARITY (*also* APPEARANCE, ARROGANCE, REPUTATION)

A prophet is not without honor, except in his own country, among his own relatives, and in his own house.

Mark 6:4 (Matthew 13:57) NKJV

You disobey God's commands in order to obey what humans have taught. You are good at rejecting God's commands so that you can follow your own teachings!

Mark 7:8–9 (Matthew 15:3–6) CEV

But many who are first, will be last; and the last, first.

Mark 10:31 (Matthew 19:30) (Matthew 20:16) (Luke 13:30) NASB

You will certainly want to tell me this saying, "Doctor, first make yourself well." You will tell me to do the same things here in my own hometown that you heard I did in Capernaum. But you can be sure that no prophets are liked by the people of their own hometown.   *Luke 4:23 CEV*

But woe to you who are rich, for you are receiving your comfort in full. Woe to you who are well-fed now, for you shall be hungry. Woe to you who laugh now, for you shall mourn and weep. Woe to you when all men speak well of you, for in the same way their fathers used to treat the false prophets.   *Luke 6:24–26 NASB*

For all who exalt themselves will be humbled, and those who humble themselves will be exalted.

Luke 14:11 (Matthew 23:12) (Luke 18:14) NRSV

You are always making yourselves look good, but God sees what is in your heart. The things that most people think are important are worthless as far as God is concerned.

Luke 16:15 CEV

The world cannot hate you, but it hates me because I testify against it that its works are evil.   *John 7:7 NRSV*

If the world hate you, ye know that it hated me before it hated you. If ye were of the world, the world would love his own: but because ye are not of the world, but I have chosen you out of the world, therefore the world hateth you.   *John 15:18–19 KJV*

POSITION, SOCIAL POSITION (*also* POPULARITY, STATUS SYMBOLS)

And whosoever shall exalt himself shall be abased; and he that shall humble himself shall be exalted.

Matthew 23:12 KJV

If anyone wants to be first, he shall be last of all, and servant of all.   *Mark 9:35 (Matthew 20:27) (Mark 10:44) NASB*

When the two men went home, it was the tax collector and not the Pharisee who was pleasing to God. If you put yourself above others, you will be put down. But if you humble yourself, you will be honored.

Luke 18:14 (Matthew 23:12) CEV

POSSESSIONS (*also* ATTACHMENT, MATERIALISM)

For what will a man be profited, if he gains the whole world, and forfeits his soul? Or what will a man give in exchange for his soul?

Matthew 16:26 (Mark 8:36–37) (Luke 9:25) NASB

If you wish to be perfect, go, sell your possessions, and give the money to the poor, and you will have treasure in heaven; then come, follow me.

Matthew 19:21 (Mark 10:21) (Luke 18:22) NRSV

Take heed and beware of covetousness, for one's life does not consist in the abundance of the things he possesses.

Luke 12:15 NKJV

POVERTY (*also* HOMELESSNESS, HUNGER)

Then the king will say to those on his right, "My father has blessed you! Come and receive the kingdom that was prepared for you before the world was created. When I was hungry, you gave me something to eat, and when I was thirsty, you gave me something to drink. When I was a stranger, you welcomed me, and when I was naked, you gave me clothes to wear. When I was sick, you took care of me, and when I was in jail, you visited me." Then the ones who pleased the Lord will ask, "When did we give you something to eat or drink? When did we welcome you as a stranger or give you clothes to wear or visit you while you were sick or in jail?" The king will answer, "Whenever you did it for any of my people, no matter how unimportant they seemed, you did it for me."

Matthew 25:34–40 CEV

The Spirit of the Lord is in me.
This is because God chose me to tell the Good News to the poor. *Luke 4:18 NCV*

God will bless you people who are poor.
His kingdom belongs to you!
God will bless you hungry people.
You will have plenty to eat!
God will bless you people who are crying.
You will laugh! *Luke 6:20–21 CEV*

POWER (*also* ABILITY, GREATNESS, HOLY SPIRIT, STRENGTH)

And lead us not into temptation, but deliver us from evil: For thine is the kingdom, and the power, and the glory, for ever. Amen. *Matthew 6:13 (Luke 11:4) KJV*

But that ye may know that the Son of man hath power on earth to forgive sins, . . . Arise, take up thy bed, and go into thine house. *Matthew 9:6 (Mark 2:10) (Luke 5:24) KJV*

Do not fear those who kill the body but cannot kill the soul; rather fear him who can destroy both soul and body in hell.

Matthew 10:28 (Luke 12:4–5) NRSV

Any kingdom where people fight each other will end up ruined. And a town or family that fights will soon destroy itself. So if Satan fights against himself, how can his kingdom last? If I use the power of Beelzebul to force out demons, whose power do your own followers use to force them out? Your followers are the ones who will judge you. But when I force out demons by the power of God's Spirit, it proves that God's kingdom has already come to you.

Matthew 12:25–28 (Mark 3:23–25) (Luke 11:17–20) CEV

All power is given unto me in heaven and in earth.

Matthew 28:18 KJV

I saw Satan fall like lightening from heaven. Behold, I give you the authority to trample on serpents and scorpions, and over all the power of the enemy, and nothing shall by any means hurt you. Nevertheless do not rejoice in this, that the spirits are subject to you, but rather rejoice because your names are written in heaven. *Luke 10:18–20 NKJV*

Hereafter shall the Son of man sit on the right hand of the power of God. *Luke 22:69 (Matthew 26:64) (Mark 14:62) KJV*

The Father loves me, because I give up my life, so that I may receive it back again. No one takes my life from me. I give it up willingly! I have the power to give it up and the power to receive it back again, just as my Father commanded me to do. *John 10:17–18 CEV*

I will no longer talk much with you, for the ruler of this world is coming. He has no power over me; but I do as the Father has commanded me, so that the world may know that I love the Father. Rise, let us be on our way.

John 14:30–31 NRSV

Father, the hour is come; glorify thy Son, that thy Son also may glorify thee: As thou hast given him power over all flesh, and that he should give eternal life to as many as thou hast given him. *John 17:1–2 KJV*

You would have no authority at all over me, . . . if it had not been granted you from above; and therefore the deeper guilt lies with the man who handed me over to you.

John 19:11 NEB

PRACTICALITY (*also* REASON)

But everyone who hears these sayings of Mine, and does not do them, will be like a foolish man who built his house on the sand: and the rain descended, the floods came, and the winds blew and beat on that house; and it fell. And great was its fall. *Matthew 7:26–27 (Luke 6:49) NKJV*

For which one of you, when he wants to build a tower, does not first sit down and calculate the cost, to see if he has enough to complete it? Otherwise, when he has laid a foundation, and is not able to finish, all who observe it begin to ridicule him, saying, "This man began to build and was not able to finish."   *Luke 14:28–30 NASB*

PRAISE (*also* PRAYER, WORSHIP)

Yea; have ye never read, Out of the mouth of babes and sucklings thou hast perfected praise?   *Matthew 21:16 KJV*

PRAYER (*also* MEDITATION)

When you pray, don't be like those showoffs who love to stand up and pray in the meeting places and on the street corners. They do this just to look good. I promise you that they already have their reward. When you pray, go into a room alone and close the door. Pray to your Father in private. He knows what is done in private, and he will reward you. When you pray, don't talk on and on as people do who don't know God. They think God likes to hear long prayers. Don't be like them. Your Father knows what you need before you ask.   *Matthew 6:5–8 CEV*

After this manner therefore pray ye: Our Father which art in heaven, Hallowed be thy name. Thy kingdom come. Thy will be done in earth, as it is in heaven. Give us this day our daily bread. And forgive us our debts, as we forgive our debtors. And lead us not into temptation, but deliver us from evil: For thine is the kingdom, and the power, and the glory, for ever. Amen. For if ye forgive men their trespasses, your heavenly Father will also forgive you: But if ye forgive not men their trespasses, neither will your Father forgive your trespasses.   *Matthew 6:9–15 (Luke 11:2–4) KJV*

Ask, and you will receive. Search, and you will find. Knock, and the door will be opened for you. Everyone who asks will receive. Everyone who searches will find. And the door will be opened for everyone who knocks.

Matthew 7:7–8 (Luke 11:9–10) CEV

Truly I tell you, whatever you bind on earth will be bound in heaven, and whatever you loose on earth will be loosed in heaven. Again, truly I tell you, if two of you agree on earth about anything you ask, it will be done for you by my Father in heaven. For where two or three are gathered in my name, I am there among them   *Matthew 18:18–20 NRSV*

I tell you the truth. If you have faith and do not doubt, you will be able to do what I did to this tree. And you will be able to do more. You will be able to say to this mountain, 'Go, mountain, fall into the sea.' And if you have faith, it will happen. If you believe, you will get anything you ask for in prayer.   *Matthew 21:21–22 (Mark 11:23–24) NCV*

And whenever you stand praying, if you have anything against anyone, forgive him, that your Father in heaven may also forgive you your trespasses. But if you do not forgive, neither will your Father in heaven forgive your trespasses.   *Mark 11:25–26 (Matthew 6:14) NKJV*

As soon as you enter a home, say, "God bless this home with peace." If the people living there are peace-loving, your prayer for peace will bless them. But if they are not peace-loving, your prayer will return to you.

Luke 10:5–6 (Matthew 10:11–13) CEV

Father, I thank thee; thou hast heard me. I knew already that thou always hearest me, but I spoke for the sake of the people standing round, that they might believe that thou didst send me.   *John 11:41–42 NEB*

If ye abide in me, and my words abide in you, ye shall ask what ye will, and it shall be done unto you.   *John 15:7 KJV*

And in that day ye shall ask me nothing. Verily, verily, I say unto you, Whatsoever ye shall ask the Father in my name, he will give it you. Hitherto have ye asked nothing in my name: ask, and ye shall receive, that your joy may be full.   *John 16:23–24 KJV*

PREJUDICE (*also* BIGOTRY, DISCRIMINATION)

Don't judge other people, and you will not be judged. You will be judged in the same way that you judge others. And the forgiveness you give to others will be given to you.

Matthew 7:1–2 (Luke 6:37–38) NCV

Two men went into the temple to pray. One was a Pharisee and the other a tax collector. The Pharisee stood over by himself and prayed, "God, I thank you that I am not greedy, dishonest, and unfaithful in marriage like other people. And I am really glad that I am not like that tax collector over there. I go without eating for two days a week, and I give you one tenth of all I earn." The tax collector stood off at a distance and did not think he was good enough even to look upward to heaven. He was so sorry for what he had done that he pounded his chest and prayed, "God, have pity on me! I am such a sinner." When the two men went home, it was the tax collector and not the Pharisee who was pleasing to God. If you put yourself above others, you will be put down. But if you humble yourself, you will be honored.

Luke 18:10–14 CEV

A new commandment I give to you, that you love one another, even as I have loved you, that you also love one another. By this all men will know that you are My disciples, if you have love for one another.

John 13:34–35 NASB

PRIDE (*also* SELF-RESPECT, SIN)

Therefore I say to you, do not worry about your life, what you will eat or what you will drink; nor about your body, what you will put on. Is not life more than food and the body more than clothing? Look at the birds of the air, for they neither sow nor reap nor gather into barns; yet your heavenly Father feeds them. Are you not of more value than they? Which of you by worrying can add one cubit to his stature?

Matthew 6:25–27 (Luke 12:22–25) NKJV

Whoever is the greatest should be the servant of others. If you put yourself above others, you will be put down. But if you humble yourself, you will be honored.

Matthew 23:11–12 (Luke 14:11) (Luke 18:14) CEV

Whoever wants to be first must be last of all and servant of all.　　　*Mark 9:35 (Matthew 20:27) (Mark 10:44) NRSV*

Foreign kings order their people around, and powerful rulers call themselves everyone's friends. But don't be like them. The most important one of you should be like the least important, and your leader should be like a servant. Who do people think is the greatest, a person who is served or one who serves? Isn't it the one who is served? But I have been with you as a servant.

Luke 22:25–27 (Matthew 20:25–28) (Mark 10:42–45) CEV

PRINCIPLES (*see* COMMANDMENTS, VIRTUE)

PRIORITIES (*also* CHOICE, GOALS)

Don't store treasures for yourselves here on earth. Moths and rust will destroy treasures here on earth. And thieves can break into your house and steal the things you have. So store your treasure in heaven. The treasures in heaven cannot be destroyed by moths and rust. And thieves cannot break in and steal that treasure. Your heart will be where your treasure is　　　*Matthew 6:19–21 (Luke 12:33–34) NCV*

Therefore do not worry, saying, "What will we eat?" or "What will we drink?" or "What will we wear?" For it is the gentiles who strive for all these things; and indeed your heavenly Father knows that you need all these things. But strive first for the kingdom of God and his righteousness, and all these things will be given to you as well.

Matthew 6:31–33 (Luke 12:29–31) NRSV

Do not fear those who kill the body but cannot kill the soul; rather fear him who can destroy both soul and body in hell.

Matthew 10:28 (Luke 12:4–5) NRSV

If you love your father or mother or even your sons and daughters more than me, you are not fit to be my disciples.

And unless you are willing to take up your cross and come with me, you are not fit to be my disciples. If you try to save your life, you will lose it. But if you give it up for me, you will surely find it. *Matthew 10:37–39 (Luke 14:26–27, 17:33) CEV*

You surely have read what David did when he and his followers were hungry. He went into the house of God and took the sacred loaves of bread that only priests were supposed to eat. He not only ate some himself, but even gave some to his followers . . . . The Son of Man is Lord over the Sabbath.   *Luke 6:3–5 (Matthew 12:3–8) (Mark 2:25–26, 27) CEV*

Martha, Martha, you are worried and bothered about so many things; but only a few things are necessary, really only one, for Mary has chosen the good part, which shall not be taken away from her.   *Luke 10:41–42 NASB*

There is one thing you still need to do. Go and sell everything you own! Give the money to the poor, and you will have riches in heaven. Then come and be my follower.   *Luke 18:22 (Matthew 19:21) (Mark 10:21) CEV*

It is the Spirit who gives life; the flesh profits nothing; the words that I have spoken to you are spirit and are life.

John 6:63 NASB

PROCESS, LIFE AS PROCESS (*also* NATURE, TIME)

Give us the food we need for each day.
Forgive the sins we have done, just as we have forgiven those who did wrong to us.

Matthew 6:11–12 (Luke 11:3–4) NCV

But more than anything else, put God's work first and do what he wants. Then all other things will be yours as well. Don't worry about tomorrow. It will take care of itself. You have enough to worry about today.

Matthew 6:33–34 (Luke 12:31) CEV

His lord said to him, "Well done, good and faithful servant; you have been faithful over a few things, I will make you ruler over many things. Enter into the joy of your lord."

Matthew 25:23 (Luke 19:17) NKJV

You cannot tell by observation when the kingdom of God comes. There will be no saying, "Look, here it is!" or "there it is!"; for in fact the kingdom of God is among you.

Luke 17:20–21 (Matthew 24:23) (Mark 13:21) NEB

So the Lord is not the God of the dead, but of the living. This means that everyone is alive as far as God is concerned.   *Luke 20:38 (Matthew 22:32) (Mark 12:37) CEV*

In your patience possess ye your souls.

Luke 21:19 (Matthew 24:12) (Mark 13:13) KJV

The wind blows where it wants to go. You hear the wind blow. But you don't know where the wind comes from or where it is going. It is the same with every person who is born from the Spirit.   *John 3:8 NCV*

But the hour is coming, and now is, when the true worshipers will worship the Father in spirit and truth; for the Father is seeking such to worship Him. God is Spirit, and those who worship Him must worship in spirit and truth.   *John 4:23–24 NKJV*

I am the true vine; my Father is the gardener. He cuts off every branch of mine that does not produce fruit. But he trims and cleans every branch that does produces fruit so that it will produce even more fruit.   *John 15:1–2 NCV*

PROCRASTINATION (see RESPONSIBILITY)

PROMISCUITY (also LUST, SEX)

If any of you have never sinned, then go ahead and throw the first stone at her!

Where is everyone? Isn't there anyone left to accuse you?

I am not going to accuse you either. You may go now, but don't sin anymore.   *John 8:7, 10, 11 CEV*

PROOF (also FAITH)

Why doth this generation seek after a sign? verily I say unto you, There shall no sign be given unto this generation.

Mark 8:12 (Matthew 12:28) (Matthew 16:14) (Luke 11:29) KJV

But the rich man said, "Abraham, then please send Lazarus to my Father's home. Let them warn my five brothers, so they won't come to this horrible place," Abraham answered, "Your brothers can read what Moses and the prophets wrote. They should pay attention to that." Then the rich man said, "No, that's not enough! If only someone from the dead would go to them, they would listen and return to God." So Abraham said, "If they don't pay attention to Moses and the prophets, they won't listen even to someone who comes back from the dead."

Luke 16:27-31 CEV

If you disbelieve me when I talk to you about things on earth, how are you to believe if I should talk about the things of heaven? *John 3:12 NEB*

Unless you people see signs and wonders, you will by no means believe. *John 4:48 NKJV*

If I do not the works of My Father, do not believe Me; but if I do, though you do not believe Me, believe the works, that you may know and believe that the Father is in Me, and I in Him. *John 10:37-38 NKJV*

Believe me that I am in the Father and the Father is in me; but if you do not, then believe me because of the works themselves. *John 14:11 NRSV*

Anyone who resolves to do the will of God will know whether the teaching is from God or whether I am speaking on my own. Those who speak on their own seek their own glory; but the one who seeks the glory of him who sent him is true, and there is nothing false in him. *John 7:17-18 NRSV*

Thomas, because thou hast seen me, thou hast believed: blessed are they that have not seen, and yet have believed.

John 20:29 KJV

PROPHECY (*also* END TIMES, PROPHETS)

Many will say to me in that day, Lord, Lord, have we not prophesied in thy name? and in thy name have cast out devils? and in thy name done many wonderful works? And then will I profess unto them, I never knew you: depart from me, ye that work iniquity.

Matthew 7:22–23 (Luke 13:26–27) KJV

I must go to Jerusalem. There the nation's leaders, the chief priests, and the teachers of the Law of Moses will make me suffer terribly. I will be killed, but three days later I will rise to life.   *Matthew 16:21 (Mark 8:31) (Luke 9:22) CEV*

Go into the village ahead of you, and immediately you will find a donkey tied, and a colt with her; untie them and bring them to me.   *Matthew 21:2 (Mark 11:2) (Luke 19:30) NRSV*

I have much more to say to you, but right now it would be more than you could understand. The Spirit shows what is true and will come and guide you into the full truth. The Spirit does not speak on his own. He will tell you only what he has heard from me, and he will let you know what is going to happen.   *John 16:12–13 CEV*

PROPHETS (*also* FALSE PROPHETS, HEBREW SCRIPTURE)

In everything do to others as you would have them do to you; for this is the law and the prophets.

Matthew 7:12 (Luke 6:31) NRSV

Ever since the coming of John the Baptist the kingdom of Heaven has been subjected to violence and violent men are seizing it. For all the prophets and the Law foretold things to come until John appeared, and John is the destined Elijah, if you will but accept it. If you have ears, then hear.

Matthew 11:12–15 NEB

And you are nothing but showoffs! Isaiah the prophet was right when he wrote that God had said,

>"All of you praise me with your words
>but you never really think about me.
>It is useless for you to worship me,
>when you teach rules made up by humans."

Matthew 15:7–9 (Mark 7:6–8) CEV

Love the Lord your God with all your heart, soul, and mind. This is the first and most important commandment. The second most important commandment is like this one. And it is, "Love others as much as you love yourself." All the Law of Moses and the Books of the Prophets are based on these two commandments.

Matthew 22:37–40 (Mark 12:29–31) CEV

A prophet is not without honor except in his home town and among his own relatives and in his own household.

Mark 6:4 (Matthew 13:57) NASB

What kind of person did you go out to the desert to see? Was he like tall grass blown about by the wind? What kind of man did you really go out to see? Was he someone dressed in fine clothes? People who wear expensive clothes and live in luxury are in the king's palace. What then did you go out to see? Was he a prophet? He certainly was! I tell you that he was more than a prophet. In the Scriptures, God calls John his messenger and says, "I am sending my messenger ahead of you to get things ready for you." No one ever born on this earth is greater than John. But whoever is least important in God's kingdom is greater than John.

Luke 7:24–28 CEV

This is an evil generation: they seek a sign; and there shall no sign be given it, but the sign of Jonas the prophet. For as Jonas was a sign unto the Ninevites, so shall the Son of man be to this generation.

Luke 11:29–30 (Matthew 12:38–40) KJV

Woe to you! For you build the tombs of the prophets whom you ancestors killed. So you are witnesses and approve of the deeds of your ancestors; for they killed them, and you build their tombs. Therefore also the Wisdom of God said, "I will send them prophets and apostles, some of whom they will kill and persecute," so that this generation may be charged with the blood of all the prophets shed since the foundation of the world, from the blood of Abel to the blood of Zechariah, who perished between the altar and the sanctuary. Yes, I tell you, it will be charged against this generation.

Luke 11:47–51 NRSV

There will be weeping and gnashing of teeth there when you see Abraham and Isaac and Jacob and all the prophets in the kingdom of God, but yourselves being cast out. And they will come from east and west, and from north and south, and will recline at the table in the kingdom of God. And behold, some are last who will be first and some are first who will be last.   *Luke 13:28–30 (Matthew 8:11–12) NASB*

O Jerusalem, Jerusalem, which killest the prophets, and stonest them that are sent unto thee; how often would I have gathered thy children together, as a hen doth gather her brood under her wings, and ye would not!

Luke 13:34 (Matthew 23:37) KJV

The law and the prophets were until John: since that time the kingdom of God is preached, and every man presseth into it.   *Luke 16:16 (Matthew 11:12–13) KJV*

PROSPERITY (*see* POSSESSIONS, WEALTH)

PROVIDENCE (*also* CIRCUMSTANCE)

But I say to you, love your enemies, and pray for those who persecute you in order that you may be sons of your Father who is in heaven; for He causes His sun to rise on the evil and the good, and sends rain on the righteous and the unrighteous.   *Matthew 5:44–45 (Luke 6:35–36) NASB*

PSYCHIC PHENOMENA (*see* FAITH, MIRACLES)

PSYCHOLOGY (*see* GUILT, FEAR, FORGIVENESS, LOVE)

PUBLIC OPINION (*see* POPULARITY, REPUTATION)

PURIFICATION (*also* BODY, FASTING)

Blessed are the pure in heart: for they shall see God.

Matthew 5:8 KJV

However, this kind does not go out except by prayer and fasting.   *Matthew 17:21 (Mark 9:29) NKJV*

You blind Pharisee, first clean the inside of the cup and of the dish, so that the outside of it may become clean also.

Matthew 23:26 (Luke 11:40–41) NASB

I am the true vine, and my Father is the gardener. He cuts away every branch of mine that does not produce fruit. But he trims clean every branch that does produce fruit, so that it will produce even more fruit.   *John 15:1–2 CEV*

PURPOSE—CHRIST'S (also MOTIVATION)

The Spirit of the Lord is upon me, because he hath anointed me to preach the gospel to the poor; he hath sent me to heal the broken hearted, to preach deliverance to the captives, and recovering of sight to the blind, to set at liberty them that are bruised.   *Luke 4:18 KJV*

I must preach the kingdom of God to the other cities also, because for this purpose I have been sent.

Luke 4:43 (Mark 1:38) NKJV

I came to bring fire to the earth, and how I wish it were already kindled! I have a baptism with which to be baptized, and what stress I am under until it is completed!

Luke 12:49–50 NRSV

Indeed, God did not send the Son into the world to condemn the world, but in order that the world might be saved through him. Those who believe in him are not condemned; but those who do not believe are condemned already, because they have not believed in the name of the only Son of God.   *John 3:17–18 NRSV*

But I came to give life—life in all its fullness.

John 10:10 NCV

You are saying that I am a king.
I was born into this world to tell about the truth. And everyone who belongs to the truth knows my voice.

John 18:37 CEV

QUESTIONS (see SPIRITUAL SEARCHING)

QUIETNESS (see MEDITATION, MYSTICISM, PEACE)

RACE RELATIONS (also COMMUNITY, PREJUDICE)

Therefore, however you want people to treat you, so treat them, for this is the Law and the Prophets.

Matthew 7:12 (Luke 6:31) NASB

These things I command you, that you love one another.

John 15:17 NKJV

REALITY (see KINGDOM OF GOD, TRUTH)

REASON (also INTELLECTUALISM)

Why do you reason because you have no bread? Do you not yet perceive nor understand? Is your heart still hardened? Having eyes, do you not see? And having ears, do you not hear? And do you not remember?

Mark 8:17–18 (Matthew 16:8–9) NKJV

You hypocrites! You know how to analyze the appearance of the earth and the sky, but why do you not analyze this present time? And why do you not even on your own initiative judge what is right?

Luke 12:56–57 (Matthew 16:2) NASB

REBELLION (see CONFORMITY, CYNICISM)

REBIRTH, SPIRITUAL BIRTH (also SELF-TRANSCEN-DENCE)

For nation will arise against nation, and kingdom against kingdom; there will be earthquakes in various places; there will also be famines. These things are merely the beginning of birth pangs.

Mark 13:8 (Matthew 24:7–8) (Luke 21:10–11) NASB

I tell you for certain that you must be born from above before you can see God's kingdom!   *John 3:3 CEV*

I tell you the truth. Unless one is born from water and the Spirit, he cannot enter God's kingdom. A person's body is born from his human parents. But a person's spiritual life is born from the Spirit. Don't be surprised when I tell you, "You must all be born again." The wind blows where it wants to go. You hear the wind blow. But you don't know where the wind comes from or where it is going. It is the same with every person who is born from the Spirit.

John 3:5–8 NCV

It is the Spirit who gives life; the flesh profits nothing. The words that I speak to you are spirit, and they are life. But there are some of you who do not believe.

John 6:63–64 NKJV

The time has come for the Son of Man to be given his glory. I tell you for certain that a grain of wheat that falls on the ground will never be more than one grain unless it dies. But if it dies, it will produce lots of wheat. If you love your life, you will lose it. If you give it up in this world, you will be given eternal life.

John 12:23–25 CEV

RECONCILIATION (also FORGIVENESS)

Therefore if you bring your gift to the altar, and there remember that your brother has something against you, leave your gift there before the altar, and go your way. First be reconciled to your brother, and then come and offer your gift. Agree with your adversary quickly, while you are on the way with him, lest your adversary deliver you to the judge, the judge hand you over to the officer, and you be thrown into prison.

Matthew 5:23–25 (Luke 12:58) NKJV

And if your brother sins, go and reprove him in private; if he listens to you, you have won your brother. But if he does not listen to you, take one or two more with you, so that by the mouth of two or three witnesses every fact may be confirmed. And if he refuses to listen to them, tell it to the church; and if he refuses to listen even to the church, let him be to you as a Gentile and a tax-gatherer.

Matthew 18:15–18 (Luke 17:3) NASB

I will leave and go to my father and say to him, "Father, I have sinned against God in heaven and against you. I am no longer good enough to be called your son. Treat me like one of your workers." The younger son got up and started back to his father. But when he was still a long way off, his father saw him and felt sorry for him. He ran to his son and hugged and kissed him. "But we should be glad and celebrate! Your brother was dead, but now he is alive. He was lost and has now been found."

Luke 15:18–20 CEV

REDEMPTION (*also* SALVATION)

For this is my blood of the new testament, which is shed for many for the remission of sins.

Matthew 26:28 (Mark 14:24) (Luke 22:20) KJV

For even the Son of Man did not come to be served, but to serve, and to give His life a ransom for many.

Mark 10:45 (Matthew 20:28) NKJV

But when these things begin to take place, straighten up and lift up your heads, because your redemption is drawing near.   *Luke 21:28* NASB

REGENERATION (*see* REBIRTH, SPIRITUALITY)

REJECTION (*also* UNBELIEF)

Whoever listens to you listens to me, and whoever rejects you rejects me, and whoever rejects me rejects the one who sent me.   *Luke 10:16 (Matthew 10:40)* NRSV

If you tell others that you belong to me, the Son of Man will tell God's angels that you are my followers. But if you reject me, you will be rejected in front of them.

Luke 12:8–9 (Matthew 10:32–33) CEV

And if any man hear my words, and believe not, I judge him not: for I came not to judge the world, but to save the world. He that rejecteth me, and receiveth not my words, hath one that judgeth him: the word that I have spoken, the same shall judge him in the last day.

John 12:47–48 (John 3:17) KJV

RELATIONSHIPS (*also* CELIBACY, ONENESS)

Always treat others as you would like them to treat you: that is the Law and the prophets.

Matthew 7:12 (Luke 6:31) NEB

Don't think that I came to bring peace to the earth! I came to bring trouble, not peace. I came to turn sons against their fathers, daughters against their mothers, and daughters-in-law against their mothers-in-law. Your worst enemies will be in your own family. If you love your father or mother or even your sons and daughters more than me, you are not fit to be my disciples. And unless you are willing to take up your cross and come with me, you are not fit to be my disciples. If you try to save your life, you will lose it. But if you give it up for me, you will surely find it. *Matthew 10:34–39 (Luke 12:51–53, 14:26–27, 17:33) CEV*

Love the Lord your God with all your heart, soul, and mind. This is the first and most important commandment. The second most important commandment is like this one. And it is, "Love others as much as you love yourself." All the Law of Moses and the Books of the Prophets are based on these two commandments.

Matthew 22:37–40 (Mark 12:29–31) CEV

RELIGION (*also* SPIRITUALITY)

I use stories when I speak to them because when they look, they cannot see, and when they listen, they cannot hear or understand. *Matthew 13:13 (Mark 4:11) (Luke 8:10) CEV*

The kingdom of God cometh not with observation: Neither shall they say, Lo here! or, Lo there! for, behold, the kingdom of God is within you.

Luke 17:20–21 (Matthew 24:23) (Mark 13:21) KJV

You search the scriptures because you think that in them you have eternal life; and it is they that testify on my behalf. Yet you refuse to come to me to have life. I do not accept glory from human beings. *John 5:39–41 NRSV*

If you love me, you will do as I command. *John 14:15 CEV*

When the Advocate comes, whom I will send to you from the Father, the Spirit of truth who comes from the Father, he will testify on my behalf. You also are to testify because you have been with me from the beginning. I have said these things to you to keep you from stumbling.

John 15:26–16:1 NRSV

RELIGIOSITY (*also* APPEARANCE, HYPOCRISY, SUPERFICIALITY, WORLDLINESS)

When you pray, don't be like those showoffs who love to stand up and pray in the meeting places and on the street corners. They do this just to look good. I promise you that they already have their reward. When you pray, go into a room alone and close the door. Pray to your Father in private. He knows what is done in private, and he will reward you. When you pray, don't talk on and on as people do who don't know God. They think God likes to hear long prayers. Don't be like them. Your Father knows what you need before you ask. *Matthew 6:5–8 CEV*

No one can serve two masters; for either he will hate the one and love the other, or else he will be loyal to the one and despise the other. You cannot serve God and mammon. *Matthew 6:24 (Luke 16:13) NKJV*

So then, you will know them by their fruits. Not everyone who says to Me, "Lord, Lord," will enter the kingdom of heaven; but he who does the will of My Father who is in heaven. *Matthew 7:20–21 (Luke 6:44, 46) NASB*

For John came neither eating nor drinking, and they say, "He has a demon." The Son of Man came eating and drinking, and they say, "Look, a glutton and a winebibber, a friend of tax collectors and sinners!" But wisdom is justified by her children.

Matthew 11:18–19 (Luke 7:33–35) NKJV

You Pharisees and teachers are showoffs, and you're in for trouble! You wash the outside of your cups and dishes, while inside there is nothing but greed and selfishness. You blind Pharisee! First clean the inside of a cup, and then the outside will also be clean. *Matthew 23:25 (Luke 11:39) CEV*

The Sabbath was made for man, and not man for the Sabbath. Consequently, the Son of Man is Lord even of the Sabbath. *Mark 2:27–28 (Matthew 12:8) (Luke 6:5) NASB*

You disobey God's commands in order to obey what humans have taught. You are good at rejecting God's commands so that you can follow your own teachings!

Mark 7:8–9 (Matthew 15:3–6) CEV

The Pharisee stood and prayed thus with himself, "God, I thank You that I am not like other men—extortioners, unjust, adulterers, or even as this tax collector. I fast twice a week; I give tithes of all that I possess." And the tax collector, standing afar off, would not so much as raise his eyes to heaven, but beat his breast, saying, "God be merciful to me a sinner!" I tell you, this man went down to his house justified rather than the other; for everyone who exalts himself will be humbled, and he who humbles himself will be exalted. *Luke 18:11–14 NKJV*

Beware of the scribes, who like to walk around in long robes, and love respectful greetings in the market places, and chief seats in the synagogues, and places of honor at banquets, who devour widow's houses, and for appearance's sake offer long prayers; these will receive greater condemnation.

Luke 20:46–47 (Mark 12:38–40) NASB

Take these things away! Do not make My Father's house a house of merchandise! *John 2:16 NKJV*

I came to judge the people of this world. I am here to give sight to the blind and to make blind everyone who sees.
If you were blind, you would not be guilty. But now that you claim to see, you will keep on being guilty.

John 9:39, 41 CEV

RENUNCIATION (*also* ASCETICISM)

If anyone wants to follow me, he must say 'no' to the things he wants. He must be willing to die on a cross, and he must follow me. Whoever wants to save his life will give up true life. But whoever gives up his life for me and for the Good News will have true life forever. It is worth nothing for a person to have the whole world, if he loses his soul. A person could never pay enough to buy back his soul.

Mark 8:34–37 (Matthew 16:24–26) (Luke 9:23–25) NCV

One thing you lack: Go your way, sell whatever you have and give to the poor, and you will have treasure in heaven; and come, take up the cross, and follow Me.

Mark 10:21 (Matthew 19:21) (Luke 12:33) NKJV

So therefore, none of you can become my disciple if you do not give up all your possessions. *Luke 14:33 NRSV*

You can be sure that anyone who gives up home or wife or brothers or family or children because of God's kingdom will be given much more in this life. And in the future world they will have eternal life.

Luke 18:29–30 (Matthew 19:29) (Mark 10:29–30) CEV

Those who love their life lose it, and those who hate their life in this world will keep it for eternal life. *John 12:25 NRSV*

REPENTANCE (*also* FORGIVENESS)

Repent, for the kingdom of heaven is at hand.

Matthew 4:17 (Mark 1:15) NKJV

The time is fulfilled, and the kingdom of God is at hand; repent and believe in the gospel. *Mark 1:15 (Mark 4:17) NASB*

Those who are well have no need of a physician, but those who are sick. I did not come to call the righteous, but sinners, to repentance.

Mark 2:17 (Matthew 9:12–13) (Luke 5:31–32) NKJV

Do you think that these people were worse sinners than everyone else in Galilee just because of what happened to them? Not at all! But you can be sure that if you don't turn back to God, every one of you will also be killed. What about those eighteen people who died when the tower in Siloam fell on them? Do you think they were worse than everyone else in Jerusalem? Not at all! But you can be sure that if you don't turn back to God, every one of you will also die. *Luke 13:2–5 CEV*

What man among you, if he has a hundred sheep and has lost one of them, does not leave the ninety-nine in the open pasture, and go after the one which is lost, until he finds it? And when he has found it, he lays it on his shoulders, rejoicing. And when he comes home, he calls together his friends and his neighbors, saying to them, "Rejoice with me, for I have found my sheep which was lost!" I tell you that in the same way, there will be more joy in heaven over one sinner who repents, than over ninety-nine righteous persons who need no repentance.

Luke 15:4–7 (Matthew 18:12–13) NASB

I say unto you, that likewise joy shall be in heaven over one sinner that repenteth, more than over ninety and nine just persons, which need no repentance. Either what woman having ten pieces of silver, if she lose one piece, doth not light a candle, and sweep the house, and seek diligently till she find it? And when she hath found it, she calleth her friends and her neighbours together, saying, Rejoice with me; for I have found the piece which I had lost. Likewise, I say unto you, there is joy in the presence of the angels of God over one sinner that repenteth.

Luke 15:7–10 (Matthew 18:14) KJV

I will arise and go to my father, and will say to him, "Father, I have sinned against heaven and before you, and I am no longer worthy to be called your son. Make me like one of your hired servants." And he arose and came to his father. But when he was still a great way off, his father saw him and had compassion, and ran and fell on his neck and kissed him. *Luke 15:18–19 NKJV*

The tax collector stood off at a distance and did not think he was good enough to look up toward heaven. He was so sorry for what he had done that he pounded his chest and prayed, "God, have pity on me! I am such a sinner." When the two men went home, it was the tax collector and not the Pharisee who was pleasing to God. If you put yourself above others, you will be put down. But if you humble yourself, you will be honored. *Luke 18:13–14 CEV*

Thus it is written, and thus it was necessary for the Christ to suffer and to rise from the dead the third day, and that repentance and remission of sins should be preached in His name to all nations, beginning at Jerusalem.

Luke 24:46–47 NKJV

REPUTATION (*also* POPULARITY, SUCCESS)

Blessed are you when they revile and persecute you, and say all kinds of evil against you falsely for My sake. Rejoice and be exceedingly glad, for great is your reward in heaven, for so they persecuted the prophets who were before you. *Matthew 5:11–12 (Luke 6:22–23) NKJV*

John the Baptist did not go around eating and drinking, and you said, "That man has a demon in him!" But the Son of Man goes around eating and drinking, and you say, "That man eats and drinks too much! He is even a friend of tax collectors and sinners." Yet Wisdom is shown to be right by what it does. *Matthew 11:18–19 (Luke 7:33–35) CEV*

A prophet is not without honor except in his home town and among his own relatives and in his own household.

Mark 6:4 (Matthew 13:57) NASB

When you are having a party for lunch or supper, do not invite your friends, your brothers or other relations, or your rich neighbors; they will only ask you back again and so you will be repaid. But when you give a party, ask the poor, the crippled, the lame, and the blind; and so find happiness. For they have no means of repaying you; but you will be repaid on the day when good men rise from the dead.

Luke 14:12–14 NEB

I don't want praise from men. But I know you—I know that you don't have God's love in you. I have come from my Father—I speak for him. But you don't accept me. But when another person comes, speaking only for himself, you will accept him. You like to have praise from each other. But you never try to get the praise that comes from the only God. So how can you believe? *John 5:41–44 NCV*

RESPECT *(also* HONOR, LOVE)
Why do you disobey God and follow your own teaching? Didn't God command you to respect your father and mother?. . . But you let people get by without helping their parents when they should. You let them say that what they have has been offered to God. Is this any way to show respect to your parents? You ignore God's commands in order to follow your own teaching.

Matthew 15:3–6 (Mark 7:8–13) CEV

RESPONSIBILITY (also STEWARDSHIP)

Is there anyone among you who, if your child asks for bread will give a stone? Or if the child asks for a fish, will give a snake? If you then, who are evil, know how to give good gifts to your children, how much more will your Father in heaven give good things to those who ask him! In everything do to others as you would have them do to you; for this is the law and the prophets.

Matthew 7:9–12 (Luke 6:31) NRSV

I promise you that on the day of judgment, everyone will have to account for every careless word they have spoken. On that day they will be told that they are either innocent or guilty because of the things they have said.

Matthew 12:36–37 (Luke 6:45) CEV

His lord said to him, "Well done, good and faithful servant; you have been faithful over a few things, I will make you ruler over many things. Enter into the joy of your lord."

Matthew 25:23 (Luke 19:17) NKJV

And the King will answer and say to them, "Truly I say to you, to the extent that you did it to one of these brothers of Mine, even the least of them, you did it to Me."

Matthew 25:40 NASB

He that is faithful in that which is least is faithful also in much: and he that is unjust in the least is unjust also in much. If therefore ye have not been faithful in the unrighteous mammon, who will commit to your trust the true riches? And if ye have not been faithful in that which is another man's, who shall give you that which is your own?

Luke 16:10–12 KJV

There will always be something that causes people to sin. But anyone who causes them to sin is in for trouble. A person who causes even one of my little followers to sin would be better off thrown into the ocean with a heavy stone tied around the neck. So be careful what you do.

Correct any followers of mine who sin, and forgive the ones who say they are sorry.

Luke 17:1–3 (Matthew 18:6–7) (Mark 9:42) CEV

REST (also SABBATH)

If you are tired from carrying heavy burdens, come to me and I will give you rest. Take the yoke I give you. Put it on your shoulders and learn from me. I am gentle and humble, and you will find rest. This yoke is easy to bear, and this burden is light. *Matthew 11:28–30 CEV*

The Sabbath was made for man, and not man for the Sabbath. Consequently, the Son of Man is Lord even of the Sabbath. *Mark 2:27–28 (Matthew 12:8) (Luke 6:5) NASB*

Come ye yourselves apart into a desert place, and rest a while. *Mark 6:31 KJV*

RESURRECTION (also ETERNAL LIFE, IMMORTALITY)

For in the resurrection they neither marry nor are given in marriage, but are like angels of God in heaven. But concerning the resurrection of the dead, have you not read what was spoken to you by God, saying, "I am the God of Abraham, the God of Isaac, and the God of Jacob"? God is not the God of the dead, but of the living.

Matthew 22:30–32 (Mark 12:21–22) (Luke 20:35–38) NKJV

The Son of Man is being betrayed into the hands of men, and they will kill him. And after He is killed, He will rise the third day. *Mark 9:31 (Matthew 17:22-23) (Luke 9:44) NKJV*

But when you give a feast, invite the poor, the maimed, the lame, the blind. And you will be blessed, because they cannot repay you; for you shall be repaid at the resurrection of the just. *Luke 14:13–14 NKJV*

Thus it is written, and thus it was necessary for the Christ to suffer and to rise from the dead the third day, and that repentance and remission of sins should be preached in His name to all nations, beginning at Jerusalem.

Luke 24:46–47 NKJV

Destroy this temple, . . . and in three days I will build it again.   *John 2:19 CEV*

Do not marvel at this; for an hour is coming, in which all who are in the tombs shall hear His voice, and shall come forth; those who did the good deeds to a resurrection of life, those who committed the evil deeds to a resurrection of judgment.   *John 5:28–29 NASB*

Everyone who sees the Son and believes in him has eternal life. I will raise him up on the last day. This is what my Father wants.   *John 6:40 NCV*

The Father loves me, because I give up my life, so that I may receive it back again. No one takes my life from me. I give it up willingly! I have the power to receive it back again, just as my Father commanded me to do.
    John 10:17-18 CEV

I am the resurrection and the life; he who believes in Me shall live even if he dies, and everyone who lives and believes in Me shall never die. Do you believe this?
    John 11:25–26 NASB

In a little while the world will no longer see me, but you will see me; because I live, you also will live. On that day you will know that I am in my Father, and you in me, and I in you.   *John 14:19–20 NRSV*

RETALIATION (*see* FIGHTING, REVENGE)

REVELATION, PROGRESSIVE (*also* HOLY SPIRIT, INTUITION, VISION(S))

Ask, and it shall be given you; seek, and ye shall find; knock, and it shall be opened unto you: For every one that asketh receiveth; and he that seeketh findeth; and to him that knocketh it shall be opened.

    Matthew 7:7–8 (Luke 11:9–10) KJV

Therefore do not fear them, for there is nothing covered that will not be revealed, and hidden that will not be known.   *Matthew 10:26 (Luke 12:2) NASB*

But blessed are your eyes for they see, and your ears for they hear; for assuredly I say to you, that many prophets and righteous men desired to see what you see, and did not see it, and to hear what you hear, and did not hear it.

Matthew 13:16–17 NKJV

I have much more to say to you, but right now it would be more than you could understand. The Spirit shows what is true and will come and guide you into the full truth. The Spirit does not speak on his own. He will tell you only what he has heard from me, and he will let you know what is going to happen.

John 16:12–13 CEV

REVENGE (*also* FIGHTING, TEMPER, VIOLENCE)

You have heard that it was said, "An eye for an eye and a tooth for a tooth." But I say to you, Do not resist an evildoer. But if anyone strikes you on the right cheek, turn the other also; and if anyone wants to sue you and take your coat, give your cloak as well; and if anyone forces you to go one mile, go also the second mile.

Matthew 5:38–41 (Luke 6:29) NRSV

REWARD (*also* BLESSINGS, SUCCESS)

God will bless you when people insult you, mistreat you, and tell all kinds of evil lies about you because of me. Be happy and excited! You will have a great reward in heaven. People did these same things to the prophets who lived long ago.

Matthew 5:11–12 (Luke 6:22–23) CEV

For if you love those who love you, what reward have you? Do not even the tax collectors do the same?

Matthew 5:46 (Luke 6:32) NKJV

Be careful! When you do good things, don't do them in front of people to be seen by them. If you do that, then you will have no reward from your Father in heaven.

Matthew 6:1 NCV

But when you pray, go into a room by yourself, shut the door, and pray to your Father who is there in the secret place; and your Father who sees what is secret will reward you.

Matthew 6:6 NEB

For the Son of Man is to come with his angels in the glory of his Father, and then he will repay everyone for what has been done. Truly I tell you, there are some standing here who will not taste death before they see the Son of Man coming in his kingdom.

Matthew 16:27-28 (Mark 8:38) (Luke 9:26) NRSV

His lord said unto him, Well done, thou good and faithful servant: thou hast been faithful over a few things, I will make thee ruler over many things: enter thou into the joy of thy Lord. *Matthew 25:21 (Luke 19:17) KJV*

Then the king will say to those on his right, "My father has blessed you! Come and receive the kingdom that was prepared for you before the world was created. When I was hungry, you gave me something to eat, and when I was thirsty, you gave me something to drink. When I was a stranger, you welcomed me, and when I was naked, you gave me clothes to wear. When I was sick, you took care of me, and when I was in jail, you visited me."

Matthew 25:34–36 CEV

For he who is not against us is for us. For whoever gives you a cup of water to drink because of your name as followers of Christ, truly I say to you, he shall not lose his reward. *Mark 9:40–41 NASB*

One thing you lack: Go your way, sell whatever you have and give to the poor, and you will have treasure in heaven; and come, take up the cross, and follow Me.

Mark 10:21 (Matthew 19:21) (Luke 12:33) NKJV

You can be sure that anyone who gives up home or brothers or sisters or mother or father or children or land for me and for the good news will be rewarded.

Mark 10:29–30 (Matthew 19:29) (Luke 18:29–30) CEV

But love your enemies, do good, and lend, hoping for nothing in return; and your reward will be great, and you will be sons of the Most High. *Luke 6:35 (Matthew 5:44) NKJV*

Instead when you give a feast, invite the poor, the crippled, the lame, and the blind. Then you will be blessed, because they cannot pay you back. They have nothing. But you will be rewarded when the good people rise from death.

Luke 14:13–14 NCV

RICHES (*also* MATERIALISM)

The seeds that fell among the thorn bushes are also people who hear the message. But they start worrying about the needs of this life and are fooled by the desire to get rich. So the message gets choked out, and they never produce anything. *Matthew 13:22 (Mark 4:18–19) (Luke 8:14) CEV*

Assuredly I say to you that it is hard for a rich man to enter the kingdom of heaven. And again I say to you, it is easier for a camel to go through the eye of a needle than for a rich man to enter the kingdom of God.

With men this is impossible, but with God all things are possible.

Matthew 19:23–24, 26 (Mark 10:23–25, 27) (Luke 18:24–25, 27) NKJV

But you rich people are in for trouble.
You have already had an easy life!
You well-fed people are in for trouble.
You will go hungry!
You people who are laughing now are in for trouble.
You are going to cry and weep! *Luke 6:24–25 CEV*

Be careful and guard against all kind of greed. A man's life is not measured by the many things he owns.

Luke 12:15 NCV

You are those who justify yourselves in the sight of others; but God knows your hearts; for what is prized by human beings is an abomination in the sight of God.

Luke 16:15 NRSV

RIGHTEOUSNESS (*also* COMMANDMENTS)

Blessed are those who hunger and thirst for righteousness, For they shall be filled. *Matthew 5:6 (Luke 6:21) NKJV*

Blessed are the pure in heart: for they shall see God.

Matthew 5:8 KJV

Whoever then annuls one the least of these commandments, and so teaches others, shall be called least in the kingdom of heaven; but whoever keeps and teaches them, he shall be called great in the kingdom of heaven. For I say to you, that unless your righteousness surpasses that of the scribes and Pharisees, you shall not enter the kingdom of heaven.

Matthew 5:19–20 NASB

For all who do evil hate the light and do not come to the light, so that their deeds may not be exposed. But those who do what is true come to the light, so that it may be clearly seen that their deeds have been done in God.

John 3:20–21 NRSV

RIGHTS, HUMAN RIGHTS   (*also* JUSTICE)

Then the king will say to those on his right, "My father has blessed you! Come and receive the kingdom that was prepared for you before the world was created. When I was hungry, you gave me something to eat, and when I was thirsty, you gave me something to drink. When I was a stranger, you welcomed me, and when I was naked, you gave me clothes to wear. When I was sick, you took care of me, and when I was in jail, you visited me."

Matthew 25:37–40 CEV

Do for other people what you want them to do for you.

Luke 6:31 (Matthew 7:12) NCV

RITUALS   (*see* BAPTISM, COMMUNION)

ROLE MODELS   (*also* EXAMPLE)

The Son of Man did not come to be served, but to serve, and to give His life a ransom for many.

Matthew 20:28 (Mark 10:45) NKJV

But do not be called Rabbi; for One is your Teacher, and you are all brothers. And do not call anyone on earth your father; for One is your Father, He who is in heaven. And do not be called leaders; for One is your Leader, that is, Christ.

Matthew 23:8–10 NASB

A certain man was going down from Jerusalem to Jericho; and he fell among robbers, and they stripped him and beat him, and went off leaving him half dead. And by chance a certain priest was going down on that road, and when he saw him, he passed by on the other side. And likewise a Levite also, when he came to the place and saw him, passed by on the other side. But a certain Samaritan, who was on a journey, came upon him; and when he saw him, he felt compassion, and came to him, and bandaged up his wounds, pouring oil and wine on them; and he put him on his own beast, and brought him to an inn, and took care of him. And on the next day he took out two denarii and gave them to the innkeeper and said, "Take care of him; and whatever more you spend, when I return, I will repay you." Which of these three do you think proved to be a neighbor to the man who fell into the robbers' hands?

Go and do the same.   *Luke 10:30–36, 37 NASB*

I am the light of the world. Whoever follows me will never walk in darkness but will have the light of life.

John 8:12 NRSV

SABBATH (*also* REST)

Or have you not read in the law that on the Sabbath the priests in the temple profane the Sabbath, and are blameless? Yet I say to you that in this place there is One greater than the temple. But if you had known what this means, "I desire mercy and not sacrifice," you would not have condemned the guiltless. For the Son of Man is Lord even of the Sabbath.

Matthew 12:5–8 (Mark 2:25–27) (Luke 6:5) NKJV

What man shall there be among you, that shall have one sheep, and if it will fall into a pit on the sabbath day, will he not lay hold on it, and lift it out? How much then is a man better than a sheep? Wherefore it is lawful to do well on the sabbath days.

Matthew 12:11–12 (Luke 13:15–16) (Luke 14:5) KJV

The Sabbath was made for man, and not man for the Sabbath. Consequently, the Son of Man is Lord even of the Sabbath. *Mark 2:27–28 (Matthew 12:8) (Luke 6:5) NASB*

I ask you, is it lawful to do good or to do harm on the sabbath, to save life or to destroy it?

Luke 6:9 (Matthew 12:12) (Mark 3:4) NRSV

You hypocrites, does not each of you on the Sabbath untie his ox or his donkey from the stall, and lead him away to water him? And this woman, a daughter of Abraham as she is, whom Satan has bound for eighteen long years, should she not have been released from this bond on the Sabbath day?

Luke 13:15–16 (Matthew 12:11–12) (Luke 14:5) NASB

Which of you shall have an ass or an ox fallen into a pit, and will not straightway pull him out on the sabbath day?

Luke 14:5 KJV

I worked one miracle, and it amazed you. Moses commanded you to circumcise your sons. But it wasn't really Moses who gave this command. It was your ancestors, and even on the Sabbath you circumcise your sons in order to obey the Law of Moses. Why are you angry with me for making someone completely well on the Sabbath? Don't judge by appearances. Judge by what is right. *John 7:21–24 CEV*

SACRAMENTS (*see* BAPTISM, COMMUNION)

SACRIFICE (*also* MARTYRDOM, RENUNCIATION)

Those who are well have no need of a physician, but those who are sick. But go and learn what this means: "I desire mercy and not sacrifice." For I did not come to call the righteous, but sinners, to repentance.

Matthew 9:12–13 (Mark 2:17) (Luke 5:31–32) NKJV

Of a truth I say unto you, that this poor widow hath cast in more than they all: For all these have of their abundance cast in unto the offerings of God: but she of her penury hath cast in all the living that she had.

Luke 21:3–4 (Mark 12:43–44) KJV

Remember Lot's wife. Whoever seeks to keep his life shall lose it, and whoever loses his life shall preserve it.

Luke 17:32–33 (Matthew 10:39) (Matthew 16:25) (Mark 8:35) (Luke 9:24) NASB

I am the good shepherd. The good shepherd gives His life for the sheep. But a hireling, he who is not the shepherd, one who does not own the sheep, sees the wolf coming and leaves the sheep and flees; and the wolf catches the sheep and scatters them. The hireling flees because he is a hireling and does not care about the sheep. I am the good shepherd; and I know My sheep, and am known by My own. As the Father knows Me, even so I know the Father; and I lay down My life for the sheep.   *John 10:11–15 NKJV*

The Father loves me because I give my life. I give my life so that I can take it back again. No one takes it away from me. I give my own life freely. I have the right to give my life, and I have the right to take it back. This is what my Father commanded me to do.   *John 10:17–18 NCV*

SAFETY (*see* SECURITY)

SALVATION (*also* ATONEMENT, REDEMPTION)

If you forgive others for the wrongs they do to you, your Father in heaven will forgive you. But if you don't forgive others, your Father will not forgive your sins.

Matthew 6:14-15 (Mark 11:25–26) CEV

I tell you the truth. You must change and become like little children. If you don't do this, you will never enter the kingdom of heaven. The greatest person in the kingdom of heaven is the one who makes himself humble like this child. Whoever accepts a little child in my name accepts me.   *Matthew 18:3–5 (Mark 10:15) (Luke 18:17) NCV*

Take heed that you do not despise one of these little ones, for I say to you that in heaven their angels always see the face of My Father who is in heaven. For the Son of Man has come to save that which was lost.   *Matthew 18:10–11 NKJV*

If any of you want to be my followers, you must forget about yourself. You must take up your cross and follow me.

If you want to save your life, you will destroy it. But if you give up your life for me and for the good news, you will save it. What will you gain , if you own the whole world but destroy yourself? What could you give to get back your soul? *Mark 8:34–37 (Matthew 16:24–26) (Luke 9:23–25) CEV*

Zacchaeus, make haste and come down, for today I must stay at your house.

Today salvation has come to this house, because he also is a son of Abraham; for the Son of Man has come to seek and to save that which was lost. *Luke 19:5, 9–10 NKJV*

For God so loved the world, that he gave his only begotten Son, that whosoever believeth in him should not perish, but have everlasting life. For God sent not his Son into the world to condemn the world; but that the world through him might be saved. *John 3:16–17 KJV*

I am the gate. All who come in through me will be saved. Through me they will come and go and find pasture. A thief comes only to rob, kill, and destroy. I came so that everyone would have life, and have it in its fullest.

John 10:9–10 CEV

I am the resurrection, and the life: he that believeth in me, though he were dead, yet shall he live. *John 11:25 KJV*

SANCTITY (*also* DIVINITY)

Are not two sparrows sold for a farthing? and one of them shall not fall on the ground without your Father. But the very hairs of your head are all numbered. Fear ye not therefore, ye are of more value than many sparrows.

Matthew 10:29–31 (Luke 12:6–7) KJV

You blind fools! Which is greater, the gold or the temple that makes the gold sacred? You also teach that it doesn't matter if a person swears by the altar. But you say that it does matter if someone swears by the gift on the altar. Are you blind? Which is more important, the gift or the altar that makes the gift sacred?

Matthew 23:17–19 (Mark 12:40) (Luke 20:47) CEV

SATAN (*also* DEVIL(S))

Go away from me, Satan! You are not helping me! You don't care about the things of God. You care only about things that men think are important.

Matthew 16:23 (Mark 8:33) (Luke 4:8) NCV

I saw Satan fall like lightning from heaven. Behold, I give you the authority to trample on serpents and scorpions, and over all the power of the enemy, and nothing shall by any means hurt you. Nevertheless do not rejoice in this, that the spirits are subject to you, but rather rejoice because your names are written in heaven. *Luke 10:18–20* NKJV

Simon, Simon! Indeed, Satan has asked for you, that he may sift you as wheat. But I have prayed for you, that your faith should not fail; and when you have returned to Me, strengthen your brethren. *Luke 22:31–32* NKJV

SCIENCE (*also* MYSTICISM)

My Father, Lord of heaven and earth, I am grateful that you hid all this from the wise and educated people and showed it to ordinary people. Yes, Father, that is what pleased you.

Luke 10:21 (Matthew 11:25–26) CEV

You hypocrites! You know how to analyze the appearance of the earth and the sky, but why do you not analyze this present time? And why do you not even on your own initiative judge what is right?

Luke 12:56–57 (Matthew 16:2) NASB

SCRIPTURE (*see* HEBREW SCRIPTURES, WORD)
SECOND COMING OF CHRIST (*see* END TIMES, FALSE PROPHETS, FINAL JUDGMENT)
SECRECY (*also* MYSTERY)

Don't be afraid of anyone! Everything that is hidden will be found out, and every secret will be known. Whatever I say to you in the dark, you must tell in the light. And you must announce from the housetops whatever I have whispered to you. *Matthew 10:26–27 (Luke 12:2–3)* CEV

SECURITY (*also* INSECURITY)

Don't store up treasures on earth! Moths and rust can destroy them, and thieves can break in and steal them. Instead, store up your treasures in heaven, where moths and rust cannot destroy them, and thieves cannot break in and steal them. Your heart will always be where your treasure is. *Matthew 6:19–21 (Luke 12:33–34) CEV*

Do not fear those who kill the body but cannot kill the soul; rather fear him who can destroy both soul and body in hell.
Matthew 10:28 (Luke 12:4–5) NRSV

Then I can say to myself, "I have enough good things stored to last for many years. Rest, eat, drink, and enjoy life!" But God said to that man, "Foolish man! Tonight you will die. So who will get those things you have prepared for yourself?" This is how it will be for anyone who stores things up only for himself and is not rich toward God.
Luke 12:19–21 NCV

Very truly, I tell you, whoever keeps my word will never see death. *John 8:51 NRSV*

Peace is my parting gift to you, my own peace, such as the world cannot give. Set your troubled hearts at rest, and banish your fears. *John 14:27 NEB*

SELF-ACTUALIZATION (*also* ALTRUISM, REBIRTH, SELF-TRANSCENDENCE)

But seek first the kingdom of God and His righteousness, and all these things shall be added to you. Therefore do not worry about tomorrow, for tomorrow will worry about its own things. Sufficient for the day is its own trouble.
Matthew 6:33–34 (Luke 12:31) NKJV

Ask, and you will receive. Search, and you will find. Knock, and the door will be opened for you. Everyone who asks will receive. Everyone who searches will find. And the door will be opened for everyone who knocks.
Matthew 7:7–8 (Luke 11:9–10) CEV

But love your enemies, do good, and lend, hoping for nothing in return; and your reward will be great, and you will be sons of the Most High. For He is kind to the unthankful and evil. Therefore be merciful, just as your Father also is merciful.

Luke 6:35–36 (Matthew 5:44–45) NKJV

Don't work for food that spoils. Work for food that gives eternal life. The Son of Man will give you this food, because God the Father has given him the right to do so.

John 6:27 CEV

While you have the light, believe in the light, that you may become sons of light. *John 12:36 NKJV*

But when the Spirit of truth comes, he will lead you into all truth. He will not speak his own words, but he will speak only what he hears, and he will tell you what is to come.

John 16:13 NCV

SELF-CONTROL (*see* SELF-TRANSCENDENCE)

SELF-DEFENSE (*see* DEFENSE)

SELFISHNESS (*also* EGO, SECURITY, WORLDLINESS)

You Pharisees and teachers are showoffs, and you're in for trouble! You wash the outside of your cups and dishes, while inside there is nothing but greed and selfishness. You blind Pharisee! First clean the inside of a cup, and then the outside will also be clean. *Matthew 23:25 (Luke 11:39) CEV*

And if you do good to those who do good to you, what credit is that to you? For even sinners do the same. And if you lend to those from whom you expect to receive, what credit is that to you? Even sinners lend to sinners, in order to receive back the same amount.

Luke 6:33–34 (Matthew 5:47) NASB

Woe to you lawyers! For you have taken away the key of knowledge. You did not enter in yourselves, and those who were entering in you hindered.

Luke 11:52 (Matthew 23:13) NKJV

SELFLESSNESS (*also* SPIRITUALITY)

If you wish to be perfect, go, sell your possessions, and give the money to the poor, and you will have treasure in heaven; then come, follow me.

Matthew 19:21 (Mark 10:21) (Luke 18:22) NRSV

Give to everyone who asks and don't ask people to return what they have taken from you. Treat others just as you want to be treated.   *Luke 6:30–31 (Matthew 5:42, 7:12) CEV*

If anyone wishes to come after Me, let him deny himself, and take up his cross daily, and follow Me. For whoever wishes to save his life shall lose it, but whoever loses his life for My sake, he is the one who will save it.

Luke 9:23–24 (Matthew 16:24–25) (Mark 8:34–35) NASB

SELF-RESPECT (*also* INSECURITY, LOVE)

If you forgive others for the wrongs they do to you, your Father in heaven will forgive you. But if you don't forgive others, your Father will not forgive your sins.

Matthew 6:14-15 (Mark 11:25–26) CEV

The most important command is this: "Listen, people of Israel! The Lord our God, he is the only Lord. Love the Lord your God. Love him with all your heart, all your soul, all your mind, and all your strength." The second most important command is this: "Love your neighbor as you love yourself." These two commands are the most important commands.

Mark 12:29–31 (Matthew 22:37–40) NCV

Five sparrows are sold for just two pennies, but God does not forget a one of them. Even the hairs on your head are counted. So don't be afraid! You are worth much more than many sparrows.   *Luke 12:6–7 (Matthew 10:29–31) CEV*

SELF-RIGHTEOUSNESS (*also* LEGALISM, PRIDE)

Beware of the yeast of the Pharisees, that is, their hypocrisy. Nothing is covered up that will not be uncovered, and nothing secret that will not become known. Therefore whatever you have said in the dark will be heard in the light, and what you have whispered behind closed doors will be proclaimed from the housetops.

Luke 12:1–3 (Matthew 10:26–27) NRSV

Two men went up to the temple to pray, one a Pharisee and the other a tax collector. The Pharisee stood and prayed thus with himself, "God, I thank You that I am not like other men—extortioners, unjust, adulterers, or even as this tax collector. I fast twice a week; I give tithes of all that I possess." And the tax collector, standing afar off, would not so much as raise his eyes to heaven, but beat his breast, saying, "God be merciful to me a sinner!" I tell you, this man went down to his house justified rather than the other; for everyone who exalts himself will be humbled, and he who humbles himself will be exalted.   *Luke 18:10–14 NKJV*

SELF-SACRIFICE *(see* SACRIFICE)
SELF-TRANSCENDENCE   *(also* ASCETICISM)

He that loveth father or mother more than me is not worthy of me: and he that loveth son or daughter more than me is not worthy of me. And he that taketh not his cross, and followeth after me, is not worthy of me. He that findeth his life shall lose it: and he that loseth his life for my sake shall find it.   *Matthew 10:37–39 (Luke 14:26–27, 17:33) KJV*

For their are eunuchs who were born that way from their mother's womb; and there are eunuchs who were made eunuchs by men; and there are also eunuchs who made themselves eunuchs for the sake of the kingdom of heaven. He who is able to accept this, let him accept it.

Matthew 19:12 NASB

So therefore, none of you can become my disciple if you do not give up all your possessions.   *Luke 14:33 NRSV*

SENSUALITY   *(also* PLEASURE)

Now these are the ones sown among thorns; they are the ones who hear the word, and the cares of this world, the deceitfulness of riches, and the desires for other things entering in choke the word, and it becomes unfruitful.

Mark 4:18–19 (Matthew 13:22) (Luke 8:14) NKJV

That which proceeds out of the man, that is what defiles the man. For from within, out of the heart of men, proceed evil thoughts, fornications, thefts, murders, adulteries, deeds of coveting and wickedness, as well as deceit, sensuality, envy, slander, pride and foolishness. All these evil things proceed from within and defile the man.

Mark 7:20–23 (Matthew 15:19–20) NASB

What is born of the flesh is flesh, and what is born of the Spirit is spirit.   *John 3:6 NRSV*

It is the spirit that gives life; the flesh is useless. The words that I have spoken to you are spirit and life. But among you there are some who do not believe.   *John 6:63–64 NRSV*

SENTIMENTALISM

Don't store up treasures on earth! Moths and rust can destroy them, and thieves can break in and steal them. Instead, store up your treasures in heaven, where moths and rust cannot destroy them, and thieves cannot break in and steal them. Your heart will always be where your treasure is.   *Matthew 6:19–21 (Luke 12:33–34) CEV*

God is not God of the dead but of the living; for him all are alive.   *Luke 20:38 (Matthew 22:32) (Mark 12:27) NEB*

SERVICE (*also* ALTRUISM, CHARITY, SOCIAL ACTION)

And whoever gives one of these little ones only a cup of cold water in the name of a disciple, assuredly, I say to you, he shall by no means lose his reward.

Matthew 10:42 (Mark 9:41) NKJV

It is written, "Worship the Lord your God, and serve only him."   *Luke 4:8 (Matthew 4:10) NRSV*

Give, and it shall be given unto you; good measure, pressed down, and shaken together, and running over, shall men give into your bosom. For with the same measure that ye mete withal it shall be measured to you again.

Luke 6:38 (Matthew 7:1–2) KJV

The harvest is plentiful, but the laborers are few; therefore ask the Lord of the harvest to send out laborers into his harvest. *Luke 10:2 (Matthew 9:37) NRSV*

Be ready and keep your lamps burning just like those servants who wait up for their master to return from a wedding feast. As soon as he comes and knocks, they open the door for him. Servants are fortunate if their master finds them awake and ready when he comes! I promise you that he will get ready and have his servants sit down so he can serve them. *Luke 12:35–37 CEV*

No servant can be the slave of two masters; for either he will hate the first and love the second, or he will be devoted to the first and think nothing of the second. You cannot serve God and Money. *Luke 16:13 (Matthew 6:24) NEB*

Who is more important: the one sitting at the table or the one serving him? You think the one at the table is more important. But I am like a servant among you! *Luke 22:27 (Matthew 20:27–28) (Mark 10:44–45) NCV*

Do you understand what I have done? You call me your teacher and Lord, and you should, because that is who I am. And if your Lord and teacher has washed your feet, you should do the same for each other. I have set the example, and you should do for each other exactly what I have done for you. I tell you for certain that servants are not greater than their master, and messengers are not greater than the one who sent them. You know these things, and God will bless you, if you do them. *John 13:12–17 CEV*

SEX (also CELIBACY, DESIRE, MARRIAGE)

Ye have heard that it was said by them of old time, Thou shalt not commit adultery: But I say unto you, That whosoever looketh on a woman to lust after her hath committed adultery with her already in his heart.

Matthew 5:27–28 KJV

Furthermore it has been said, "Whoever divorces his wife, let him give her a certificate of divorce." But I say to you that whoever divorces his wife for any reason except sexual immorality causes her to commit adultery; and whoever marries a woman who is divorced commits adultery.

Matthew 5:31–32 (Matthew 19:9) (Mark 10:11–12) (Luke 16:18) NKJV

SEXISM, SEXUAL HARASSMENT
(*also* DISCRIMINATION)

I promise you that on the day of judgment, everyone will have to account for every careless word they have spoken. On that day they will be told that they are either innocent or guilty because of the things they have said.

Matthew 12:36–37 (Luke 6:45) CEV

And the King will anwer them "Truly I tell you, just as you did it to one of the least of these who are members of my family, you did it to me." *Matthew 25:40* NRSV

Do to others as you would have them do to you.

Luke 6:31 (Matthew 7:12) NRSV

For with the same measure that you use, it will be measured back to you. *Luke 6:38 (Matthew 7:2)* NKJV

A worker should be given his pay.

Luke 10:7 (Matthew 10:10) NCV

SHARING (*see* CHARITY, COOPERATION)
SIGNS (*also* MIRACLES, PROOF, WORKS)

When it is evening you say, "It will be fair weather for the sky is red"; and in the morning, "It will be foul weather today, for the sky is red and threatening." Hypocrites! You know how to discern the face of the sky, but you cannot discern the signs of the times. A wicked and adulterous generation seeks after a sign, and no sign shall be given to it except the sign of the prophet Jonah.

Matthew 16:2–4 (Mark 8:12) (Luke 12:54–56) NKJV

And these signs will accompany those who have believed: in My name they will cast out demons, they will speak with new tongues; they will pick up serpents, and if they drink any deadly poison, it shall not hurt them; they will lay hands on the sick, and they will recover.

Mark 16:17–18 NASB

Did I not say to you that if you would believe you would
see the glory of God?

Father, I thank You that You have heard Me.

And I know that You always hear Me, but because of the
people who are standing by I said this, that they may
believe that You sent Me.   *John 11:40,41, 42 NKJV*

SIMPLICITY, SIMPLE LIVING (*also* MONEY, SPEECH)

When you pray, go into a room alone and close the door.
Pray to your Father in private. He knows what is done in
private, and he will reward you. When you pray, don't talk
on and on as people do who don't know God. They think
God likes to hear long prayers. Don't be like them. Your
Father knows what you need before you ask.

Matthew 6:6–8 CEV

Don't store up treasures on earth! Moths and rust can
destroy them, and thieves can break in and steal them.
Instead, store up your treasures in heaven, where moths
and rust cannot destroy them, and thieves cannot break in
and steal them. Your heart will always be where your
treasure is.   *Matthew 6:19–21 (Luke 12:33–34) CEV*

Therefore take no thought, saying, What shall we eat? or,
What shall we drink? or, Wherewithal shall we be clothed?
(For after all these things do the Gentiles seek:) for your
heavenly Father knoweth that ye have need of all these
things. But seek ye first the kingdom of God, and his
righteousness; and all these things shall be added unto you.
Take therefore no thought for the morrow: for the morrow
shall take thought for the things of itself. Sufficient unto the
day is the evil thereof.   *Matthew 6:31–34 (Luke 12:29–31) KJV*

And as you go, preach, saying, "The kingdom of heaven is
at hand." Heal the sick, raise the dead, cleanse the lepers,
cast out demons; freely you received, freely give. Do not
acquire gold, or silver, or copper for your money belts, or
a bag for your journey, or even two tunics, or sandals, or a
staff; for the worker is worthy of his support.

Matthew 10:7–10 (Mark 6:8–9) (Luke 10:4) NASB

If you wish to be perfect, go, sell your possessions, and give the money to the poor, and you will have treasure in heaven; then come, follow me.

Matthew 19:21 (Mark 10:21) (Luke 18:22) NRSV

Now these are the ones sown among thorns; they are the ones who hear the word, and the cares of this world, the deceitfulness of riches, and the desires for other things entering in choke the word, and it becomes unfruitful.

Mark 4:18–19 (Matthew 13:22) (Luke 8:14) NKJV

What kind of person did you go out to the desert to see? Was he like tall grass blown about by the wind? What kind of man did you really go out to see? Was he someone dressed in fine clothes? People who wear expensive clothes and live in luxury are in the king's palace. What then did you go out to see? Was he a prophet? He certainly was! I tell you that he was more than a prophet. In the Scriptures, God calls John his messenger and says, "I am sending my messenger ahead of you to get things ready for you." No one ever born on this earth is greater than John. But whoever is least important in God's kingdom is greater than John.

Luke 7:24–28 CEV

Martha, Martha, you are worried and bothered about so many things; but only a few things are necessary, really only one, for Mary has chosen the good part, which shall not be taken away from her.

Luke 10:41–42 NASB

So therefore, none of you can become my disciple if you do not give up all your possessions.

Luke 14:33 NRSV

SIN (*also* FORGIVENESS)

For whether is easier, to say, Thy sins be forgiven thee; or to say, Arise, and walk? But that ye may know that the Son of man hath power on earth to forgive sins, . . . Arise, take up thy bed, and go unto thine house.

Matthew 9:5–6 (Mark 2:9–11) (Luke 5:24) KJV

Healthy people don't need a doctor, but sick people do. Go and learn what the Scriptures mean when they say, "Instead of offering sacrifices to me, I want you to be

merciful to others." I did not come to invite good people to
be my followers. I came to invite sinners.

Matthew 9:12–13 (Mark 2:17) (Luke 5:31–32) CEV

For from within, out of the heart of men, proceed evil
thoughts, adulteries, fornications, murders, thefts,
covetousness, wickedness, deceit, lewdness, an evil eye,
blasphemy, pride, foolishness. All these evil things come
from within and defile a man.

Mark 7:21–23 (Matthew 15:19–20) NKJV

And forgive us our sins; for we also forgive every one that
is indebted to us. And lead us not into temptation; but
deliver us from evil.   *Luke 11:4 (Matthew 6:12–13)* KJV

There will always be something that causes people to sin. But
anyone who causes them to sin is in for trouble. A person who
causes even one of my little followers to sin would be better
off thrown into the ocean with a heavy stone tied around the
neck. So be careful what you do. Correct any followers of mine
who sin, and forgive the ones who say they are sorry. Even if
one of them mistreats you seven times in one day and says, "I
am sorry," you should still forgive that person.

Luke 17:1–4 (Matthew 18:6–7) (Mark 9:42) CEV

I tell you the truth. Everyone who lives in sin is a slave to
sin. A slave does not stay with a family forever, but a son
belongs to the family forever. So if the Son makes you free,
then you will be truly free.   *John 8:34–36* NCV

Neither this man nor his parents sinned, but that the works
of God should be revealed in him.   *John 9:3* NKJV

If I had not come and spoken to them, they would not be
guilty of sin. But now they have no excuse for their sin.
Everyone who hates me also hates my Father. I have done
things that no one else has ever done. If they had not seen
me do these things, they would not be guilty. But they did
see me do these things, and they still hate me and my Father
too.   *John 15:22–24* CEV

SINCERITY *(see* AUTHENTICITY)

SISTERHOOD *(also* LOVE, ONENESS)

Who is my mother and who are my brothers?. . . These are
my mother and my brothers! Anyone who obeys my Father
in heaven is my brother or sister or mother.

Matthew 12:48–50 (Mark 3:33–35) (Luke 8:21) CEV

But you must not be called 'Teacher.' You are all brothers
and sisters together. You have only one Teacher.

Matthew 23:8 NCV

SLANDER *(see* GOSSIP)

SLEEP *(also* REST)

Therefore, be on the alert—for you do not know when the
master of the house is coming, whether in the evening, at
midnight, at cockcrowing, or in the morning—lest he come
suddenly and find you asleep. And what I say to you I say
to all, "Be on the alert!"   *Mark 13:35–37 (Matthew 24:42)* NASB

Why sleep ye? rise and pray, lest ye enter into temptation.

Luke 22:46 (Matthew 26:41) (Mark 14:38) KJV

SOCIAL ACTION *(also* ACTION, CHARITY, COMPASSION, HUNGER, MERCY, PEACE)

God blesses those people who are merciful.
They will be treated with mercy!
God blesses those people who make peace.
They will be called his children!
God blesses those people who are treated badly
   for doing right.
They belong to the kingdom of heaven.

Matthew 5:7, 9–10 CEV

And as you go, preach, saying, "The kingdom of heaven is
at hand." Heal the sick, raise the dead, cleanse the lepers,
cast out demons; freely you received, freely give.

Matthew 10:7–8 NASB

For whosoever shall give you a cup of water to drink in my
name, because ye belong to Christ, verily I say unto you,
he shall not lose his reward.   *Mark 9:41 (Matthew 10:42)* KJV

Give to everyone who asks and don't ask people to return what they have taken from you. Treat others just as you want to be treated. *Luke 6:30–31 (Matthew 5:42, 7:12)* CEV

Give, and it will be given to you; good measure, pressed down, shaken together, running over, they will pour into your lap. For by your standard of measure it will be measured to you in return.

Luke 6:38 (Matthew 7:2) (Mark 4:24) NASB

More than that, blessed are those who hear the word of God and keep it! *Luke 11:28* NKJV

In a certain city there was a judge who neither feared God nor had respect for people. In that city there was a widow who kept coming to him and saying, "Grant me justice against my opponent." For a while he refused; but later he said to himself, "Though I have no fear of God and no respect for anyone, yet because this widow keeps bothering me, I will grant her justice, so that she may not wear me out by continually coming." *Luke 18:2–5* NRSV

SOCIAL CHANGE (*see* CHANGE, NEW COVENANT)

SOCIAL RESPONSIBILITY (*also* CHARITY, COMPASSION, PRIORITIES, SOCIAL ACTION)

And whoever shall force you to go one mile, go with him two. Give to him who asks of you, and do not turn away from him who wants to borrow from you.

Matthew 5:41–42 (Luke 6:30) NASB

Don't condemn others, and God will not condemn you. God will be as hard on you as you are on others! He will treat you exactly as you treat them.

Matthew 7:1–2 (Luke 6:37–38) CEV

You will know these false prophets by what they do. Not all those who say that I am their Lord will enter the kingdom of heaven. The only people who will enter the kingdom of heaven are those who do what my Father in heaven wants. *Matthew 7:20–21 (Luke 6:44, 46)* NCV

Healthy people don't need a doctor, but sick people do. Go and learn what the scriptures mean when they say, "Instead of offering sacrifices to me, I want you to be merciful to others." I did not come to invite good people to be my followers. I came to invite sinners.

Matthew 9:12–13 (Mark 2:17) (Luke 5:31–32) CEV

Why do you disobey God and follow your own teaching? Didn't God command you to respect your father and mother? . . . But you let people get by without helping their parents when they should. You let them say that what they have has been offered to God. Is this any way to show respect to your parents? You ignore God's commands in order to follow your own teaching.

Matthew 15:3–6 (Mark 7:9–13) CEV

The Spirit of the LORD is upon Me,
Because He has anointed Me
To preach the gospel to the poor;
He has sent Me to heal the brokenhearted,
To proclaim liberty to the captives and recovery of sight to the blind,
To set at liberty those who are oppressed.

Luke 4:18 NKJV

Give to everyone who asks and don't ask people to return what they have taken from you. Treat others just as you want to be treated. *Luke 6:30–31 (Matthew 5:42, 7:12) CEV*

But love your enemies, do good, and lend, hoping for nothing in return; and your reward will be great, and you will be sons of the Most High. For He is kind to the unthankful and evil. Therefore be merciful, just as your Father also is merciful. *Luke 6:35–36 (Matthew 5:44–45) NKJV*

A certain man went down from Jerusalem to Jericho, and fell among thieves, which stripped him of his raiment, and wounded him, and departed, leaving him half dead. And by chance there came down a certain priest that way: and when he saw him, he passed by on the other side. And likewise a Levite, when he was at the place, came and looked on him, and passed by on the other side. But a certain Samaritan, as he journeyed, came where he was: and when he saw him, he had compassion on him. And went to him, and bound up his wounds, pouring in oil and wine, and set him on his own beast, and brought him to an inn, and took care of him. And on the morrow when he departed, he took out two pence, and gave them to the host, and said unto him, Take care of him; and whatsoever thou spendest more, when I come again, I will repay thee. Which now of these three, thinkest thou, was neighbour unto him that fell among the thieves?

Luke 10:30–36 KJV

SOCIALISM (*see* ECONOMICS)

SOCIETY (*also* COMMUNITY, MATERIALISM)

Satan, get away from me! You're in my way because you think like everyone else and not like God.

Matthew 16:23 (Mark 8:33) (Luke 4:8) CEV

But woe unto you that are rich! for ye have received your consolation. Woe unto you that are full! for ye shall hunger. . . .

Luke 6:24-25 KJV

You are those who justify yourselves in the sight of others; but God knows your hearts; for what is prized by human beings is an abomination in the sight of God.

Luke 16:15 NRSV

SOLITUDE (*also* MEDITATION)

When you pray, go into a room alone and close the door. Pray to your Father in private. He knows what is done in private, and he will reward you. When you pray, don't talk on and on as people do who don't know God. They think God likes to hear long prayers. Don't be like them. Your Father knows what you need before you ask.

Matthew 6:6–8 CEV

Come with me. We will go to a quiet place to be alone. There we will get some rest.

Mark 6:31 NCV

SORROW (see GRIEF)

SOUL (also SPIRITUALITY)

Do not fear those who kill the body but cannot kill the soul; rather fear him who can destroy both soul and body in hell.

Matthew 10:28 (Luke 12:4–5) NRSV

The most important one says: "People of Israel, you have only one Lord and God. You must love him with all your heart, soul, mind, and strength."

Mark 12:29–30 (Matthew 22:37) CEV

In your patience possess ye your souls.

Luke 21:19 (Matthew 24:12) (Mark 13:13) KJV

SPEECH (also ANGER, GOSSIP, OATHS, TESTIMONY)

Say only "yes" if you mean "yes," and say only "no" if you mean "no." If you must say more than "yes" or "no," it is from the Evil One. *Matthew 5:37 NCV*

You are a bunch of evil snakes, so how can you say anything good? Your words show what is in your hearts. Good people bring good things out of their hearts, but evil people bring evil things out of their hearts.

Matthew 12:34 CEV

And I say to you, that every careless word that men shall speak, they shall render account for it in the day of judgment. For by your words you shall be justified, and by your words you shall be condemned.

Matthew 12:36–37 (Luke 6:45) NASB

I don't speak on my own. I say only what the Father who sent me has told me to say. I know that his commands will bring eternal life. That is why I tell you exactly what the Father has told me. *John 12:49–50 CEV*

SPIRIT   (see HOLY SPIRIT)

SPIRITUAL INSENSITIVITY (also CYNICISM, WORLD-LINESS)

The eye is the lamp of the body. So, if your eye is healthy, your whole body will be full of light; but if your eye is unhealthy, your whole body will be full of darkness. If then the light in you is darkness, how great is the darkness!

Matthew 6:22–23 (Luke 11:34–36) NRSV

Then they also will answer, "Lord, when was it that we saw you hungry or thirsty or a stranger or naked or sick or in prison, and did not take care of you?" Then he will answer them, "Truly I tell you, just as you did not do it to one of the least of these, you did not do it to me.

Matthew 25:44–45 NRSV

Why are you so fearful? How is it that you have no faith?

Mark 4:40 (Luke 8:25) NKJV

A prophet is not without honor except in his home town and among his own relatives and in his own household.

Mark 6:4 (Matthew 13:57) NASB

Why do you reason because you have no bread? Do you not yet perceive nor understand? Is your heart still hardened? Having eyes, do you not see? And having ears, do you not hear? And do you not remember?

Mark 8:17–18 (Matthew 16:8–9) NKJV

It is said, "Do not put the Lord your God to the test."

Luke 4:12 (Matthew 4:7) NRSV

Unless you people see signs and wonders, you will by no means believe.   *John 4:48 NKJV*

I am come in my Father's name, and ye receive me not: if another shall come in his own name, him ye will receive. How can ye believe, which receive honour one of another, and seek not the honour that cometh from God only?

John 5:43–44 KJV

I have told you, and you refused to believe me. The things I do by my Father's authority show who I am. But since you are not my sheep, you don't believe me.   *John 10:25–26 CEV*

SPIRITUAL SEARCHING (*also* EFFORT, SPIRITUALITY)

Blessed are those who hunger and thirst for righteousness, For they shall be filled.   *Matthew 5:6 (Luke 6:21) NKJV*

But strive first for the kingdom of God and his righteousness, and all these things will be given to you as well. So do not worry about tomorrow, for tomorrow will bring worries of its own. Today's trouble is enough for today.   *Matthew 6:33–34 (Luke 12:31–32) NRSV*

Ask, and it shall be given to you; seek, and you shall find; knock, and it shall be opened to you: For every one who asks receives, and he who seeks finds, and to him who knocks it shall be opened.   *Matthew 7:7–8 (Luke 11:9–10) NASB*

My Father, Lord of heaven and earth, I am grateful that you hid all this from the wise and educated people and showed it to ordinary people. Yes, Father, that is what pleased you.
    Luke 10:21 (Matthew 11:25–26) CEV

If you love me, you will do the things I command. I will ask the Father, and he will give you another Helper. He will give you this Helper to be with you forever. The Helper is the Spirit of truth. The world cannot accept him because it does not see him or know him. But you know him. He lives with you and he will be in you.   *John 14:15–17 NCV*

SPIRITUALITY (*also* CHRIST, HOLY SPIRIT, RELIGION, SPIRITUAL SEARCHING)

Keep watching and praying, that you may not enter into temptation; the spirit is willing, but the flesh is weak.
    Matthew 26:41 (Mark 14:38) (Luke 22:46) NASB

For what shall it profit a man, if he shall gain the whole world, and lose his own soul?
    Mark 8:36 (Matthew 16:26) (Luke 9:25) KJV

Father, "Into Your hands I commit My spirit."

Luke 23:46 NKJV

But the hour is coming, and now is, when the true worshipers will worship the Father in spirit and truth; for the Father is seeking such to worship Him. God is Spirit, and those who worship Him must worship in spirit and truth. *John 4:23–24 NKJV*

It is the Spirit that gives life; the flesh is useless. The words that I have spoken to you are spirit and life. *John 6:63 NRSV*

There is still much that I could say to you, but the burden would be too great for you now. However, when he comes who is the Spirit of truth, he will guide you into all the truth.

John 16:12 –13 NEB

Father, I am on my way to you. But I say these things while I am still in the world, so that my followers will have the same complete joy that I do. I have told them your message. But the people of this world hate them, because they don't belong to this world, just as I don't. Father, I don't ask you to take my followers out of the world, but keep them safe from the evil one. They don't belong to this world, and neither do I. Your word is the truth. So let this truth make them completely yours. *John 17:13–17 CEV*

STATUS SYMBOLS (*also* APPEARANCE, POSITION, TITLES)

Don't store up treasures on earth! Moths and rust can destroy them, and thieves can break in and steal them. Instead, store up your treasures in heaven, where moths and rust cannot destroy them, and thieves cannot break in and steal them. Your heart will always be where your treasure is. *Matthew 6:19–21 (Luke 12:33–34) CEV*

No one can serve two masters; for either he will hate the one and love the other, or else he will be loyal to the one and despise the other. You cannot serve God and mammon. *Matthew 6:24 (Luke 16:13) NKJV*

For what will it profit them if they gain the whole world but forfeit their life? Or what will they give in return for their life?   *Matthew 16:26 (Mark 8:36–37) (Luke 9:25)* NRSV

Yet lackest thou one thing: sell all that thou hast, and distribute unto the poor, and thou shalt have treasure in heaven: and come, follow me.

Luke 18:22 (Matthew 19:21) (Mark 10:21) KJV

STEWARDSHIP (*also* SOCIAL RESPONSIBILITY)

The kingdom is also like what happened when a man went away and put his three servants in charge of all he owned. The man knew what each servant could do. So he handed five thousand coins to the first servant, two thousand to the second, and one thousand to the third. Then he left the country. As soon as the man had gone, the servant with the five thousand coins used them to earn five thousand more. The servant who had two thousand coins did the same with his money and earned two thousand more. But the servant with one thousand coins dug a hole and hid his master's money in the ground. Some time later the master of those servants returned. He called them in and asked what they had done with his money. The servant who had been given five thousand coins brought them in with the five thousand he had earned. He said, "Sir, you gave me five thousand coins, and I have earned five thousand more." "Wonderful!" his master replied, "You are a good and faithful servant. I left you in charge of only a little, but now I will put you in charge of much more. Come and share in my happiness!"   *Matthew 25:14–21 (Luke 19:12–17)* CEV

A rich man's farm produced a big crop, and he said to himself, "What can I do? I don't have a place large enough to store everything." Later, he said, "Now I know what I'll do. I'll tear down my barns and build bigger ones, where I can store all my grain and other goods. Then I'll say to myself. "You have stored up enough good things to last for years to come. Live it up! Eat, drink, and enjoy yourself." But God said to him, "You fool! Tonight you will die. Then who will get what you have stored up?" This is what happens to people who store up everything for themselves, but are poor in the sight of God.   *Luke 12:16–21 CEV*

There was a rich man who had a manager, and charges were brought to him that this man was squandering his property. So he summoned him and said to him, "What is this that I hear about you? Give me an accounting of your management, because you cannot be my manager any longer." Then the manager said to himself, "What will I do, now that my master is taking the position away from me? I am not strong enough to dig, and I am ashamed to beg. I have decided what to do so that, when I am dismissed as manager, people may welcome me into their homes." So, summoning his master's debtors one by one, he asked the first, "How much do you owe my master?" He answered, "A hundred jugs of olive oil." He said to him, "Take your bill, sit down quickly, and make it fifty." Then he asked another, "And how much do you owe?" He replied, "A hundred containers of wheat." He said to him, "Take your bill and make it eighty." And his master commended the dishonest manager because he acted shrewdly; for the children of this age are more shrewd in dealing with their own generation than are the children of light. And I tell you, make friends for yourselves by means of dishonest wealth so that when it is gone, they may welcome you into the eternal homes.   *Luke 16:1–9 NRSV*

STRENGTH (*also* ABILITY, GREATNESS, POWER)

Therefore whosoever heareth these sayings of mine, and doeth them, I will liken him unto a wise man, which built his house upon a rock; And the rain descended, and the floods came, and the winds blew, and beat upon that house; and it fell not: for it was founded upon a rock.

Matthew 7:24–25 (Luke 6:47–48) KJV

Be on guard, that your hearts may not be weighted down with dissipation and drunkenness and the worries of life, and that day come on you suddenly like a trap; for it will come upon all those who dwell on the face of all the earth. But keep on the alert at all times, praying in order that you may have strength to escape all these things that are about to take place, and to stand before the Son of Man.

Luke 21:34–36 NASB

I cannot do anything on my own. The Father sent me, and he is the one who told me how to judge. I judge with fairness, because I obey him, and I don't just try to please myself. *John 5:30 CEV*

STRESS (*also* ANXIETY, WORLDLINESS, WORRY)

Therefore do not worry, saying, "What will we eat?" or "What will we drink?" or "What will we wear?" For it is the Gentiles who strive for all these things; and indeed your heavenly Father knows that you need all these things. But strive first for the kingdom of God and his righteousness, and all these things will be given to you as well. So do not worry about tomorrow, for tomorrow will bring worries of its own. Today's trouble is enough for today.

Matthew 6:31–34 (Luke 12:29–31) NRSV

I came to bring fire to the earth, and how I wish it were already kindled! I have a baptism with which to be baptized, and what stress I am under until it is completed!

Luke 12:49–50 NRSV

These things I have spoken to you, that in Me you may have peace. In the world you will have tribulation; but be of good cheer; I have overcome the world. *John 16:33 NKJV*

SUCCESS (*also* AMBITION, APPEARANCE, REWARD, WORLDLINESS, WORRY)

But many who are now first will be last, and many who are now last will be first.

Mark 10:31 (Matthew 19:30) (Matthew 20:16) (Luke 13:30) CEV

You make yourselves look good in front of people. But God knows what is really in your hearts. The things that are important to people are worth nothing to God.

Luke 16:15 NCV

But don't act like them. If you want to be great, you must be the servant of all the others. And if you want to be first, you must be everyone's slave. The Son of Man did not come to be a slave master, but a slave who will give his life to rescue many people.

Mark 10:43–44 (Matthew 20:26–27) (Luke 22:26) CEV

SUFFERING (*also* PERSECUTION, TROUBLE)

Ye know not what ye ask. Are ye able to drink of the cup that I shall drink of, and to be baptized with the baptism that I am baptized with? *Matthew 20:22 (Mark 10:38) KJV*

> The Spirit of the LORD is upon Me,
> Because he has anointed Me
> To preach the gospel to the poor;
> He has sent Me to heal the brokenhearted,
> To proclaim liberty to the captives
> And recovery of sight to the blind,
> To set at liberty those who are oppressed.

Luke 4:18 NKJV

If you love your life, you will lose it. If you give it up in this world, you will be given eternal life. If you serve me, you must go with me. My servants will be with me wherever I am. If you serve me, my Father will honor you. Now I am deeply troubled, and I don't know what to say. But I must not ask my Father to keep me from this time of suffering. In fact, I came into the world to suffer. *John 12:25–27 CEV*

SUICIDE (*also* COMMANDMENTS, DEATH)

It is not those who are healthy who need a physician, but those who are sick. But go and learn what this means, "I desire compassion, and not sacrifice," for I did not come to call the righteous, but sinners.

Matthew 9:12–13 (Mark 2:17) (Luke 5:31–32) NASB

Do not murder. Be faithful in marriage. Do not steal. Do not tell lies about others. Respect your father and mother. And love others as much as you love yourself.

Matthew 19:18–19 (Mark 10:19) (Luke 18:20) CEV

And the king will answer them, "Truly I tell you, just as you did it to one of the least of these who are members of my family, you did it to me." *Matthew 25:40 NRSV*

Five sparrows are sold for just two pennies, but God does not forget a one of them. Even the hairs on your head are counted. So don't be afraid! You are worth much more than many sparrows.   *Luke 12:6–7 (Matthew 10:29–31) CEV*

SUPERFICIALITY (*also* APPEARANCE, RELIGIOSITY)

And what is the seed that fell on rocky ground? That seed is like the person who hears the teaching and quickly accepts it with joy. But he does not let the teaching go deep into his life. He keeps it only a short time. When trouble or persecution comes because of the teaching he accepted, then he quickly gives up.

Matthew 13:20–21 (Mark 4:16–17) (Luke 8:13) NCV

Don't any of you know what I am talking about by now? Don't you know that the food you put into your mouth goes into your stomach and then out of your body? But the words that come out of your mouth come from your heart. And they are what make you unfit to worship God. Out of your heart come evil thoughts, murder, unfaithfulness in marriage, vulgar deeds, stealing, telling lies, and insulting others. These are what make you unclean. Eating without washing your hands will not make you unfit to worship God.   *Matthew 15:16–20 (Mark 7:18–23) CEV*

For you pay tithe of mint and anise and cumin, and have neglected the weightier matters of the law: justice and mercy and faith. These you ought to have done, without leaving the others undone. Blind guides, who strain out a gnat and swallow a camel!

Matthew 23:23–24 (Luke 11:42) NKJV

TALENT (*see* ABILITY, RESPONSIBILITY)

TAX   (*also* MONEY)

What thinkest thou, Simon? of whom do the kings of the earth take custom or tribute? of their own children, or of strangers?

Then are the children free? Notwithstanding, lest we should offend them, go thou to the sea, and cast an hook, and take up the fish that first cometh up; and when thou hast opened his mouth, thou shalt find a piece of money: that take, and give unto them for me and thee.

Matthew 17:25–27 KJV

Render therefore to Caesar the things that are Caesar's, and to God the things that are God's.

Matthew 22:21 (Mark 12:17) (Luke 20:25) NKJV

TEACHING (*also* EDUCATION, EVANGELISM, EXAMPLE)

Therefore, whoever breaks one of the least of these commandments, and teaches others to do the same, will be called least in the kingdom of heaven; but whoever does them and teaches them will be called great in the kingdom of heaven. *Matthew 5:19 NRSV*

But you must not be called 'Teacher.' You are all brothers and sisters together. You have only one Teacher.

Matthew 23:8 NCV

No one can come to me unless drawn by the Father who sent me; and I will raise that person up on the last day. It is written in the prophets, "And they shall all be taught by God." Everyone who has heard and learned from the Father comes to me. *John 6:44–45 NRSV*

But the Holy Spirit will come and help you, because the Father will send the Spirit to take my place. The Spirit will teach you everything and will remind you of what I said while I was with you. *John 14:26 CEV*

I spoke openly to the world. I always taught in synagogues and in the temple, where the Jews always meet, and in secret I have said nothing. *John 18:20 NKJV*

TECHNOCRACY (*see* BUREAUCRACY, MATERIALISM)

TEMPER (*also* ANGER, VIOLENCE)

Blessed are the gentle for they shall inherit the earth.
Blessed are the peacemakers, for they shall be called sons of God. *Matthew 5:5, 9 NASB*

This is what I say to all who will listen to me: Love your enemies, and be good to everyone who hates you. Ask God to bless anyone who curses you, and pray for everyone who is cruel to you. If someone slaps you on one cheek, don't stop that person from slapping you on the other cheek. If someone wants to take your coat, don't try to keep back your shirt. Give to everyone who asks and don't ask people to return what they have taken from you. Treat others just as you want to be treated.

Luke 6:27–31 (Matthew 5:39–42, 44) CEV

In your patience possess ye your souls.

Luke 21:19 (Matthew 24:12) (Mark 13:13) KJV

TEMPTATION (*also* WORLDLINESS)

Watch and pray, lest you enter into temptation. The spirit indeed is willing, but the flesh is weak.

Matthew 26:41 (Mark 14:38) (Luke 22:46) NKJV

Get thee behind me, Satan: for it is written, Thou shalt worship the Lord thy God, and him only shalt thou serve. . . . It is said, Thou shalt not tempt the Lord thy God.

Luke 4:8, 12 (Matthew 4:10, 7) KJV

And forgive us our sins; for we also forgive every one that is indebted to us. And lead us not into temptation; but deliver us from evil. *Luke 11:4 (Matthew 6:12–13)* KJV

There will always be something that causes people to sin. But anyone who causes them to sin is in for trouble. A person who causes even one of my little followers to sin would be better off thrown into the ocean with a heavy stone tied around the neck. So be careful what you do. Correct any followers of mine who sin, and forgive the ones who say they are sorry. Even if one of them mistreats you seven times in one day and says, "I am sorry," you should still forgive that person.

Luke 17:1–4 (Matthew 18:6–7) (Mark 9:42) CEV

Why are you sleeping? Rise and pray that you may not enter into temptation. *Luke 22:46* NASB

TERRITORIALISM (*also* PATRIOTISM)

My kingdom is not from this world. If my kingdom were from this world, my followers would be fighting to keep me from being handed over to the Jews. But as it is, my kingdom is not from here.   *John 18:36 NRSV*

TESTIMONY (*also* EVANGELISM)

I do choose. Be made clean! See that you say nothing to anyone; but go, show yourself to the priest, and offer the gift that Moses commanded, as a testimony to them.

Matthew 8:3, 4 (Mark 1:41, 44) (Luke 5:13, 14) NRSV

Because of me, you will be dragged before rulers and kings to tell them and the Gentiles about your faith. But when someone arrests you, don't worry about what you will say or how you will say it. At that time you will be given the words to say. But you will not really be the one speaking. The Spirit from your Father will tell you what to say.

Matthew 10:18–20 CEV

Go and tell John the things you have seen and heard: that the blind see, the lame walk, the lepers are cleansed, the deaf hear, the dead are raised, the poor have the gospel preached to them. And blessed is he who is not offended because of Me.

Luke 7:22–23 (Matthew 11:4–6) NKJV

Very truly, I tell you, we speak of what we know and testify to what we have seen; yet you do not receive our testimony. If I have told you about earthly things, and you do not believe, how can you believe if I tell you about heavenly things?   *John 3:11–12 NRSV*

But I have a testimony greater than John's. The works that the Father has given me to complete, the very works that I am doing, testify on my behalf that the Father has sent me.

John 5:36 NRSV

Didn't I tell you that if you had faith, you would see the glory of God?

Father, I thank you for answering my prayer. I know that you always answer my prayers. But I said this, so that the people here would believe that you sent me.

Lazarus, come out! *John 11:40, 41–42, 43 CEV*

When the Advocate comes, whom I will send to you from the Father, the Spirit of truth who comes from the Father, he will testify on my behalf. You also are to testify because you have been with me from the beginning. I have said these things to you to keep you from stumbling.

John 15:26–16:1 NRSV

THANKFULNESS (*see* GRATITUDE, HUMILITY)

THEFT, THIEVES (*also* DECEIT)

Don't store up treasures on earth! Moths and rust can destroy them, and thieves can break in and steal them. Instead, store up your treasures in heaven, where moths and rust cannot destroy them, and thieves cannot break in and steal them. Your heart will always be where your treasure is. *Matthew 6:19–21 (Luke 12:33–34) CEV*

For out of the heart proceed evil thoughts, murders, adulteries, fornications, thefts, false witness, blasphemies.

Matthew 15:19 (Mark 7:21–22) NKJV

Is it not written, My house shall be called of all nations the house of prayer? but ye have made it a den of thieves.

Mark 11:17 (Matthew 21:13) (Luke 19:46) KJV

THIRST (*also* DESIRE, HUNGER, NEED)

For I was an hungered, and ye gave me meat: I was thirsty, and ye gave me drink: I was a stranger, and ye took me in.

Matthew 25:35 KJV

If you knew the gift of God, and who it is who says to you, "Give Me a drink," you would have asked Him, and He would have given you living water. *John 4:10 NKJV*

Everyone who drinks of this water shall thirst again; but whoever drinks of the water that I shall give him shall never thirst; but the water that I shall give him shall become in him a well of water springing up to eternal life.

John 4:13–14 NASB

If you are thirsty, come to me and drink! Have faith in me, and you will have life-giving water flowing from deep inside you, just as the Scriptures say. *John 7:37–38 CEV*

THOUGHT (*also* INTELLECTUALISM)

Which of you by taking thought can add one cubit unto his stature? *Matthew 6:27 (Luke 12:25) KJV*

Go your way; and as you have believed, so let it be done for you. *Matthew 8:13 NKJV*

TITLES (*also* AMBITION, STATUS SYMBOLS, WINNING)

But you must not be called, 'Teacher.' You are all brothers and sisters together. You have only one Teacher. And don't call any person on earth 'Father.' You have one Father. He is in heaven. And you should not be called 'Master.' You have only one Master, the Christ. *Matthew 23:8–10 NCV*

I have come with my Father's authority, and you have not welcomed me. But you will welcome people who come on their own. How could you possibly believe? You like to have your friends praise you, and you don't care about praise that the only God can give! *John 5:43–44 CEV*

TOLERANCE (*also* INCLUSIVENESS)

You have heard that it was said, "You shall love your neighbor, and hate your enemy." But I say to you, love your enemies, and pray for those who persecute you in order that you may be sons of your Father who is in heaven; for He causes His sun to rise on the evil and the good, and sends rain on the righteous and the unrighteous.

Matthew 5:43–45 (Luke 6:27–28) NASB

And why do you look at the speck that is in your brother's eye, but do not notice the log that is in your own eye? Or how can you say to your brother, "Let me take the speck out of your eye," and behold, the log is in your own eye?

You hypocrite, first take the log out of your own eye, and then you will see clearly to take the speck out of your brother's eye. *Matthew 7:3–5 (Luke 6:41–42) NASB*

Do not stop him; for no one who does a deed of power in my name will be able soon afterward to speak evil of me. Whoever is not against us is for us. For truly I tell you, whoever gives you a cup of water to drink because you bear the name of Christ will by no means lose the reward. *Mark 9:39–41 (Luke 9:50) NRSV*

Don't judge other people, and you will not be judged. Don't accuse others of being guilty, and you will not be accused of being guilty. Forgive other people, and you will be forgiven. *Luke 6:37 (Matthew 7:1–2) NCV*

TRADITION (*also* REVELATION)

You know that you have been taught, "An eye for an eye and a tooth for a tooth." But I tell you not to try to get even with a person who has done something to you. When someone slaps your right cheek, turn and let that person slap your other cheek. *Matthew 5:38-39 (Luke 6:29) CEV*

Satan get away from me! You're in my way because you think like everyone else and not like God.

Matthew 16:23 (Mark 8:33) (Luke 4:8) CEV

No one sews a patch of unshrunk cloth on an old garment; otherwise the patch pulls away from it, the new from the old, and a worse tear results. And no one puts new wine into old wineskins; otherwise the wine will burst the skins, and the wine is lost, and the skins as well; but one puts new wine into fresh wineskins.

Mark 2:21–22 (Matthew 9:16–17) (Luke 5:36–37) NASB

Well hath Esias prophesied of you hypocrites, as it is written, This people honoureth me with their lips, but their heart is far from me. Howbeit in vain do they worship me, teaching for doctrine the commandments of men. For laying aside the commandment of God, ye hold the tradition of men, as the washing of pots and cups: and many other such like things ye do. And he said unto them, full well ye reject the commandment of God, that ye may keep your own tradition. *Mark 7:6–9 (Matthew 15:6–9) KJV*

You search the scriptures because you think that in them you have eternal life; and it is they that testify on my behalf. Yet you refuse to come to me to have life. I do not accept glory from human beings. But I know that you do not have the love of God in you. *John 5:39–42 NRSV*

I have come with my Father's authority, and you have not welcomed me. But you welcome people who come on their own. How could you possibly believe? You like to have your friends praise you, and you don't care about praise that the only God can give! *John 5:43–44 CEV*

TRAINING (see EDUCATION)

TRANSCENDENCE (also FREEDOM, LIBERATION, SELF-TRANSCENDENCE, TROUBLE)

Because of your little faith. For truly I tell you, if you have faith the size of a mustard seed, you will say to this mountain, "Move from here to there," and it will move; and nothing will be impossible for you.

Matthew 17:20 (Luke 17:6) NRSV

If you continue in my word, you are truly my disciples; and you will know the truth, and the truth will make you free. *John 8:31–32 NRSV*

Father, I don't ask you to take my followers out of the world, but keep them safe from the evil one. They don't belong to this world, and neither do I. Your word is the truth. So let this truth make them completely yours.

John 17:15–17 CEV

TRIBULATION (see END TIMES, FINAL JUDGEMENT, TROUBLE)

TROUBLE (also AFFLICTION, WORLDLINESS)

But seek first the kingdom of God and His righteousness, and all these things shall be added to you. Therefore do not worry about tomorrow, for tomorrow will worry about its own things. Sufficient for the day is its own trouble.

Matthew 6:33–34 (Luke 12:31) NKJV

Let not your heart be troubled; you believe in God, believe also in Me. *John 14:1 NKJV*

I give you peace, the kind of peace that only I can give. It is not like the peace that this world can give. So don't be worried or afraid. *John 14:27 CEV*

These things I have spoken to you, that in Me you may have peace. In the world you will have tribulation; but be of good cheer; I have overcome the world. *John 16:33 NKJV*

TRUST (*also* FAITH)

Anyone who can be trusted in little matters can also be trusted in important matters. But anyone who is dishonest in little matters will be dishonest in important matters. If you cannot be trusted with this wicked wealth, who will trust you with true wealth? And if you cannot be trusted with what belongs to someone else, who will give you something that will be your own? *Luke 16:10–12 CEV*

Let not your heart be troubled; you believe in God, believe also in Me. In My Father's house are many mansions; if it were not so, I would have told you. I go to prepare a place for you. And if I go and prepare a place for you, I will come again and receive you to Myself; that where I am , there you may be also. And where I go you know, and the way you know. *John 14:1–4 NKJV*

TRUTH (*also* DISCERNMENT, UNDERSTANDING, WILL)

Ask, and you will receive. Search, and you will find. Knock, and the door will be opened for you. Everyone who asks will receive. Everyone who searches will find. And the door will be opened for everyone who knocks.

Matthew 7:7–8 (Luke 11:9–10) CEV

Go your way; let it be done to you as you have believed.

Matthew 8:13 NASB

Beware of the yeast of the Pharisees, that is, their hypocrisy. Nothing is covered up that will not be uncovered, and nothing secret that will not become known. Therefore whatever you have said in the dark will be heard in the light, and what you have whispered behind closed doors will be proclaimed from the housetops.

Luke 12:1–3 (Matthew 10:26–27) (Mark 4:22) (Luke 8:17) NRSV

And this is the judgment, that the light is come into the world, and men loved the darkness rather than the light; for their deeds were evil. For everyone who does evil hates the light, and does not come to the light, lest his deeds should be exposed. But he who practices the truth comes to the light, that his deeds may be manifested as having been wrought in God. *John 3:19–21 NASB*

God is a Spirit: and they that worship him must worship him in spirit and in truth. *John 4:24 KJV*

If I speak for myself, there is no way to prove I am telling the truth. But there is someone else who speaks for me, and I know what he says is true. You sent messengers to John, and he told them the truth. *John 5:31–33 CEV*

If you continue to obey my teaching, you are truly my followers. Then you will know the truth. And the truth will make you free. *John 8:31–32 NCV*

Why can't you understand what I am talking about? Can't you stand to hear what I am saying? Your father is the devil, and you do exactly what he wants. He has always been a murderer and a liar. There is nothing truthful about him. He speaks on his own, and everything he says is a lie. Not only is he a liar himself, but he is also the father of all lies. Everything I have told you is true, and you still refuse to have faith in me. Can any of you accuse me of sin? If you cannot, why won't you have faith in me? After all, I am telling you the truth. *John 8:43–46 CEV*

I am the way, and the truth, and the life. No one comes to the Father except through me. If you know me, you will know my Father also. From now on you do know him and have seen him. *John 14:6–7 NRSV*

I have much more to say to you, but right now it would be more than you could understand. The Spirit shows what is true and will come and guide you into the full truth. *John 16:12 CEV*

I do not pray that You should take them out of the world, but that You should keep them from the evil one. They are not of the world, just as I am not of the world. Sanctify them by Your truth. Your word is truth. As You sent Me into the world, I also have sent them into the world. And for their sakes I sanctify Myself, that they also may be sanctified by the truth. *John 17:15–19 NKJV*

You are saying that I am a king.
I was born into this world to tell about the truth. And everyone who belongs to the truth knows my voice. *John 18:37 CEV*

TYRANNY (see OPPRESSION)

UNBELIEF (also CYNICISM, SPIRITUAL INSENSITIVITY, WILL)

Therefore speak I to them in parables; because while seeing they do not see, and while hearing they do not hear, nor do they understand.
Matthew 13:13 (Mark 4:11–12) (Luke 8:10) NASB

Now the parable is this: The seed is the word of God. Those by the wayside are the ones who hear; then the devil comes and takes away the word out of their hearts, lest they should believe and be saved.
Luke 8:11–12 (Matthew 13:18–19) (Mark 4:13–15) NKJV

You people are stubborn and don't have any faith! How much longer must I be with you? Why do I have to put up with you? *Luke 9:41 (Matthew 17:17) (Mark 9:19) CEV*

O Jerusalem, Jerusalem, which killest the prophets, and stonest them that are sent unto thee; how often would I have gathered thy children together, as a hen doth gather her brood under her wings, and ye would not!
Luke 13:34 (Matthew 23:37) KJV

If I tell you, you will by no means believe. And if I also ask you, you will by no means answer Me or let Me go.

Luke 22:67–68 NKJV

O fools, and slow of heart to believe all that the prophets have spoken.   *Luke 24:25 KJV*

Indeed, God did not send the Son into the world to condemn the world, but in order that the world might be saved through him. Those who believe in him are not condemned; but those who do not believe are condemned already, because they have not believed in the name of the only Son of God.   *John 3:17–18 NRSV*

And you do not have His word abiding in you, for you do not believe Him whom He sent.

Do not think that I will accuse you before the Father; the one who accuses you is Moses, in whom you have set your hope. For if you believed Moses, you would believe Me; for he wrote of Me. But if you do not believe his writings, how will you believe My words?   *John 5:45–47 NASB*

It is the spirit that gives life; the flesh is useless. The words that I have spoken to you are spirit and life. But among you there are some who do not believe. . . . .   *John 6:63–64 NRSV*

You are from below, but I am from above. You belong to this world, but I don't. That is why I said you will die with your sins unforgiven. If you don't have faith in me for who I am, you will die, and your sins will not be forgiven.

John 8:23–24 CEV

But because I tell the truth, you do not believe me. Which of you convicts me of sin? If I tell the truth, why do you not believe me?   *John 8:45–46 NRSV*

If I do not do the works of My Father, do not believe Me; but if I do, though you do not believe Me, believe the works, that you may know and believe that the Father is in Me, and I in Him.   *John 10:37–38 NKJV*

UNDERSTANDING (alsoDISCERNMENT, MYSTICISM, TRUTH, WILL)

I have explained the secrets about the kingdom of heaven to you, but not to others. Everyone who has something will be given more. But people who don't have anything will lose even what little they have. I use stories when I speak to them because when they look, they cannot see, and when they listen, they cannot hear or understand. So God's promise came true, just as the prophet Isaiah had said,

> "These people will listen and listen, but never understand.
> They will look and look, but never see.
> All of them have stubborn minds!
> Their ears are stopped up, and their eyes are covered.
> They cannot see or hear or understand.
> If they could, they would turn to me, and I would heal them."
>
> *Matthew 13:11–15 (Mark 4:11–12) (Luke 8:10) CEV*

Therefore hear the parable of the sower. When anyone hears the word of the kingdom, and does not understand it, then the wicked one comes and snatches away what was sown in his heart. This is he who received seed by the wayside. *Matthew 13:18–19 (Mark 4:13–15) (Luke 8:11–12) NKJV*

But he that received seed into the good ground is he that heareth the word, and understandeth it; which also beareth fruit, and bringeth forth, some an hundredfold, some sixty, some thirty. *Matthew 13:23 (Mark 4:20) (Luke 8:15) KJV*

UNITY (also INCLUSIVENESS, ONENESS)

But do not be called Rabbi; for One is your Teacher, and you are all brothers. *Matthew 23:8 NASB*

How can Satan cast out Satan? If a kingdom is divided against itself, that kingdom cannot stand. And if a house is divided against itself, that house will not be able to stand. And if Satan has risen up against himself and is divided, he cannot stand, but his end has come.

Mark 3:23–26 (Matthew 12:25–26) (Luke 11:17–18) NRSV

I am the good shepherd. I know my sheep, and they know me. Just as the Father knows me, I know the Father, and I give up my life for my sheep. I have other sheep that are not in this sheep pen. I must bring them together too, when they hear my voice. Then there will be one flock of sheep and one shepherd.

John 10:14–16 CEV

And now I am no longer in the world, but they are in the world, and I am coming to you. Holy Father, protect them in your name that you have given me, so that they may be one, as we are one.

John 17:11 NRSV

And the glory which You gave Me I have given them, that they may be one just as We are one: I in them, and You in Me; that they may be made perfect in one, and that the world may know that You have sent Me, and have loved them as You have loved Me.

John 17:22–23 NKJV

And I have declared unto them thy name, and will declare it: that the love wherewith thou hast loved me may be in them, and I in them.

John 17:26 KJV

UNSELFISHNESS (*see* SELFLESSNESS)

USURY (*also* GREED)

You cannot be the slave of two masters. You will like one more than the other or be more loyal to one than the other. You cannot serve God and money.

Luke 16:13 (Matthew 6:24) CEV

And if you lend to those from whom you hope to receive back, what credit is that to you? For even sinners lend to sinners to receive as much back. But love your enemies, do good, and lend, hoping for nothing in return; and your reward will be great, and you will be sons of the Most High. For He is kind to the unthankful and evil.

Luke 6:34–35 NKJV

VALUES (*also* COMMANDMENTS, SPIRITUALITY)

Always treat others as you would like them to treat you: that is the Law and the prophets.

Matthew 7:12 (Luke 6:31) NEB

Don't think that I came to bring peace to the earth! I came to bring trouble, not peace. I came to turn sons against their fathers, daughters against their mothers, and daughters-in-law against their mothers-in-law. Your worst enemies will be in your own family. If you love your father or mother or even your sons and daughters more than me, you are not fit to be my disciples. And unless you are willing to take up your cross and come with me, you are not fit to be my disciples. If you try to save your life, you will lose it. But if you give it up for me, you will surely find it.

Matthew 10:34–39 (Luke 12:51–53, 14:26–27, 17:33) CEV

You know the commandments: "Do not commit adultery," "Do not murder," "Do not steal," "Do not bear false witness," "Do not defraud," "Honor your father and mother."

Mark 10:19 (Matthew 19:17–19) (Luke 18:20) NKJV

There is one thing you still need to do. Go and sell everything you own! Give the money to the poor, and you will have riches in heaven. Then come and be my follower.

Luke 18:22 (Matthew 19:21) (Mark 10:21) CEV

Earthly food spoils and ruins. So don't work to get that kind of food. But work to get the food that stays good always and gives you eternal life. The Son of Man will give you that food. God the Father has shown that he is with the Son of Man.

John 6:27 NCV

VANITY (*also* APPEARANCE, ARROGANCE, PRIDE)

Which of you by taking thought can add one cubit unto his stature?

Matthew 6:27 (Luke 12:25) KJV

The Pharisees and the teachers of the Law are experts in the Law of Moses. So obey everything they teach you, but don't do as they do. After all, they say one thing and do something else. They pile heavy burdens on people's shoulders and won't lift a finger to help them. Everything they do is just to show off in front of others. They even make a big show of wearing Scripture verses on their foreheads and arms, and they wear big tassels for everyone to see. They love the best seats at banquets and the front seats in the meeting places. And when they are in the market, they like to have people greet them as their teachers.

Matthew 23:2–7 (Luke 11:43, 46) CEV

And whoever exalts himself will be humbled, and he who humbles himself will be exalted.　　*Matthew 23:12 NKJV*

Now you Pharisees clean the outside of the cup and of the dish, but inside you are full of greed and wickedness. You fools! Did not the one who made the outside make the inside also? So give for alms those things that are within; and see, everything will be clean for you.

Luke 11:39–41 (Matthew 23:25–26) NRSV

VENGEANCE (see REVENGE)

VIGILANCE (also ALERTNESS)

Watch therefore: for ye know not what hour your Lord doth come. But know this, that if the goodman of the house had known in what watch the thief would come, he would have watched, and would not have suffered his house to be broken up.　　*Matthew 24:42–43 (Luke 12:39) KJV*

Therefore you also be ready, for the Son of Man is coming at an hour you do not expect. Who then is a faithful and wise servant, whom his master made ruler over his household, to give them food in due season. Blessed is that servant whom his master, when he comes, will find so doing.　　*Matthew 24:44–46 (Luke 12:40–43) NKJV*

Blessed are those servants, whom the lord when he cometh shall find watching: verily I say unto you, that he shall gird himself, and make them to sit down to meat, and will come forth and serve them.　　*Luke 12:37 KJV*

Why are you sleeping? Rise and pray that you may not enter into temptation.　　*Luke 22:46 NASB*

VIOLENCE (*also* FEAR, REVENGE, WAR)

And fear not them which kill the body, but are not able to kill the soul: but rather fear him which is able to destroy both soul and body in hell. *Matthew 10:28 (Luke 12:4–5)* KJV

From the time of John the Baptist until now, violent people have been trying to take over the kingdom of heaven by force. All the Books of the Prophets and the Law of Moses told what was going to happen up to the time of John. And if you believe them, John is Elijah, the prophet you are waiting for. If you have ears, pay attention!

Matthew 11:12–15 CEV

And the King will answer and say to them, "Assuredly, I say to you, inasmuch as you did it to one of the least of these My brethren, you did it to Me." *Matthew 25:40* NKJV

Put your sword away. Anyone who lives by fighting will die by fighting. Don't you know that I could ask my Father, and right away he would send me more than twelve armies of angels? But then, how could the words of the Scriptures come true, which say this must happen?

Matthew 26:52–54 CEV

VIRGINITY (*see* CELIBACY, SEX)

VIRTUE (*also* JUSTICE, LOVE)

Blessed are the poor in spirit: for theirs is the kingdom of heaven.

Blessed are they that mourn: for they shall be comforted.

Blessed are the meek: for they shall inherit the earth.

Blessed are they which do hunger and thirst after righteousness: for they shall be filled.

Blessed are the merciful: for they shall obtain mercy.

Blessed are the pure in heart: for they shall see God.

Blessed are the peacemakers: for they shall be called the children of God.

Blessed are they which are persecuted for righteousness' sake: for theirs is the kingdom of heaven.

Blessed are ye, when men shall revile you, and persecute you, and shall say all manner of evil against you falsely, for my sake.

Rejoice, and be exceeding glad: for great is your reward in heaven: for so persecuted they the prophets which were before you.   *Matthew 5:3–12 (Luke 6:20–23) KJV*

Why do you ask me about what is good? There is only one who is good. If you wish to enter into life, keep the commandments.   *Matthew 19:17 (Mark 10:18) (Luke 18:19) NRSV*

VISION(S) (*also* PERCEPTION, REVELATION)

Blessed are the pure in heart, for they will see God.

Matthew 5:8 NRSV

To you it has been granted to know the mysteries of the kingdom of heaven, but to them it has not been granted. For whoever has, to him shall more be given, and he shall have an abundance; but whoever does not have, even what he has shall be taken away from him.

Matthew 13:11–12 (Mark 14:11–12) (Luke 8:10) NASB

I saw Satan fall like from heaven like a flash of lightning. I have given you the power to trample on snakes and scorpions, and to defeat the power of your enemy Satan. Nothing can harm you. But don't be happy because evil spirits obey you. Be happy that your names are written in heaven."   *Luke 10:18-20 CEV*

Very truly, I tell you, no one can see the kingdom of God without being born from above.   *John 3:3 NRSV*

VOCATION (*see* CALLING, CAREER, LABOR)

WAGES (*also* REWARD)

So when evening had come, the owner of the vineyard said to his steward, "Call the laborers and give them their wages, beginning with the last to the first." And when those came who were hired about the eleventh hour, they each received a denarius. But when the first came, they supposed that they would receive more; and they likewise received each a denarius. And when they had received it, they complained against the landowner, saying, "These last men have worked only one hour, and you made them equal to us who have borne the burden and the heat of the day." But he answered one of them and said, "Friend, I am doing you no wrong. Did you not agree with me for a denarius? Take what is yours and go your way. I wish to give to this last man the same as to you. Is it not lawful for me to do what I wish with my own things? Or is your eye evil because I am good?" So the last will be first, and the first last. For many are called, but few chosen.

Matthew 20:8–16 NKJV

Stay in the peaceful house. Eat and drink what the people there give you. A worker should be given his pay. Don't move from house to house.   *Luke 10:7 (Matthew 9:10) NCV*

WAITING (see PATIENCE)

WANTS (also DESIRE, NEED)

But more than anything else, put God's work first and do what he wants. Then all other things will be yours as well. Don't worry about tomorrow. It will take care of itself. You have enough to worry about today.

Matthew 6:33–34 (Luke 12:31) CEV

Take heed and beware of covetousness, for one's life does not consist in the abundance of the things he possesses.

Luke 12:15 NKJV

WAR (also FIGHTING, PACIFISM)

You have heard that it was said, "You shall love your neighbor and hate your enemy." But I say to you, love your enemies, bless those who curse you, do good to those who hate you, and pray for those who spitefully use you and persecute you, that you may be sons of your Father in heaven; for He makes His sun rise on the evil and on the good, and sends rain on the just and on the unjust.

Matthew 5:43–45 (Luke 6:27–28) NKJV

For nation shall rise up against nation, and kingdom against kingdom; there will be earthquakes in various places; there will also be famines. These things are merely the beginning of birth pangs.

Mark 13:8 (Matthew 24:7–8) (Luke 21:10–11) NASB

WASTE (also STEWARDSHIP)

Give not that which is holy unto the dogs, neither cast ye your pearls before swine, lest they trample them under their feet, and turn again and rend you.   *Matthew 7:6 KJV*

Gather up the leftover fragments, that nothing may be lost.
John 6:12 NASB

WEAKNESS (also STRENGTH)

Watch and pray, lest you enter into temptation. The spirit indeed is willing, but the flesh is weak.

Matthew 26:41 (Mark 14:38) (Luke 22:46) NKJV

WEALTH (also BLESSINGS, POSSESSIONS, RICHES)

It is written, "Man shall not live by bread alone, but by every word that proceeds from the mouth of God."

Matthew 4:4 (Luke 4:4) NKJV

Don't store up treasures on earth! Moths and rust can destroy them, and thieves can break in and steal them. Instead, store up your treasures in heaven, where moths and rust cannot destroy them, and thieves cannot break in and steal them. Your heart will always be where your treasure is.   *Matthew 6:19–21 (Luke 12:33–34) CEV*

But woe to you who are rich,
  for you have received your consolation.

Luke 6:24 NRSV

A rich man's farm produced a big crop, and he said to himself, "What can I do? I don't have a place large enough to store everything." Later, he said, "Now I know what I'll do. I'll tear down my barns and build bigger ones, where I can store all my grain and other goods. Then I'll say to myself. 'You have stored up enough good things to last for years to come. Live it up! Eat, drink, and enjoy yourself.'" But God said to him, "You fool! Tonight you will die. Then who will get what you have stored up?" This is what happens to people who store up everything for themselves, but are poor in the sight of God.   *Luke 12:16–21 CEV*

No slave can serve two masters; for a slave will either hate the one and love the other, or be devoted to the one and despise the other. You cannot serve God and wealth.

Luke 16:13 (Matthew 6:24) NRSV

WHOLENESS (*also* FAITH, HEALTH, MENTAL HEALTH)

Go your way; and as you have believed, so let it be done for you. *Matthew 8:13 NKJV*

They that be whole need not a physician, but they that are sick. But go ye and learn what that meaneth, I will have mercy, and not sacrifice: for I am not come to call the righteous, but sinners to repentance.

Matthew 9:12–13 (Mark 2:17) (Luke 5:31–32) KJV

Wilt thou be made whole?
Rise, take up thy bed, and walk.
Behold, thou art made whole: sin no more, lest a worse thing come unto thee. *John 5:6, 8, 14 KJV*

Stay joined to me, and I will stay joined to you. Just as a branch cannot produce fruit unless it stays joined to the vine, you cannot produce fruit unless you stay joined to me. I am the vine, and you are the branches. If you stay joined to me, and I stay joined to you, then you will produce lots of fruit. But you cannot do anything without me.

John 15:4–5 CEV

WICKEDNESS (*see* EVIL)

WILL (*also* PURPOSE)

Your will be done
On earth as it is in heaven. *Luke 11:2 (Matthew 6:9–10) NKJV*

Not every one that saith unto me, Lord, Lord, shall enter into the kingdom of heaven; but he that doeth the will of my Father which is in heaven. *Matthew 7:21 (Luke 6:46) KJV*

For whoever does the will of my Father in heaven is my brother and sister and mother.

Matthew 12:50 (Mark 3:35) (Luke 8:21) NRSV

My food is to do the will of him who sent me and to complete his work.   *John 4:34 NRSV*

I cannot do anything on my own. The Father sent me, and he is the one who told me how to judge. I judge with fairness, because I obey him, and I don't just try to please myself.   *John 5:30 CEV*

For I came down from heaven, not to do mine own will, but the will of him that sent me. And this is the Father's will which hath sent me, that of all which he hath given me I should lose nothing, but should raise it up again at the last day. And this is the will of him that sent me, that every one which seeth the Son, and believeth on him, may have everlasting life: and I will raise him up at the last day.

John 6:38–40 KJV

My teaching is not Mine, but His who sent me. If any man is willing to do His will, he shall know of the teaching, whether it is of God, or whether I speak from Myself. He who speaks from himself seeks his own glory; but He who is seeking the glory of the one who sent Him, He is true, and there is no unrighteousness in Him.   *John 7:16–18 NASB*

WINE (also COMMUNION)

The Son of Man came eating and drinking, and they say, "Look, a glutton and a winebibber, a friend of tax collectors and sinners! But wisdom is justified by her children.

Matthew 11:19 (Luke 7:34–35) NKJV

Take this and drink it. This is my blood, and with it God makes his agreement with you. It will be poured out, so that many people will have their sins forgiven. From now on I am not going to drink any wine, until I drink new wine with you in my Father's kingdom.

Matthew 26:27–29 (Mark 24:23–25) (Luke 22:17–18) CEV

No one sews a piece of unshrunk cloth on an old garment; or else the new piece pulls away from the old, and the tear is made worse. And no one puts new wine into old wineskins; or else the new wine bursts the wineskins, the wine is spilled, and the wineskins are ruined. But new wine must be put into new wineskins.

Mark 2:21–22 (Matthew 9:16–17) (Luke 5:36–37) NKJV

WINNING (*also* AMBITION, APPEARANCE, REWARD)

If anyone wants to be first, he shall be last of all, and servant of all.

Mark 9:35 (Matthew 20:26–27) (Mark 10:43–44) (Luke 22:26) NASB

But many who are first will be last, and the last will be first.

Mark 10:31 (Matthew 19:30) (Matthew 20:16) (Luke 13:30) NRSV

WISDOM (*also* SPIRITUALITY, WORKS)

Ask, and it shall be given to you; seek, and you shall find; knock, and it shall be opened to you: For every one who asks receives, and he who seeks finds, and to him who knocks it shall be opened. *Matthew 7:7–8 (Luke 11:9–10)* NASB

Listen! I am sending you out, and you will be like sheep among wolves. So be as smart as snakes. But also be like doves and do nothing wrong. *Matthew 10:16* NCV

In your patience possess ye your souls.

Luke 21:19 (Matthew 24:12) (Mark 13:13) KJV

I have much more to say to you, but right now it would be more than you could understand. The Spirit shows what is true and will come and guide you into the full truth.

John 16:12 CEV

WITNESS (*see* EVANGELISM, MISSIONS, TESTIMONY)

WOMEN (*also* EQUALITY)

O woman, great is your faith! Let it be to you as you desire.

Matthew 15:28 NKJV

Have you not read that the one who made them at the beginning "made them male and female," and said, "For this reason a man shall leave his father and mother and be joined to his wife, and the two shall become one flesh"? So they are no longer two, but one flesh. Therefore what God has joined together, let no one separate.

Matthew 19:4–6 (Mark 10:6–9) NRSV

Let her alone; why trouble ye her? she hath wrought a good work on me. For ye have the poor with you always, whensoever ye will ye may do them good: but me ye have not always. She hath done what she could: she is come aforehand to anoint my body to the burying. Verily I say unto you, Wheresoever this gospel shall be preached throughout the whole world, this also that she hath done shall be spoken of for a memorial of her.

Mark 14:6–9 (Matthew 26:10–13) (John 12:7–8) KJV

Have you noticed this woman? When I came into your home, you didn't give me any water so I could wash my feet. But she has washed my feet with her tears and dried them with her hair. You didn't greet me with a kiss, but from the time I came in, she has not stopped kissing my feet. You didn't even pour olive oil on my head, but she has poured expensive perfume on my feet. So I tell you that all her sins are forgiven, and that is why she has shown great love. But anyone who has been forgiven only a little will show only a little love. Your sins are forgiven.

Luke 7:44–48 CEV

Of a truth I say unto you, that this poor widow hath cast in more than they all: For all these have of their abundance cast in unto the offerings of God: but she of her penury hath cast in all the living that she had.

Luke 21:3–4 (Mark 12:43–44) KJV

If any of you have never sinned, then go ahead and throw the first stone at her!

Where is everyone? Isn't there anyone left to accuse you?

I am not going to accuse you either. You may go now, but don't sin anymore.   *John 8:7, 10, 11* CEV

When a woman gives birth to a baby, she has pain, because her time has come. But when her baby is born, she forgets the pain. She forgets because she is so happy that a child has been born into the world. It is the same with you. Now you are sad. But I will see you again and you will be happy. And no one will take away your joy.   *John 16:21-22* NCV

Woman, behold thy son!   *John 19:26 KJV*

WORD, WORD OF GOD (also CHRIST, HEBREW SCRIPTURES, TRUTH)

It is written, "Man shall not live by bread alone, but by every word that proceeds from the mouth of God."

Matthew 4:4 (Luke 4:4) NKJV

Therefore, however you want people to treat you, so treat them, for this is the Law and the Prophets.

Matthew 7:12 (Luke 6:31) NASB

Everyone then who hears these words of mine and acts on them will be like a wise man who built his house on rock. The rain fell, the floods came, and the winds blew and beat on that house, but it did not fall, because it had been founded on rock.   *Matthew 7:24–5 (Luke 6:47–48) NRSV*

Heaven and earth will pass away, but my words will not pass away.   *Mark 13:31 (Matthew 24:35) (Luke 21:33) NRSV*

My mother and My brothers are these who hear the word of God and do it.   *Luke 8:21 (Matthew 12:50) (Mark 3:35) NKJV*

More than that, blessed are those who hear the word of God and keep it!   *Luke 11:28 NKJV*

If you continue in my word, you are truly my disciples; and you will know the truth, and the truth will make you free.

John 8:31–32 NRSV

Yet you have not known Him, but I know Him. And if I say, "I do not know Him," I shall be a liar like you; but I do know Him and keep His word.   *John 8:55 NKJV*

If anyone loves Me, he will keep My word; and My Father will love him, and We will come to him, and make Our abode with him. He who does not love Me does not keep My words; and the word which you hear is not Mine, but the Father's who sent Me.   *John 14:23–24 NASB*

I have much more to say to you, but right now it would be more than you could understand. The Spirit shows what is true and will come and guide you into the full truth. The Spirit does not speak on his own. He will tell you only what he has heard from me, and he will let you know what is going to happen. *John 16:12–13 CEV*

Sanctify them in the truth; Thy word is truth.

John 17:17 NASB

WORDS (*see* SPEECH)

WORKS (*also* ALTRUISM, SOCIAL ACTION)

You will know them by their fruits. Grapes are not gathered from thorn bushes, nor figs from thistles, are they? Even so, every good tree bears good fruit; but the bad tree bears bad fruit. *Matthew 7:16–17 (Matthew 12:33) (Luke 6:43–44) NASB*

You can tell who the false prophets are by their deeds. Not everyone who calls me their Lord will get into the kingdom of heaven. Only the ones who obey my Father in heaven will get in. *Matthew 7:20–21 (Luke 6:44, 46) CEV*

Many will say to me in that day, Lord, Lord, have we not prophesied in thy name? and in thy name have cast out devils? and in thy name done many wonderful works? And then will I profess unto them, I never knew you: depart from me, ye that work iniquity.

Matthew 7:22–23 (Luke 13:26–27) KJV

John the Baptist did not go around eating and drinking, and you said, "That man has a demon in him!" But the Son of Man goes around eating and drinking, and you say, "That man eats and drinks too much! He is even a friend of tax collectors and sinners." Yet Wisdom is shown to be right by what it does. *Matthew 11:18–19 (Luke 7:33–35) CEV*

Why do you keep calling me 'Lord, Lord'—and never do what I tell you? *Luke 6:46 (Matthew 7:21) NEB*

Don't be surprised! The time will come when all of the dead will hear the voice of the Son of Man, and they will come out of their graves. Everyone who has done good things will rise to life, but everyone who has done evil things will rise and be condemned. *John 5:28–29 CEV*

But I have a testimony greater than John's. The works that the Father has given me to complete, the very works that I am doing, testify on my behalf that the Father has sent me.

John 5:36 NRSV

I told you, and you do not believe; the works that I do in My Father's name, these bear witness of Me.

John 10:25 NASB

Believe me that I am in the Father and the Father is in me; but if you do not, then believe me because of the works themselves. Very truly, I tell you, the one who believes in me will also do the works that I do and, in fact, will do greater works than these, because I am going to the Father.

John 14:11–12 NRSV

If you love me, you will do as I command. Then I will ask the Father to send you the Holy Spirit who will help you and always be with you.

John 14:15–16 CEV

WORLDLINESS (*also* AMBITION, MATERIALISM, SOCIETY)

Now he who received seed among the thorns is he who hears the word, and the cares of this world and the deceitfulness of riches choke the word, and he becomes unfruitful.

Matthew 13:22 (Mark 4:18–19) (Luke 8:14) NKJV

But none of you should be called a teacher. You have only one teacher, and all of you are like brothers and sisters. Don't call anyone on earth your father. All of you have the same Father in heaven. None of you should be called the leader. The Messiah is your only leader. Whoever is the greatest should be the servant of the others. If you put yourself above others, you will be put down. But if you humble yourself, you will be honored.

Matthew 23:8–12 CEV

But how terrible it will be for you who are rich,
   because you have had your easy life.
How terrible it will be for you who are full now,
   because you will be hungry.

> How terrible it will be for you who are laughing now,
> because you will be sad and cry. *Luke 6:24–25 NCV*

So therefore, none of you can become my disciple if you do not give up all your possessions. Salt is good; but if salt has lost its taste, how can its saltiness be restored? It is fit neither for the soil nor for the manure pile; they throw it away. Let anyone with ears to hear listen! *Luke 14:33–35 NRSV*

The Spirit will show you what is true. The people of this world cannot accept the Spirit, because they don't see or know him. But you know the Spirit, who is with you and will keep on living in you. *John 14:17 CEV*

Most assuredly, I say to you, unless a grain of wheat falls into the ground and dies, it remains alone; but if it dies, it produces much grain. He who loves his life will lose it, and he who hates his life in this world will keep it for eternal life. *John 12:24–25 NKJV*

I will no longer talk much with you, for the ruler of this world is coming. He has no power over me; but I do as the Father has commanded me, so that the world may know that I love the Father. Rise, let us be on our way.

John 14:30–31 NRSV

If the people of this world hate you, just remember that they hated me first. If you belonged to the world, its people would love you. But you don't belong to the world. I have chosen you to leave the world behind, and that is why its people hate you. *John 15:18–19 CEV*

Father, I am on my way to you. But I say these things while I am still in the world, so that my followers will have the same complete joy that I do. I have told them your message. But the people of this world hate them, because they don't belong to this world, just as I don't. Father, I don't ask you to take my followers out of the world, but keep them safe from the evil one. They don't belong to this world, and neither do I. Your word is the truth. So let this truth make them completely yours. *John 17:13–17 CEV*

My kingdom does not belong to this world. If it did, my followers would be fighting to save me from arrest by the Jews. My kingly authority comes from elsewhere.

John 18:36 NEB

WORRY (*also* ANXIETY, MATERIALISM, STRESS)

And can any of you by worrying add a single hour to your span of life? And why do you worry about clothing? Consider the lilies of the field, how they grow; they neither toil nor spin, yet I tell you, even Solomon in all his glory was not clothed like one of these.

Matthew 6:27–29 (Luke 12:25–27) NRSV

But when they deliver you up, do not worry about how or what you should speak. For it will be given to you in that hour what you should speak; for it is not you who speak, but the Spirit of your Father who speaks in you.

Matthew 10:19–20 NKJV

Don't spend all of your time thinking about eating or drinking or worrying about life. If you do, the final day will suddenly catch you like a trap. That day will surprise everyone on earth. *Luke 21:34–35 CEV*

WORSHIP (*also* PRAISE, PRAYER)

Well hath Esaias prophesied of you hypocrites, as it is written, This people honoureth me with their lips, but their heart is far from me. Howbeit in vain do they worship me, teaching for doctrines the commandments of men. For laying aside the commandment of God, ye hold the tradition of men, as the washing of pots and cups: and many other such like things ye do.

Mark 7:6–9 (Matthew 15:7–9) KJV

Ask, and it will be to given you; search, and you will find; knock, and the door will be opened for you. For everyone who asks receives, and everyone who searches finds, and for everyone who knocks, the door will be opened.

Matthew 7:7–8 (Luke 11:9–10) NRSV

You can tell who the false prophets are by their deeds. Not everyone who calls me their Lord will get into the kingdom of heaven. Only the ones who obey my Father in heaven will get in. *Matthew 7:20–21 (Luke 6:44, 46) CEV*

What comes from your heart is what makes you unclean. Out of your heart come evil thoughts, vulgar deeds, stealing, murder, unfaithfulness in marriage, greed, meanness, deceit, indecency, envy, insults, pride, and foolishness. All of these come from your heart, and they are what make you unfit to worship God.

Mark 7:20–23 (Matthew 15:19–20) CEV

It is written in the Scriptures, "My Temple will be a house where people from all nations will pray." But you are changing God's house into a "hideout for robbers."

Mark 11:17 (Matthew 21:13) (Luke 19:46) NCV

It is written, "You shall worship the Lord your God and serve Him only." *Luke 4:8 (Matthew 4:10) NASB*

The kingdom of God cometh not with observation: Neither shall they say, Lo here! or, Lo there! for, behold, the kingdom of God is within you.

Luke 17:20–21 (Matthew 24:23) (Mark 13:21) KJV

But the hour is coming, and now is, when the true worshipers will worship the Father in spirit and truth; for the Father is seeking such to worship Him. God is Spirit, and those who worship Him must worship in spirit and truth. *John 4:23–24 NKJV*

YEARNING (*also* DESIRE, HUNGER)

God blesses those people who depend only on him,
They belong to the kingdom of heaven!
God blesses those people who want to obey him
more than to eat or drink.
They will be given what they want! *Matthew 5:3, 6 CEV*

Everyone who drinks of this water shall thirst again; but whoever drinks of the water that I shall give him shall never thirst; but the water that I shall give him shall become in him a well of water springing up to eternal life.

John 4:13–14 NASB

YOUTH   (*see* CHILDREN)
ZEAL   (*also* MOTIVATION)

You are the light of the world. A city set on an hill cannot be hidden. Nor do men light a lamp, and put it under the peck-measure, but on the lampstand; and it gives light to all who are in the house. Let your light shine before men in such a way that they may see your good works, and glorify your Father who is in heaven.

Matthew 5:14–16 (Mark 4:21) (Luke 8:16) (Luke 11:33) NASB

I must work the works of Him who sent Me while it is day; the night is coming when no one can work. As long as I am in the world, I am the light of the world.   *John 9:4–5 NKJV*

INDEX